Enjoy my love

xxE

WILD WITHIN

ALSO BY MELISSA HART

Gringa: A Contradictory Girlhood
101 Ways to Love a Book

WILD WITHIN
How Rescuing Owls Inspired a Family

MELISSA HART

LYONS PRESS
Guilford, Connecticut
An imprint of Globe Pequot Press

Pages 137–38: Excerpt from "The Panther," Rainer Maria Rilke (translated by Stephen Mitchell), © 1989 Vintage. (From *The Selected Poetry of Rainer Maria Rilke,* translated by Stephen Mitchell.) Page 161: Excerpt from "A Narrow Fellow in the Grass," Emily Dickinson, © 1998 Belknap Press of Harvard University Press. (From *The Poems of Emily Dickinson,* edited by Thomas H. Johnson.)

Project editor: Meredith Dias
Layout: Melissa Evarts

Library of Congress Cataloging-in-Publication Data is available on file.

ISBN 978-0-7627-9680-9

Printed in the United States of America

At the request of some individuals mentioned in this book, the author has changed names and identifying characteristics. Dialogue is remembered to the best of her ability, representing people (and raptors) as accurately as possible. The rehabilitation and training procedures described here have since been updated at the Cascades Raptor Center to reflect the current research on wildlife care and enrichment of transient and permanent raptor residents.

For Jonathan—my best friend, always

CONTENTS

CONTENTS

I rejoice that there are owls.

—Henry David Thoreau

Foreword

I have been so hawk-addled and owl-absorbed and falcon-haunted and eagle-maniacal since I was a little kid that it was a huge shock to me to discover that there are people who couldn't care less about the clan of raptor—those arrows and bolts of razor-fingered fury in the sky, those masters of the air, those gleaners of meat in bushes and fields. I couldn't get over it. There were kids who did not think that seeing a sparrow hawk helicoptering over an empty lot and then dropping like a tiny anvil and, oh my God, *coming up with wriggling lunch* wasn't the coolest thing ever?

I mean, who could possibly not be awed by a tribe whose various members could see a rabbit clearly from a mile away (eagles), who could fly sideways though tree branches like intent feathered fighter planes (wood hawks), who looked like tiny brightly colored football linebackers (kestrels, with their cool gray helmets), who hunted absolutely silently *while on the wing* (owls), who moved faster than *any other being on earth* (falcons), and who could spot a whopping trout from fifty feet in the air, gauge piscine speed and direction, and nail the dive and light refraction and wind gust and trout startle so perfectly that they snagged three fish a day each (our friends the ospreys)? Not to mention they *looked* cool—they were seriously large, they had muscles on their muscles, they were stone-cold efficient hunters with built-in butchery tools, they weren't afraid of anything or anyone, and all of them had this stern *I could kick your ass but I am busy* look, which took me years to discover was not a general simmer of testiness but a result of the supraorbital ridge protecting their eyes.

To me, as a child and ever after, they were more *adamant* than other birds—lovely and amazing as their many cousins were, from the gawky glory of herons to the speed-freak entertainment of wrens and bushtits. They arrested your attention. You saw a hawk, you stopped what you were doing and paid attention to a master of its craft, who commanded the horizon until he or she was done with the moment and drifted airily away. You saw an eagle, you gaped; you heard the piercing whistle of an osprey along the river, you stood still and listened with reverence; you saw an owl launch at dusk, like a burly gray dream against the russet dusk, you flinched a little, and were awed, and counted yourself lucky and blessed.

They inspire fear, too—that should be said. They are hunters, they carry switchblades and know how to use them, they back down from no one, and there are endless stories of eagles carrying away babies left unattended for a fateful moment in meadows and clearings, of falcons shearing off the eyebrows of idiots climbing to their nests, of hawks and owls swooping in to snatch appetizer-size kittens, and of owls casually biting off the fingers of people who discover that Fluffy is ferocious. A friend of mine deep in the Oregon forest, for example, tells the story of watching a gyrfalcon descend upon his chickens and grab a fat one with a daggered fist as big as my friend's fist but with better weaponry, and rise again easily into the fraught and holy air, while glaring at my friend with the clear message, as my friend says, with something like reverence, *I am taking this chicken, and you are not going to be a fool and mess with me.* You wouldn't *believe* how clear and articulate the message was, says my friend, who still tells this story with awe in his voice, and he is a burly guy who has messed with bears and cougars and lived to tell stories about those disagreements.

I suppose what I am talking about here really is awe and reverence and some kind of deep thrumming respect for beings who are very good at what they do and fit into their world with admirable grace. I suppose another word for that is love. I suppose what Melissa's book is about really is awe and love. Even these most astonishing aeronautical masters, even these extraordinary creatures who fit so deftly into their wild world, crash and fall, and need help, and are cared for and sometimes healed and sometimes saved by compassionate human beings; and in Melissa's book we are granted a rare access and intimacy with some of those fallen masters, remarkable characters and personalities in their own right.

We are all punctured, in the end, bruised and battered and broken in various ways, and we seek always to rise again and fit deftly and gracefully into the world. Melissa was bruised early and often, by her parents' broken marriage and then by her own first try, and by many other scratches and wounds; yet she rose again, and in some way that she had to write about as honestly and passionately as she could, the clan of raptor was and is at the heart of her rebirth, resurrection, restoration. So it is that you hold in your hand a book I can happily call *raptorous*; and there are many days when I do not think I can summon a cooler adjective for a book, or a writer, or a human being.

—Brian Doyle, Portland, Oregon

Brian Doyle is the author of many books, among them the sprawling Oregon novel Mink River.

Prologue

"Clip Me"

"Are you sure you want to do this?"

The urologist with the slicked-back hair and tawny soul patch regarded me perched on a stool beside my husband in his chilly white office. The man's latex-sheathed fingers held the stainless steel scalpel with practiced ease, the way Jonathan wielded a syringe before tube-feeding electrolytes to an emaciated hawk. The doctor was maybe in his early forties, healthy and cheerful like us—but sober in the face of our request.

"You've got to assume you won't be able to conceive a child after your vasectomy." His eyes sought Jonathan's, and then mine. "You need to treat this surgery as irreversible."

He emphasized the last word; it hung in the disinfected air a moment before dissipating. Jonathan and I traded raised brows. The doctor's gaze dropped discreetly to the floor, then lifted slightly to focus on the great horned owl tattooed on my ankle, just visible beneath the rolled-up cuff of my Levi's.

Irreversible. I remembered how the artist's needle had punched permanent black-and-brown feathers into my skin, the stinging exhilaration of each jab to commemorate my transition from Los Angeles urbanite to Oregon nature girl. No going back.

Perfect.

My husband lay down on the exam table, sheet pulled to his waist. He reached for my hand, and his T-shirt sleeve stretched up to reveal the outspread wings of a hawk inked on one bicep. He entwined his fingers in mine and grinned so that I could see his crooked right incisor, subtle but sharp as the tomial tooth a falcon uses to sever the vertebrae of its prey.

"Now I know how the raptors feel when we're about to do a procedure," he told me.

For years Jonathan had suffered from epididymitis—infections that rendered him mute with fever and achingly swollen testicles. We celebrated our third date in the ER, my hand gripping his as a nurse ran an ultrasound wand over his groin. A vasectomy would remove the path by which the infection traveled.

An easy outpatient surgery, the doctor informed us. "I do several a day." His scalpel glowed under fluorescent light.

I pondered the gravity of the moment, but only just. Never to be pregnant, never to give birth, never to see the curious amalgamation of his-nose-my-eyes-his-chin-my-mouth—all of this felt irrelevant as long as I could spare Jonathan further physical pain.

I squeezed his hand. He looked up at the urologist with that deferential gratitude he'd reserved for all medical professionals since breaking his back in a car accident fourteen years before. Then he issued his humble mandate to the doctor.

"Clip me."

Satisfied that the local anesthesia had taken effect, the doctor pulled back the sheet. He bent and made a swift incision in the delicate skin of Jonathan's scrotum.

Jonathan vice-gripped my fingers. I fixed my eyes on the scalpel and fought the desire to bolt.

Five years before, I'd skittered out of town to avoid being present at my grandmother's death. Though I'd helped my mom and her partner guide our red-haired matriarch through the vulgar final stages of uterine cancer, I'd fled terrified from the moment of her passing, leaving my mother to navigate the transformation of seventy-four years of tap-dancing, show tune–singing merriment into *nada*.

This time, however, I wouldn't give in to cowardice. No one was dying here—I could watch this operation.

In five minutes the urologist had done the deed. He slipped out a gleaming loop of vas deferens and clipped off a piece, then tucked the severed vas back under the skin. He cauterized the cut, and the smell of burnt flesh rose like the nauseating odor of scorched feathers. The quarter-inch muscle of vas lay on a piece of gauze on the table beside me like a tiny taupe worm. I couldn't look away.

This was the fragment responsible for so much joy and so much angst in the world. This minuscule filament marked the difference between a bun in the oven and the ability to head out spontaneously for dinner and a movie, for a trip to Europe unencumbered by a diaper bag and stroller. Without it we'd never gaze together at my belly swollen with life, never feel the gentle kick of a child inside of me, never experience the euphoric panic of ruptured waters and a crowned head.

I felt fine with that.

The urologist clipped the vas on the other testicle and pulled up the sheet, then moved to the sink to deglove and scrub his hands. Behind the door I heard a man groan. Somewhere, another man chuckled.

What manner of wild indignities and triumphs surrounded us here in this office on the river? Who else behind closed doors had made the decision to forgo fathering a child? Who'd just been diagnosed with something unspeakable, forced into words?

Jonathan struggled to sit up. "Thanks, Doctor." He winced, and the urologist turned to his prescription pad.

"Vicodin?"

"Nah, ibuprofen's fine."

The man turned back to us, his round cheeks pink. "Take it easy a couple weeks. No strenuous activity, if you know what I mean?"

We gazed up at him like teenagers admonished for hanky-panky behind the gym. "Okay," we chorused.

He walked out and—laughter being my default response to stress—I burst into a fit of hysterical giggling. "He means we can't have sex!"

Jonathan's mouth stretched into weak amusement as he zipped up his Carhartts. "Too bad. I'll take you out to dinner instead."

I took his hand and helped him down the hall, out through the lobby, and into the parking lot. That week, Eugene, Oregon, had burst into a bacchanal of spring. Nubile cherry blossoms beckoned pink and white from silver branches. Male osprey dove on bent wings toward the undulating greenish waters of the Willamette River, hoping to impress the shrieking females in their giant stick nests. Maples dangled sweet-scented flowers all around us, indisputably phallic in their display. In the shimmering light of a late afternoon rainstorm, shocking patches of daffodils thrust themselves up between sidewalk cracks. The whole world seemed primed for making love.

"But we can't have sex for weeks!" I unlocked the door and collapsed into the driver's seat of our VW Beetle.

Jonathan lowered himself into the passenger's seat, teeth clenched. "If you felt like I did, you wouldn't want to."

"Sorry." I retrieved a pair of leather welder's gloves and tossed them into the empty box in the back seat. "We've gotta put a clean towel in there for next time there's a bird rescue. Spanakopita?"

"Yeah." He reached for the bottle of ibuprofen in the glove compartment and swallowed two with the remnants of the hazelnut latte he'd ordered preclipping. "And wine."

I drove to our favorite Mediterranean restaurant—a serene, elegant eatery in South Eugene. The place reminded us of the tavernas we'd discovered in Greece, piquing our interest in Turkish adventure when we could again scrounge together enough cash for an overseas adventure.

The host, Kenne, greeted us with tulip-shaped glasses of mint tea. "Welcome! But aren't you at the raptor center Thursdays?"

"Jean's working our shift tonight." I clasped his outstretched hand. "Jonathan just had a vasectomy."

"Melissa? That's oversharing . . ."

Kenne laughed and shot Jonathan a sympathetic look. "Wine's on the house, my friend."

He lit the candle on our table, illuminating the framed photo of the cook's Italian mother on the wall above my head.

Jonathan glanced at the menu. "Still got that Montepulciano?"

"Absolutely. But first you *have* to see my dog."

He sat down beside me and flipped open his wallet to a picture of a blond midsize canine. "Isn't she beautiful?"

We admired his pet, and Kenne rewarded us with his wide, gentle smile. "Thanks, you guys. You're great."

"And now you *have* to see our owl."

I passed him a photo from my backpack—Jonathan with a great horned owl on his leather-gloved arm, talking with a group of schoolkids. "Lorax," I told Kenne and pointed out the tawny feathered triangle above her beak that made her look as if she sported a unibrow. "Just like Jonathan's!"

This elicited another groan from my husband. "Sorry. Hold on . . ." I reached into my backpack and pulled out a plastic bag holding a three-inch-long gray pellet. "This is from her—owls swallow their prey whole, but they can't digest fur and bones and feathers, so their stomach makes a pellet and they cough it up. I found this in her mew. I'm going to dry it and dissect it, see how many mouse skulls I can find."

Kenne glanced around at the other diners bent over savory plates, faces golden in the candlelight. "Yes. Well . . . I'll just go get your wine."

I put the pellet back into my backpack and passed Jonathan the plate of warm pita bread. "Well, it's done, love. Poor Mom and Annie—they'll never be grandmas. My sister says she's *not* having kids."

Jonathan plucked a briny olive from the bowl of tzatziki. "And your brother's not procreating, right?"

My brother, Tim, has Down syndrome, and while he enjoyed a romantic relationship with one longtime girlfriend—who also sported an extra piece of chromosome 21—both sets of parents chaperoned their dates, allowing them alone time only in the relative safety of movie theaters and restaurants.

"Do your moms *want* grandkids?"

I shrugged. My mother and her partner had never indicated any particular interest in grandchildren. They liked to stroll through the mall and drool over the window displays at Baby Gap, occasionally breaking down to purchase flannel and corduroy ensembles for their cocker spaniel, but they'd never requested a human toddler to dress up.

"My mother already has fourteen grandchildren." Jonathan lifted his wine glass to clink mine and took a long medicinal swig. "That's probably enough for her."

Kenne appeared again, and we ordered spanakopita and *imam bayildi*—a Turkish dish of roasted eggplant with chiles and tomatoes. "And pistachio baklava for dessert." Jonathan massaged his temples. "Two orders. I need a whole piece tonight."

"You okay?" I assessed his furrowed brow. Operations had never fazed him; he'd had five after he broke his back, and another to fix a nasty case of hammertoes. Once, with a raging foot infection after stepping on a tack, he'd helped a nurse push his hospital bed into the room they'd reserved for him. But now he looked peaked, spent. "Do we need to get home?"

"Nah." He dug into his spanakopita. "I've had a glass of wine and two ibuprofen. I feel great."

I reached across the table to hold his hand. My love for this man still shocked me five years after our first rat-and-baby-owl date. After my grandmother succumbed to uterine cancer, I'd pushed everyone away—family, childhood friends, colleagues—but from the moment I spotted Jonathan in the mud and rain, kicking a soccer ball for his little dog, I knew whatever it is you know that you don't dare explain because such folly would leave you wide open to criticism involving loathsome terms like *cliché* and *trite* and—worst of all—*meet cute*.

I stifled my ardor and plowed into my baklava.

The rain gave way to a clear night sky strewn with clouds. I pointed out the window at the gossamer streaks. "Looks like Archimedes exploded up there."

"Archimedes?" Kenne bent to clear the plates. "The mathematician?"

"The snowy owl. He's at the center, too. He likes to jump on people's tennis shoes and try to mate with their feet, barking like a dog."

Kenne nodded, pursed his lips. "Interesting."

"Yeah. It's a nonstop theater of the absurd up there. Do come visit." I stood up and weaved slightly, head fuzzed from the wine. "Can we go for a short walk before I drive home?"

Jonathan nodded. "Sure. Probably good to move around a bit."

We paid the bill and said good-bye to Kenne, pulled on jackets and promenaded the leafy neighborhood with its post–World War II bungalows and liberally bumper-stickered Subarus—the latter the official car of Eugene.

"We're free!" The Montepulciano danced through my limbs. "No more condoms, no more birth control pills, no more infections, no chance of pregnancy."

"There's a small chance." Jonathan squeezed my hand to slow my pace. "The doctor said something like one in a hundred couples still conceives."

I punted a fir cone with my sneaker, and it scuttled down the sidewalk. "That won't be us."

We walked past a red house with yellow trim, its dandelion lawn festooned with toy cars and dinosaurs and a plastic green slide. Inside, I could hear a child's high-pitched rendition of "Twinkle, Twinkle, Little Star." In high school I'd been a master babysitter, booked five nights a week with a neon pink purse full of cash. Later, I'd been a favorite aunt, buying über-cool birthday gifts for a boyfriend's nieces and chartering trips to playgrounds and the Santa Barbara Zoo.

But that was my old life, before Oregon, before I got involved with Jonathan and his frozen rats and one-eyed hawks and fell in love with mellow Lorax, with droll Archimedes. Children had no place in our life now. Still, for just an instant, my conviction wavered. "D'you . . . d'you think we've made the right choice?"

Jonathan stubbed his toe on a sidewalk crack and caught his breath. "I do." He stopped short of rubbing his aching crotch and turned back toward the car. The song within the red-and-yellow house turned suddenly to screams, and my moment of doubt evaporated. I linked my arm in his. "If we ever regret not having a kid," I quipped, referencing the bumper sticker that first brought us together, "we'll put shoes on our cats."

"Or adopt a child."

I snorted, sure he was making a joke. But he, with his passion for photographing skulls and bones, knew better than I how the sands of time can erode even the firmest matter.

Unseen in the Douglas firs, Western screech owls called in the dusk. Their bouncing ping-pong-ball cries filled the air as they prepared to hunt mice attracted by backyard garbage cans and compost piles. I'd been trained not to anthropomorphize. Even a word such as *droll* would be taboo to the more hard-core rehabilitators with whom I sometimes worked. Raptors were just raptors, building nests, mating and hunting and sounding their territorial calls with no hidden agenda.

Still, I couldn't help feeling that on this night, sweet with spring's promise, the screech owls were laughing at us.

1

Caged

ALONE IN A MILDEWING LIVING ROOM, HEAD PILLOWED ON MY DOG'S shaggy back with another mutt warming my feet, I contemplated offing myself in the gloom of an early April evening. I couldn't pull a Sylvia Plath and stick my head in the oven because mine was electric. Couldn't overdose because I lacked prescription drugs, a doctor, and health insurance. I could never remember whether to slit my wrists vertically or horizontally, and anyhow, my kitchen knives—castoffs from my ex-husband's mother—could barely sever a triangle of brie.

Finally, I washed down a handful of Benadryl with a shot of apricot brandy, dumped kibble in a bowl for the dogs, and prayed in the glow of my cat-kitsch nightlight for unconsciousness.

I knew, of course, that a little diphenhydramine did nothing to entice the grim reaper; back at home, I'd had a jaded EMT buddy who'd gone on one too many Benadryl calls and threatened to publish a handbook called *Suicide Done Right*. But I did hope that five of the cheery pink pills would grant me a few hours of respite from myself in a sort of dalliance with death, a metaphorical dinner and a movie to see if I could commit.

Everything that season loomed hateful and hopeless—the incessant gray skies that hung over my new Northwest city like a shroud and the memory of my ex-husband and his browser's tiresome history of porn, of the inevitable progression of my grandmother's disease, of my mother's obligation to sell the family property on which I'd built a small cottage and planted a vegetable garden.

Mostly, I regretted my decision to leave California. I'd betrayed my thirty-year relationship with Los Angeles—with its theaters and opera houses, its museums and hole-in-the-wall taco joints, its crowded beaches and frenetic freeways—to live in an eccentric landlocked city full of rugged environmentalists and hippies waving peace flags and football-obsessed college students and a smaller group of resilient Republicans—all of them committed to sharing a relatively peaceful existence in the cold, cold rain.

"It's too hot here," my friends from L.A. whined when they called, traffic roaring in the background, horns and sirens blaring. "Eugene sounds like heaven."

I didn't correct them; nor did I invite them to visit. Isolation infiltrated the wood-paneled walls of each room in my bungalow. My self-worth crumbled under a siege of sorrow and solitude and persistent navel-gazing. I missed my grandmother—her brassy dye jobs, her bemused chuckle, our trips to the nursery to feed her plant addiction and to the Ventura Pier for fish-and-chips. I missed my mother and her partner with their gentle bickering, their quirky gallows humor, their starchy Midwest dinners.

Pride kept me from confessing my despair. Like a bird slammed into a window, I hunkered down on the mud-stained living room carpet, stunned and immobile. At last sleep found me with my head nestled into the dirty dog bed.

—◦◦—

My ex-husband and I first visited Eugene in August. Our marriage strained under the tensions of his porn addiction and chronic dishonesty, under my fantasies about other men—men who appreciated the fact that I was more girl next door than Playboy Playmate of the Year. Still, Oregon might renew us. The Northwest air seemed permeated by the heady sweetness of blackberries, and the mild summer sun glowed welcome after California's fierce heat. Douglas firs covered gently rolling hills. Rivers rippled below. A vast Saturday market offered live music, tamales, pad thai, and berries the size of silver dollars. Tie-dyed oldsters danced with androgynous-looking toddlers to the beat of a drum circle in something called the "Free Speech Plaza." Tony and I wandered down to Alton Baker Park and braved the sentinels of geese and mallards to explore the ponds and the Willamette.

I can live here, I thought.

My grandmother had left me a small inheritance, so that fall, we purchased a cheap bungalow in the west end of town surrounded by houses on all sides and shaded by a giant cedar. October exploded in masses of scarlet and orange and yellow leaves from the dogwood and big-leaf maple trees lining the sidewalks. Southern California came in two colors—green and brown. Oregon's palette astounded me, stopped me in my tracks. "It's idyllic!" I gloated to my friends back home.

And then it began to rain.

Rain in the Northwest is not the pounding, flashing performance enjoyed by the eastern part of the nation. Nor is it the festive annual soaking I'd been used to in Southern California. Rather, it's a seven-month drizzle that darkens the sky, mildews the bath towels, and propels those already prone to depression into the dim comforts of antihistamines and a flask.

The morning after my Benadryl binge, I rose from the dog bed, fur matted to my cheek and hips aching from a night on the hard floor. My dogs whined and scratched at the door. I stumbled down the hall to let them out, and they raced around the minuscule yard in circles. Sharp yips bounced off the walls of the houses surrounding me.

"C'mon, guys," I called to them, thinking of a fenced field I'd seen near the post office, a semicircle of oaks and taller firs embracing a meadow full of dogs. My boys could run there. I swallowed two ibuprofen and reached for their leashes. "We've gotta get out of here."

<hr />

I do not think of myself as a dog person, but a needy animal of any species has proved across the decades impossible for me to ignore. My father and stepmother, finicky about their furniture, had allowed into the home one genteel orange cat named Julius who slept at the foot of my bed for years until a neighbor ran him over in the street outside our house. Devastated, my little sister and I petitioned for—and won—a reeking, flea-riddled Lhasa apso named Rags.

"We'll walk him twice a day," I promised. "And wash him every week and comb out his fur."

"And feed him." Our father's mustache twitched. "I don't want anything to do with that animal, and your stepmother's already way too busy with your brother."

"And feed him," Katie and I chorused.

But my sister's interest faded when she realized she couldn't apply lipstick and eye shadow to Rags the way she did to her macabre Barbie head mounted on a pink plastic stand. Long after the rest of the family had discarded the dog, much like the overstuffed Asian-print furniture in my stepmother's parlor—as an object to be dutifully maintained if unloved—I walked and washed and brushed Rags. But bonding with an animal that smelled of halitosis and poop, no matter how many times the vet cleaned his teeth and squeezed his anal glands, proved impossible.

"We've got to find him a better home," my father said after the dog threw up partially digested grass and Snickers bar on the parlor's ice-blue carpet.

I cried into the flea-speckled bathwater, then brushed and blow-dried Rags and tied a white ribbon around his topknot, surrendering him to the backseat of my father's Buick with the conviction that dogs were not for me.

But in my imprudent twenties, I forgot myself. I moved to my grandmother's three-acre property and built a cottage. I married a man with equal passions for video games, Playboy videos, and animals. Tony desperately wanted a dog to replace the two he'd lost in his youth, and I allowed him to take me to the Humane Society. There, we discovered two month-old black orphans nestled together in a box in one cage. Tan eyebrows gave the twins a wise and mischievous demeanor.

"We can't just take one." Tony grinned his lopsided grin, which back then still struck me as charming. The puppy with the broader face laid his chin on my sandaled foot, and I capitulated, undone by the power of a fuzzy muzzle.

The puppies—"Marley" after Bob, and "Kawliga" after an obscure Hank Williams Jr. song—grew to sixty-five pounds each. After my grandmother died and we moved to Eugene, they chafed against the chain-link boundaries of our backyard, howling until they elicited angry phone calls from our neighbors.

"You've gotta help me walk them," I pleaded with Tony.

He sighed and extracted himself from his PlayStation. An hour later, I found him still in our driveway, dogs panting and prostrate on the wet pavement as he chatted with the beautiful blond woman who lived with her boyfriend in the house in front of ours. A few weeks later, I discovered him at midnight standing on the living room futon with a pair of binoculars. I asked him to move out.

He agreed to return to California for a trial separation, leaving me two cats and the dogs as parting gifts.

I had no idea how to be a responsible pet owner according to the laws of Eugene. I'd grown up in Los Angeles suburbs before the lapdog craze hit and kids still reigned supreme. Dentists doled out lollipops post-checkup, and bank employees offered comic-wrapped bubble gum along with Mommy's cash sent through pneumatic tubes. My new city's residents showered a similar devotion upon their pets. Gas station attendants and baristas at drive-through coffee kiosks handed out Milk-Bones. Bakeries offered homemade cheesy dog biscuits alongside chocolate éclairs. Where restaurants and women's clothing stores had surrendered to recession, doggie daycares and boutiques did a brisk business for purebreds and mutts alike.

❦

I'd spotted the Morse Dog Park on my way up Crest Drive from the post office one morning in February, after mailing a care package of locally roasted coffee, chocolate, and hazelnuts to my mother in an effort to soften the blow of my moving nine hundred miles away. Leafless oak trees dripping strands of pale-green lichen flanked the grassy three-acre park bordered by a pretty white fence. Although rain spattered the windshield of my car (reason enough, in California, to hole up inside with a pot of tea and Jane Austen), Eugenians tromped through the grass in knee-high rubber boots with their dogs, who frolicked unleashed and gloriously filthy.

The scene reminded me of Hieronymus Bosch and his *Garden of Earthly Delights*, an orgy of ball chasing. Big dogs loped after Frisbees and tennis balls hurled by folks in canvas hats. Small dogs chased each other in blurry circles around picnic tables. Off in one corner, with a joy I could perceive even from the inside of my orange Isuzu, a fluffy orange-and-white dog mounted a giant, white four-legged beast.

Ferociously hungover from my brandy and Benadryl cocktail, I parked outside a white two-story house—Senator Wayne Morse's historical residence. In the 1950s and '60s, Morse had distinguished himself as a sort of political rebel. One of two senators to oppose the Gulf of Tonkin Resolution, he once filibustered for over twenty-two hours. He'd suffered some setbacks, lost some elections, but you wouldn't find him passed out in his dog's bed. Judging from the signage around his house, Morse had embraced the balance that animals can bring to a stressful life; he'd raised goats, horses, cows, Dalmatians. These days, the city maintained his farm and fenced three acres out of twenty-seven as an off-leash dog park.

Marley and Kawliga strained against their leashes, dragging me past the house and down the gravel path toward a tantalizing bouquet of canine urine and mud. Under a tree I recognized as horse-chestnut from the "Trees of Oregon" calendar tacked up in my office, Marley squatted. Unprepared, I scanned the soggy fields for a plastic bag abandoned on the ground, forgetting that in Eugene, littering is a cardinal sin.

"Here." A tall, round woman my age with bouncing purple-black curls and a tiny black terrier on a leash walked up behind me and handed me a biodegradable bag specially designed for the removal of dog poop.

"Thanks." I bent over and read the words imprinted on the plastic that instructed users to stick one hand in, scoop up the dog's waste, deftly pull the hand out, and then tie up the package like a putrid little Christmas gift.

The proximity to feces unnerved me. I scooped it out of my backyard with a long-handled shovel—breath held against the stench—and dumped it into a trash can. But such hands-on attention, especially in the presence of a stranger while my dogs, still leashed, threatened to topple me into the mess, proved as daunting as anything I'd attempted (scraping ice off my windshield, scooping sodden leaves from my gutter, navigating an eight-inch slug in my kitchen sink) since I'd moved to Eugene.

"Thank you." I stood up and addressed my benefactress in her flannel-lined raincoat and Wellingtons. "This is my first time at the dog park."

She opened the creaking metal gate with a flourish, like a seasoned coworker helping a rookie navigate an office full of cubicles. "Welcome. Let me give you the grand tour."

Her name was Selena, and she came to the park twice a day in search of a boyfriend. "You single?" She looked down at my red, raw hands.

I thought of the silver ring engraved with roses, buried at the bottom of my laundry hamper. I'd had to choose the thing and buy it myself, Tony not having had the wherewithal to perform such a prenup.

He hadn't yet indicated a date for his return to Oregon—my fault. "Come back if you want," I'd told him over the phone, "but I'm not gonna live with you."

"I'll get an apartment," he said gently, but the plan felt like a threat.

I unclipped my dogs from their leashes and looked up at Selena. "I'm . . . sort of single."

"Been there. You're in the right place." She chattered cheerfully as she unfastened her dog's leash. The terrier raced off as if wheeled. My dogs stared at each other, brown eyes manic, and took off after it.

"I find the socioeconomic demographic to be highest at this park." Selena waved one pink-mittened hand at the other patrons with their poodles and Pomeranians, most of them clad in what appeared to be Eugene's official winter outfit—blue jeans, flannel-lined raincoats, and knee-high Wellingtons. "They're all professors, psychologists, doctors, vets. That guy . . ." Selena pointed to an older gentleman in an Oregon Ducks coat plodding the muddy perimeter with a geriatric yellow Lab. "That guy makes seventy-five thousand a year as a pet sitter. But alas, he's married."

She excused herself, nodding coldly at an unattached male who clipped a pinch collar around his Rottweiler's neck and yanked his pet toward the gate. She paused to toss advice over her broad shoulder. "Remember," she said, "you can tell a lot about a man by the way he treats his dog."

⌒⌒

That first morning at Morse Park, I couldn't tell anything about anyone. I found a muddy, ripped-up tennis ball in the grass and threw it over and over for Marley and Kawliga. If someone walked near, I murmured hello and dropped my burning eyes, pretending some business with my dogs' paws or ears.

I felt as foreign as I ever have in the Pacific Northwest, in my once-white canvas tennis shoes and my flimsy rain slicker. These people were sturdy, tough. They understood outerwear and mud. I felt like a hothouse orchid in a field of brave buttercups. Why on earth had I uprooted myself?

In California I'd visited my mother's house for a sedate dinner once a week. I'd gone to foreign films with friends, met colleagues for coffee, strolled through the shops and restaurants of Santa Monica's Fifth Street Promenade with my sister and my chums from high school. I longed to fraternize with my new neighbors, to return home from the dog park to meaningful work followed by beers swilled on some rollicking pub patio downtown. But apparently, I'd forgotten how to make friends.

"Hi," someone would say to me at the park. "Nice dogs."

"Thanks," I'd mutter and shuffle on without meeting the stranger's eyes.

At last I broke down and called my mother. "There's some bird outside my bedroom window. It moans all night long. I think it's some kind of owl. I can't sleep . . ."

"Honey," she said, "come home."

I clutched the brandy bottle and peered up into the mysterious branches of my cedar. "Not yet."

Oregon had something to teach me. That much, I knew. And I couldn't head back down the I-5 until I figured out what it was.

I said good-bye to my mother and went to bed, shoving in silicone earplugs so I wouldn't have to hear the damned bird.

Exhausted from insomnia again the next morning, I hauled myself out of bed and loaded my panting, whining mutts into the car. For a week I repeated the ritual, until I began to recognize dog park regulars. Here was the retired art professor with his gentle voice and a giraffe-like stride that matched that of his elderly greyhound; the gray-haired woman who did her best to appear homeless with a ragged terrier and shapeless green coat and slouched hat but who was, in actuality, a wealthy and successful computer programmer; the beautiful young journalist from Chicago with an Australian accent and a stunning brown dog she referred to as a "French griffon" (accent on the final syllable, no hard *n*).

Most of the patrons of Morse Dog Park boasted pets of a particular breed. As I grew more comfortable and began to stammer small talk with the locals, I heard names like "teddy bear poodle" and "labradoodle" and "Portuguese water dog."

"And what breed are *your* dogs?"

Inevitably, the question worked its way into any conversation I had with these people.

Purebreds bothered me. I grew up navigating a troublesome class dichotomy—my furious, philandering father boasted a six-figure income and that parlor, while my mother toed the poverty line as the editor of a small-town, plebeian newspaper. I gravitated toward shelter dogs, abandoned cats, people who'd been kicked around a bit and lived to tell an interesting story. Privilege and entitled pedigree made me want to provoke—not a flattering trait. There's little more dreadful than a practical joker who alone thinks she's funny.

"*My* dogs," I told the next fellow to question me, "are Jamaican long-haired retrievers."

I took a sadistic pleasure in the confusion that wrinkled his face. "They're so exotic looking." He stroked his silver beard and studied Marley and Kawliga minutely. I bit my tongue to keep from grimacing. My dogs were perpetually covered in mud. Burrs marred Kawliga's flanks, and Marley had knocked out an incisor crashing headlong into the fence in pursuit of raccoons. I didn't bathe my pets, didn't brush them. Still, people wanted to believe in my breed.

A dreadlocked woman in a fabulous faux-fur, ankle-length coat with a black Newfoundland to match swore she recognized my dogs from her recent trip to Jamaica. "They've got dreads on their flanks." She bent down to examine Marley's matted fur. "I've heard they're bred like that as protection from the sun—there's more airflow on their skin that way."

"Right," I said.

My deception offered paltry comfort and a way to hide my increasing loneliness. Selena, after her initial grace, had little to say to me at the dog park, intent on pursuing her prey. I'd left Santa Barbara City College to work as an English teacher for a distance-learning high school; now my students and colleagues hailed from all over the world but appeared only via my computer, unable to meet for office hours at the local coffeehouse. I had no reason, beyond the dog park, to leave the confines of my cage.

And then I met Jonathan.

"Is that guy *kicking* his dog?" I stopped Selena on her promenade and pointed.

A tall young man with a brown ponytail stood near the vast puddle of shiny grayish-green mud comprised of dirt, canine urine, and sour fertilizer runoff from the creek that staggered through the park. He stood with his back to us. As I watched he drew back his leg and kicked, sending a soccer ball and a small orange-and-white dog flying.

"That's just not right." I marched across the field to confront him.

"Ah . . . Melissa? I think . . ."

Selena's appeals faded into the midst of my outrage. I might not be a dog person, but that didn't mean someone had the right to punt one of them across a field.

"Excuse me . . ."

The man looked up. The little dog at his heels yipped, the soccer ball gripped in its tiny teeth. "Yes? One moment . . ."

I watched as he gently extracted the ball from the animal's mouth, set it on the ground beside him, and let loose with another kick. The ball went flying; the dog raced alongside it, unharmed and barking in apparent ecstasy. The man turned to me. "You were saying?"

"Oh . . ." I bent and picked up a tennis ball soaked with greenish mud. "Sorry . . . uh . . . what breed of dog is that?"

"Got him from a shelter—Shetland sheepdog. You know, a sheltie. This is Cody." He stuck out one gloved hand. "I'm Jonathan."

I looked down at my filthy hand and wiped it on my jeans. "Sorry."

"No problem." He punted the ball across the field again. Cody let out an ear-piercing shriek and bolted after it, followed by Marley and Kawliga, who leaped and spun, delighted at this new duo of playthings.

"Looks like your guys have a lot of energy."

I nodded with studied solemnity. "It's characteristic of the breed."

My comment provoked no response. Nothing. Devoid of my cue, I began to panic.

My great-grandparents had worked as a comedy duo—"Hap Hazard, the Careless Comedian, and Mary Hart, Who Cares Less"—in vaudeville theaters throughout the 1930s and '40s. My great-grandmother worked a glamorous straight man role, feeding her husband leads to his punch lines. In the dog park Jonathan forced me to assume the roles of both straight man and comic, setting up the joke that suddenly struck me as shabby and outmoded.

Still, as my family had taught me, the show must go on.

"My dogs are Jamaican long-haired retrievers."

He narrowed his hazel eyes. "You made that up."

I sighed. "You're right. I'm not very good at all this." I waved my hand vaguely toward the field.

"Yeah . . . I love Cody, but I'm more of a cat person, myself."

I cast a rueful look at my sixty-five-pound mutts covered head to paw in mud and thought of my gray-and-brown tabbies tidily curled up at the foot of my bed. "Me, too."

He chuckled. A dark unibrow hovered boldly over his hawk-like nose. Tattoos marked his left arm—a Scottish sword, some kind of bird.

"Is that a robin?" I pointed at the feathers inked into his skin.

"Red-tailed hawk." He bent his six feet to retrieve a tennis ball and threw it for my dogs. "I volunteer as a rehabber, helping injured birds of prey."

I bobbed my head, unwilling to concede that I had no idea what he was talking about. "Do you own a hawk?"

"Ah . . . no. That's a big commitment. I'd like to be a falconer someday, but right now I just have Cody."

He pointed to his fuzzy orange-and-white dog, who launched him-self at a half-deflated soccer ball and shook it in his needle-like teeth.

"I'm at the university," he added, "getting a master's in photography."

Photography. I knew nothing of that subject, either—nothing of what made a picture fine art as opposed to, say, the adorable photo on the wall of my childhood dentist's office that showed a black kitten clinging by its paws to a curtain rod above the words "Hang in there."

"What d'you take pictures of?" I peered up at him from under my lank, dripping bangs.

"I broke my back as a teen. I'm working on a series about strength and physical pain." His unibrow furrowed, and his long hands emphasized his words, opening and closing like wings.

His interests struck me as exotic, but his quiet hazel eyes, when he glanced away from me toward the forest, seemed to hold the sadness of a person who'd known recent loss. I listened with new interest. Did Jonathan, too, spend nights huddled alone on his living room carpet with only his dog for comfort?

He pointed above the tree line. The weak spring sun shone in a pale disk behind the clouds, and two small birds darted toward a larger one in the sky. The big guy dove and spun, attempting to maneuver away from the attack, but the little birds proved persistent; they chased him from one end of the park to the other until he gave up and took off toward the hills. "Cooper's hawk," Jonathan said. "I've been hearing them call."

"Cooper's hawk? What's that?"

I'd heard of red-tails, but that was all. Birds held little interest for me beyond my mother's backyard chickens. My aunt had owned cockatiels during my childhood; she let them fly about her basement apartment, uncaged. They pooped and chewed on her vintage Beatles albums and her Grace Slick posters, and bombed her furniture and hair and clothes with flecks of millet. Her husband, my Uncle Scott, possessed a parrot named Stella—a fearsome creature from my childhood who dive-bombed me when I walked into the kitchen, and ripped buttons off my coat while letting loose a litany of curses she'd learned from her previous owner, who'd seen action in Vietnam.

Stella had ruined me for birds.

In Los Angeles I'd occasionally paused to watch a starling bathe in an oil-slick puddle after a sprinkle of rain, but the sight appealed only a little more than watching the ever-present seagulls on Manhattan Beach make off with a surfer's bag of Cheetos. Still, I attempted to share Jonathan's interest in the aerial display above the dog park.

I squinted up at the sky. "Are those smaller birds its babies?"

He shook his head. "The Cooper's eats feeder birds. It's a fast little accipiter—sorry, forest hawk—with these cool orange eyes. Those are jays mobbing the hawk; it's probably getting too close to their nest. Jays don't like raptors."

"What's a raptor?"

He blinked at me, shock superseding his chivalry. "You're kidding."

I shrugged, red-eyed. I'd barely slept the night before. A window-rattling thunderstorm had kept me awake until two in the morning. A cedar limb crashed down upon my roof, and Marley and Kawliga whimpered and cried. I'd clung to them, terrified, in the bedroom doorway until the storm subsided. This morning, I had no energy for pride. I regarded Jonathan through bleary eyes.

"No. I'm from Los Angeles."

He took pity on me. "Raptors are birds of prey—you know, they hunt with their talons and rip food apart with their beaks." He ticked off species with his fingers. "They're hawks and falcons, owls and osprey, kites and vultures and eagles. Come up to the raptor center when I'm on shift, and I'll give you a tour."

"That would be cool," I allowed.

"It is."

He told me how sometimes an injured bird appearing to be on its deathbed can take a turn for the better. Maybe it gets just the right medicine or an unusually skilled rehabilitator, or maybe it catches a glimpse of life beyond the bars of its pet carrier. "And then we can set it free."

That day at the dog park, I felt the bars of my own self-imposed cage begin to crumble. I punted the soccer ball for Cody and turned back to Jonathan. "Come here often?" I asked with a rusty grin to acknowledge the cliché.

He knelt in the mud and gently extracted a piece of gravel wedged into his pet's paw. "Eight a.m. every day. I've got to get to school now."

I smiled again, the action so unfamiliar after months of downturn that my lips hurt. "See you tomorrow, then," I called over my shoulder, and stalked over to the kiddie pool to hose down my filthy dogs.

That night, I abandoned the pathetic comforts of Benadryl and the brandy bottle. Instead, I hunched over my laptop—fingers curved talon-like over the keys—intent on hunting down everything I could find on Cooper's hawks.

2

Tooth and Talon

THAT NIGHT, I LEARNED THAT RAPTORS DOMINATE THE FOOD CHAIN, threatened by nothing but humanity with its power lines and cell phone towers, its barbed and speeding infrastructure. In spite of ourselves, birds of prey populate the fields and forests, and even suburban trees like the sprawling cedar over my bedroom.

"Western screech owl," I determined after listening for an hour to sound clips of owl calls on the computer. My very own raptor, lured, no doubt, by the trio of songbird feeders dangling from my next-door neighbor's porch and trilling out a territorial call each evening to other screech owls in other suburban trees. We attract raptors to us without knowing it, their presence obvious to anyone who cares to look up and investigate. That Cooper's hawk I'd watched above the dog park likely nested next to people's homes, as well, with a view of a supermarket and a Big 5 Sporting Goods.

The more I read, the more I realized the Cooper's was a cool little bird. Two types of hawks live in the Northwest: buteos—big, broad-winged hawks like red-tails and Swainson's that soar over open fields—and accipiters like this Cooper's guy with its short wings and a long, dark-banded tail. Thanks to its streamlined structure, it can zip through forests in pursuit of songbirds without banging up its wings.

I'd possessed such speed and strength once. Back in California, I'd bicycled a hundred miles at a time and regularly won my age division in 10Ks. Full of hubris, I wrangled firewood, cut acres of weeds, roofed my little cottage on my grandmother's property. Surely, I could retrieve what I'd lost.

The morning after my raptor research, I unearthed my Asics from the back of my closet and tied them on, testing their spring. My calf muscles felt tight, unresponsive. Dizzy from lack of sleep, eyes blurred from reading on the computer for hours in a darkened room, I staggered to my car with Marley and Kawliga and headed to Morse Family Farm. This time, I ignored the main gravel path and jogged a dirt trail down through the firs, some shrouded in swaths of English ivy. Pale-green lichen hung from tree limbs, dripping frigid water down my neck. The air smelled of wood pulp from a factory on the outskirts of town. My dogs, overjoyed to be liberated from our minuscule backyard, rolled and cavorted, then loped up to shake and spray me with flecks of disgusting mud.

I tried to mop it up with one of my newly purchased biodegradable bags, but only succeeded in spreading the muck more thoroughly over my blue jeans. "Why would anyone live in this town?" I muttered, longing for the arid running trails I'd left behind.

Selena, overhearing me as she strolled by, pointed to the evergreens towering protectively over a profusion of oaks around us, just breaking out in delicate new leaves. "Because it's gorgeous."

"It's dark at four thirty in the afternoon." I shuddered at the billowing gray clouds. "And freezing cold."

The dog park's gate creaked and Selena and I looked over, surprise lifting our brows. Jonathan staggered in with a giant black garbage bag, Cody dancing at the heels of his hiking boots.

"Hey, it's better than upstate New York, where I'm from. They're still buried in snow."

He bent to untie his bag, revealing a trove of tennis balls. "Bought 'em on eBay for five bucks." He looked up at me. "I felt sorry for you always hunting around and not being able to find any."

A slow flush rose in my cheeks. I reached for a ball and tossed it, hoping to hide my confusion, my undeniable delight. Jonathan dumped a pile of balls on the ground in front of my dogs and paused to watch them sniff and mouth each one. "I'm gonna go distribute these."

He walked off, and Selena bent to claim a ball for her terrier. "He's courting you."

I snorted, rolled my eyes. "He's courting Marley and Kawliga."

"Same thing."

She touched my reddened cheek with one gloved finger and laughed.

My failed and still-legal marriage aside, casual sex with a handsome graduate student sounded just fine to me, but a sustained relationship felt about as appealing as the gruesome photo I'd seen online the night before—some poor owl tangled in a rancher's barbed-wire fence. According to the caption, the bird had been flying along just fine when it found itself ensnared and bleeding, unable to get free without a whole lot of pain and trouble. The image seemed to me—in the midst of disentangling myself from my college sweetheart—an apt metaphor for romantic love.

"Anyhow . . ." I tossed two balls at once for my dogs. The left one sailed far beyond the fence; Marley leaped up and dragged himself over the railing, disappearing into the forest. "Anyhow, there's no way he's interested in me. I'm a disaster."

Selena moved with me toward the gate. "Well, Jonathan's hardly Mr. Happiness. I've been seeing him here for months, and he's never cracked a smile. Won't even talk to me. Before you showed up he kept to himself, just kicking that ball for his dog. I think he's in recovery."

She grabbed Kawliga's collar and held on while I opened the gate and jogged off to pursue Marley. "Recovery?" I called back.

She shrugged. "Hey, by the time we hit thirty, aren't we all?"

Over the next few weeks, I discovered that Selena had been married, too; her husband had left her with a mortgage on a dilapidated house down the road. "I don't know how I'm gonna keep it on my income," she confessed under a giant purple umbrella with her terrier at the heels of her checkered Wellingtons.

"My mom's helping me this month," I said. "It's all I can do not to ask Tony to come back."

"Don't." She shook her head so that her curls bounced. "Get a roommate."

"I guess you're right."

I'd tried never to hurt anyone, not intentionally. Now, every evening, I heard the anguish in Tony's voice as he called and apologized and begged me to move back to California or let him return to Eugene. I didn't tell him I'd been to the courthouse to inquire about divorce papers. "I need more time to think," I said and fled to the dog park to distract myself.

I found that different demographics visited the park at different times of day. Loners tended toward six in the morning, when they could pace the muddy paths with their shy spaniels unaccosted by the chatty folks who showed up at eight with their stainless steel coffee mugs, their leaping Labradors and obsequious golden retrievers. Dogs who didn't play well with others appeared midday, their owners banking on the fact that most people went to work or school. Fewer patrons meant fewer altercations with their pit bulls.

I went at eight because Jonathan took Cody there before his classes. On a whim one day, desperate to get out of the house and away from my computer, I returned to the dog park at noon. Marley and Kawliga sang a duet down the gravel path, overjoyed at the surprise of two park trips in under four hours. Only two people stood in the field. In a far corner a man in denim and flannel brandished a blue plastic lever called a Chuckit!, hurling tennis balls for his Doberman. A ponytailed woman jogged along the fence, flanked by a German shepherd. Overhead, I spied a pair of Cooper's hawks darting in and out of the fir tops. One burst out of the tree canopy and took off; I thought I recognized the flap-flap-glide flying style I'd read about on a website run by the Cornell Lab of Ornithology.

I picked up a sodden ball and threw it for my dogs, claiming a tiny corner of territory under an oak, bordered by a fenced-off section of swamp which the city had designated, apparently without irony, as a "naturally sensitive area."

Marley and Kawliga ran back and forth, chasing the ball and dropping it near my muddy tennis shoes. My right palm oozed with dog slobber and dirt; cleaning it on the grass proved futile, so I wiped it on my jeans. I half hoped I might hear the rumble of Jonathan's truck coming up Crest Drive, his sheltie yipping from the open window. What did it mean that I longed to see him, that the park seemed brighter—despite the valley's constant cloud cover—when he loped down the path?

"It means you're lonely, you idiot," I muttered. "Find some friends."

The jogger approached in a 10K race T-shirt. I moved toward her to say hello, maybe ask about upcoming races. But her shepherd stopped short when it spotted my dogs, and then launched itself full force at Kawliga.

"What the hell!" I screamed as the shepherd sunk its teeth into my dog's back.

Marley rushed to the defense of his twin. I screamed again at the sudden snarling tangle of teeth and legs.

"Hey! Get your dog!" I hollered.

The jogger paused in her trajectory. "It's okay." She tossed her head, and her ponytail flipped, a careless blond exclamation point. "They're just playing."

Then she ran on, leaving her dog's teeth embedded in Marley's neck.

Enraged, I flew at the shepherd and swung one of my leashes at it, hoping to smack it with the metal clip.

"Halt!" An older woman threw open the gate and raced by me, brandishing a spray bottle. "Halt!" she yelled again, and aimed the nozzle at the German shepherd's muzzle.

"Don't hurt my dog!" The jogger raced back to us and hauled her dog off mine by its neon-orange collar. She glared from under her Nike visor. "If Groucho's eyes are damaged, you'll foot the bill."

She clipped a leash to her pet and stalked off, snarling F-bombs over her shoulder. Trembling, I leashed up my boys.

"I was out walking and saw the whole thing." The woman, silver-haired, in yoga pants and parka, bent down to examine Marley and Kawliga, who whined and gazed up at me through pained brown eyes. "Flesh wounds. I'd get 'em home, wash these out with peroxide. Shave the fur around 'em if you can. Helps with healing."

Blood seeped from cuts under Kawliga's ear and on his back. Marley limped, puncture wounds reddening one flank. The woman picked up his paw and squeezed it gently. He whimpered.

"What was that stuff you sprayed?"

"Bitter Apple." She showed me the bottle. "Smells like hell, and dogs hate it. I've been bitten on walks through here." She tossed her long braid over her shoulder. "Stay alert. Can't always tell a dog's temperament by looking at it." She grimaced, deepening the wrinkles around her eyes. "Come back at five. Fewer feral dogs, know what I mean?"

She turned on the heel of one boot and marched off, glaring in the jogger's direction. "And fewer feral owners."

—◦—

Unsettled, I skipped the park for a day, walked my dogs on the frost-covered field beside the grammar school, and tried to jog along the icy road while they pulled me in two different directions. At five the next day, I couldn't stand their whimpering and my solitude any longer. I stopped at the pet store for a bottle of Bitter Apple and headed to Morse.

The happy-hour crowd liked to gather there after work and school. They gossiped and flirted while their dogs chased tennis balls and Frisbees until it got too dark to see.

That evening, Selena and Jonathan stood together and looked up as I pushed through the gate. "There she is." Selena nudged him. "We thought you weren't coming."

I recounted the details of the attack, and Jonathan knelt beside my dogs, carefully fingering their wounds. "I've got something that'll help. Watch Cody a minute?"

Dutifully, I kicked the deflated soccer ball for the sheltie. Jonathan pushed through the gate and strode up the hill toward the parking lot. He returned with a small tube of medicine.

"Put this on your dogs three times a day, and watch for infection. It's an herbal salve we use on birds when they come in with puncture wounds."

"Thanks . . . that's kind of you." Again, my cheeks flamed.

"I'll just be over here." Selena walked off, a wry smile twisting her lips.

I thought of the image of the owl tangled in barbed wire and fell into an awkward silence. "Do you . . ." I recalled the research I'd done on his raptor rehabilitation center. "Do you really feed baby owls?"

"Yep. Some days, if we get enough orphans, it's almost all I do my whole four-hour shift." He pointed over my shoulder. "Cooper's hawks are back."

I turned to see a small bird sailing through the trees, a flash of shrieking brown in green branches. "Nature, red in tooth and claw," I recited. "That's Tennyson."

"Actually," Jonathan said, "that Cooper's isn't hunting right now. The fledglings are playing, learning to fly."

This information cheered me. In a dog park where a German shepherd could attack a couple of innocent mutts, where a jogger could act with wild disregard for someone else's terror, there were also Cooper's hawks—not just flying, but *playing*—and a photography student willing to shell out cash for a garbage bag full of tennis balls.

That afternoon, inspired, I paused on my run to watch mallards on Amazon Creek, crows dismantling McDonald's sacks for the treasured stale fries within, blackbirds perched on fence posts—red wings flashing as they chortled a melody so lovely that I resolved to leave my iPod at home. I began to notice other flora and fauna, as well—orange-tusked nutria rats clambering around the creek bank, the curling tendrils of sword ferns, the gray-blue arrows of herons sailing across cloudy skies.

The sheer wonder of the world in which I now found myself yanked me out of pathetic narcissism and gave me something to talk about with Jonathan in the park. "Did you know that this lichen," I said, producing a handful of the feathery green stuff pulled from a branch, "is called usnea, or Old Man's Beard?" I giggled. "It's also called Backpacker's Toilet Paper."

"Better that than poison oak." He pocketed the lichen. "Might make a good photo."

We began to meet twice a day, chattering for an hour in the morning and the late afternoon while our dogs played together. I listened, brow furrowed, as he debated the merits of peregrines versus Harris's hawks, Canons versus Nikons, Camus versus Kafka, his voice full of gravitas, and sadness lurking just below his direct hazel gaze.

"What brought you to Oregon?" I asked one day, after we'd spent half an hour checking out the Cooper's hawks through his binoculars.

"Always wanted to go west and become a photographer. Got easier when my fiancée left me for another guy."

So he had known loss.

I searched my memory for something I might offer as consolation. "My ex-husband charged phone sex to my credit card and blamed it on the guys at Jiffy Lube."

Jonathan plucked at his eyebrow with a thumb and forefinger. "My apartment in New York burned down. I lost almost everything."

I hurled a tennis ball across a vast expanse of glistening green mud. "I built a cottage next to my grandmother, and she died of cancer, so I had to move."

"My dad died of melanoma when I was fifteen."

We studied each other, assessing our separate griefs. He told me how he'd driven across the country with Cody, stopping along the way to camp and take pictures at Arches National Park before moving into a studio apartment near the university. I told him how my ailing grandmother, at seventy-four, had remained cheerful in her insistence that we add rum and ice cream to her cans of Ensure as a nightcap to enjoy while watching Sesame Street's Elmo, whom she revered. "Meanwhile, I flipped out, quit my college teaching job, bought a house after two days in Eugene, and left everyone."

I paused and looked away, toward the sky. "I've never seen the campus. We could meet there for coffee sometime, and I could see your photos." I tossed the invitation over one shoulder. He could catch it, or not.

He dropped it. Across the field a couple of dogs launched into battle, and he ran to scoop up Cody before he could join the fray.

"Oh God, another fight." I leashed up Marley and Kawliga.

Suddenly, Selena flew by and shoved her terrier into my arms. "It's a cat! Those dogs have a cat!"

"What?" I began to run with her.

"*Don't.*" Jonathan took my arm and held on.

My dogs strained against their leashes. I tightened my grip on the terrier. "They caught a cat? Someone's pet? Oh, no . . ." I pictured my tabbies limp in canine jaws and closed my eyes.

Jonathan wrapped his arm around me. For a moment I leaned into the comfort of his chest. His heart beat in my ear. "It'll be okay," he said, one hand warm against my head. "Don't worry."

Other park patrons huddled by the far fence. Someone in a hooded raincoat caught up the two snarling dogs by their collars and stood apart from the group, head hung.

Serena shrugged off her raincoat and hovered over something, wrapping it up. Then she hurried across the field and out the gate with the bundle held against her chest. "I'll come get my dog later," she called out.

"I'll be here!" I stepped out of Jonathan's embrace and looked at him. "Do you really think the cat will be okay?"

He pursed his lips, blew out a stream of air. "Depends on how badly they mauled it."

The raincoated figure with the pair of dogs slunk, head still bowed, through a back gate. Jonathan set Cody on the ground. "I hate to leave you, but I've got to get up to the raptor center."

"Of course. Thanks."

I walked with him to the parking lot, both of us silent, and drove home to embrace my own cats with Tennyson's verse on repeat in my head.

—◆—

I didn't see Jonathan again for a week. Maybe he'd decided to frequent another, less violent park. We hadn't exchanged phone numbers or e-mail addresses; perhaps, in this city of one hundred forty thousand people, I'd never see him again.

"There're five dog parks in the city." I sat on Selena's couch and dipped an experimental fingertip into the glass of absinthe she'd poured me in an informal wake for the cat. "Jonathan's probably got a girl at every one. I'll bet he brings bags of tennis balls to them all."

She passed me a box of sugar cubes in her dim living room, lit only by a string of white lights tangled in a rangy philodendron. The liquor lent sparkle to her usually placid eyes. "Probably. You don't want a romantic relationship, anyway, remember?"

I remembered. Home alone that night, I berated myself for hurting Tony, for ending our marriage. I thought of calling and inviting his return, if only to ease my own guilt. We could go together to some twelve-step group and get rehabilitated; at least then I'd have some peace, and someone to watch *Seinfeld* reruns with on the long, dark evenings punctuated by the burble of my screech owl.

"Don't do it." Selena cautioned me over the phone, my unofficial sponsor. "Have another drink. Buy a vibrator. But don't call your ex. It's cruel, especially when you're in love with someone else."

"I'm not in *love*," I protested. Still, I registered how my heart danced when, the next afternoon, I heard the familiar sound of Jonathan's truck and looked up to see it climbing Crest Drive. He pulled into the parking lot beside me as I loaded up my rancid, panting dogs for the ride home. My teeth began to chatter. I mashed them into a grimace.

"Hey." Jonathan got out of his truck and sauntered over to me, smiling so that I could see how one of his front teeth curved over the other, just slightly. "I've been visiting my family in New York." He nodded at the back of my Isuzu. "Nice bumper sticker."

I ducked and rubbed dirt off the red vinyl to hide my excitement. "I bought it at the Santa Monica Promenade with my sister."

I told him how Katie and I had wandered the chic, perfumed shops, then dined on overpriced pizza at Wolfgang Puck's. "When we walked out, there was this old guy at a card table full of bumper stickers. My sister bought one that said, 'We're not human beings having a spiritual experience; we're spiritual beings having a human experience.' I liked this one."

Jonathan read it out loud: "If I wanted to hear the pitter-patter of little feet, I'd put shoes on my cat."

"Yeah . . . I'm not into babies."

I regretted the words the minute I said them. They sounded inexplicably harsh, too simple for my complicated feelings about motherhood.

I'd never wanted to be pregnant, never wanted an infant. I liked older kids, but while I was an undergraduate, a new mother hired me to babysit for her infant stricken with colic. The child erupted into violent screaming fits no matter how often I plied him with microwaved breast milk from the dozens of bags in the freezer and sang him every show tune I knew. After two weeks I confessed to his run-ragged grad student mom that I wasn't up to the task of caregiving. "I'm sorry." I relinquished her cash, red-faced. "I guess I don't like babies." She clutched her squalling son to her chest. "That's not a very nice thing to say."

"Baby animals are awesome," I said now. "And I admire other people's infants—really, I do."

Jonathan merely laughed at my confession. "You know what? I don't like babies, either. Hey, I know you've gotta get home, but I wanted to ask you . . . I have to drive up to Portland this weekend to pick up six hundred pounds of frozen rats. Wanna come?"

He delivered the invitation with a straight face, as if he'd just invited me to dinner and a movie. I wrinkled my nose. "Frozen rats?"

"We order them from a place called the Gourmet Rodent back east and thaw them out to feed to the birds."

"Oh. Um . . . interesting."

"Yeah. Next shipment comes in this weekend, and I'm heading up to get them. A fledgling owl fell out of its nest and got injured near Portland, so I'm going to pick it up, too. I know you haven't seen much of Oregon . . ."

Dead rats? I'd done my time with dying, from my grandmother's initial surgery, after which she imitated E.T. with the red-lighted pulse monitor on her index finger, to my hasty good-bye in her doorway, when pain turned her snarling and outraged as her Siamese cat. I'd moved to escape death, and, yet, here stood a man inviting me to interact with it deliberately, in field-trip form.

I looked over his shoulder at Spencer Butte, the single mountain looming more than two thousand feet above the south hills of Eugene. A Cooper's hawk shot over our heads, hot on the heels of some robin. I wasn't stupid. I knew I couldn't truly hide from death and savagery in Oregon. The sooner I accepted this, the happier I'd be.

Suddenly, my state stretched out before me, vast and pregnant with possibility. When I got home I'd fill out the divorce papers and overnight them to Tony; it had to be done, regardless of what might happen—or not happen—between Jonathan and me.

Rain began to fall, misting against my cheeks. I shivered, wrapped in my ridiculous red raincoat. Baffled by Jonathan's invitation, but sensing redemption, I offered a tentative smile.

"Okay," I said. "I'll go."

3

Disparate Species

"Never look directly into a bird's eyes like that. You'll scare it."

"Sorry."

I straightened up on the bench seat of Jonathan's truck, rigid under the featherweight cardboard pet carrier on my lap. Inside, a brown baby owl, fuzzy as a child's stuffed toy, scrabbled and clacked. I'd been trying to get a look at its beak and talons, gauging the potential for laceration should the bird bust out of its box, when Jonathan chastised me for peering into one of the airholes.

He sat hunched over the steering wheel, navigating I-5 traffic back to Eugene. The Dodge struggled against the drag of an afternoon wind and a bed weighted down with six hundred pounds of frozen rats.

"Look at that guy."

He pointed to a two-foot-tall, rust-colored bird with a buff chest. It sat on a fence post just off the highway, unflappable in the wake of a Safeway truck that thundered by. "I've counted twenty red-tailed hawks on this stretch before."

"Why here? Shouldn't they be over in that forest?"

I pointed toward a dark blur of firs. Jonathan drummed his fingertips on the steering wheel, eyes on the road. "Red-tails are soaring hawks, buteos. They can't stay in the trees—they scan open fields for rodents and smaller birds. Tractors stir up mouse and gopher homes near the roadside. See?" He pointed out a hawk in a recently plowed field; the bird flew up and over us with some small brown thing in its talons, red tail flashing in the sunlight. "Fence poles are a perfect perch to scout out prey."

This conversation thrilled me so much more than the tête-à-têtes during which Selena and I drank too much and trashed our ex-partners. The world through Jonathan's eyes began to come alive in a new and shocking way; a bird on the side of the road wasn't random after all—it possessed a whole complex story.

What on earth could I offer him in return? A meditation on the chaparral that covered the bare hills around my hometown? Perhaps those scrubby sages and buckwheats hid wonders, as well, but I'd never taken the time to notice.

Over the past three hours, Jonathan had grown more and more attractive in his knowledge of nature. My own master's degree, the fact of my educational books for children, the essay I'd sold to a national woman's magazine about my eccentric great-aunts passing off a thrift store quilt as their own and winning blue ribbons and cash—none of this seemed glamorous compared to hand-feeding baby owls.

"I'm training for the Portland Marathon." I flexed my feet, waiting for a compliment on my muscled calves.

He looked away, out the window toward a large, dark shape in the sky. "Think that might be an immature bald."

I didn't blame him for his disinterest. While I worked to build a freelance writing career in Eugene, my life mainly revolved around a trio of lackluster destinations: my dim little home office with a view of my neighbor's rotting fir fence, the local supermarket with its high-falutin' sushi station and organic free-range soup bar, and the dog park. On my runs around Pre's Trail, I felt the ghost of the university's legendary runner, Steve Prefontaine, shake his head at my nine-minute miles. I prayed I wouldn't run into Mary Decker Slaney—a fellow Eugenian I'd revered as a high school freshman during her 1984 Olympic competition—who would surely be disappointed in both my race pace and the state of my thighs. Still, the endorphin rush found me; I imagined myself a cougar loping down the trail, not in pursuit of prey, but for the pure joy of movement in the open air.

On a clear day from another path along the West Eugene wetlands, I could see the snow-dusted Coburg Hills and the Three Sisters—the trio of volcanic peaks jutting up near Bend in central Oregon—but I lacked the impetus to drive there for a closer look. Now, in Jonathan's truck, I glanced back at snowcapped Mount Hood. "Oregon's highest mountain," he told me. "Just north of a major migration route for raptors."

Apparently, birds flew south for the winter and north for the summer along some sort of windy superhighway ("They catch thermal gusts of air," Jonathan corrected me) and people spent weeks on Bonney Butte near Mount Hood, catching raptors to band for study, and then releasing them. "Volunteers from HawkWatch International," he explained. "The bands track a bird's progress and longevity. A band's a little metal bracelet around one leg," he added.

I understood jewelry. The rest of it completely baffled me, but I would have climbed Bonney Butte if he'd asked me to, and flown the migration route, as well—anything for a change of scenery alongside this man.

The morning of our Portland trip, I'd stood in front of my closet, considering my clothing options. Over the past few months, jeans and T-shirts and fleece had crept into my wardrobe, replacing flowing skirts and flimsy blouses. I'd purchased a pair of sturdy hiking boots, preferring their ankle support in the slick mud. But they wouldn't do for Portland, written up in *Sunset* as a West Coast hipster haven.

I dug a black-and-white checked sundress out of the suitcase under my bed and reached for the sandals that had cost me a couple days' salary. I tied my hair into a sparse ponytail, missing the curls I'd chopped off after my grandmother died.

In the mirror I looked awful—too skinny from what Selena called "the divorce diet." My cheeks gleamed red and raw from cold. Inexpertly, I brushed on mascara and lipstick, then scrubbed the mess away and fled the mirror to walk Marley and Kawliga around the block.

"Poor substitute for the park. Sorry, guys."

Still, crows sailed squawking overhead to land in neighbors' rows of arborvitae, and brown squirrels skittered across lawns with tantalizing chirps. My dogs strained against their leashes, taking it all in, panting with ardor. I shut them in the backyard with a box of Milk-Bones and prayed they wouldn't scale the chain-link fence and eat the neighbor's cat.

My own tabbies stayed safe inside with food and water and a corrugated cardboard scratching post replete with fresh catnip. I left them competing for claw purchase.

Jonathan wanted to head for Portland early. We'd agreed to meet at his apartment near the raptor center. He'd drawn a map to his place on the back of one of the brochures; in my car I studied the street grid, then flipped over the card to look at a picture of a brown-and-white owl. Its dark eyes glowed liquid and tranquil, but the yellow beak curved in a menacing manner, and I saw that the designer had cropped the bird's talons out of the photo in what struck me as an expert PR move.

I'd never seen an owl up close. Still, apparently they'd been present in Southern California. Screams split the night sky above my grandmother's property. My mother and I cringed as we walked across her yard in the evenings, and I covered my head with a coat, assuming the cries came from bats. Jonathan set me straight.

"Sounds like a barn owl. You say your grandmother had an old barn?"

I nodded, closed my eyes against the sting of sorrow that shot across the bridge of my nose.

"There was probably a nest in there. You say she had three acres? That's prime hunting territory—you probably had great horneds and screech owls, too. Barn owls are ghostly, with a shriek that makes your hair stand on end. Some Native American tribes say owls call out the names of people who are about to die."

"Oh."

He put his hand on my knee for an instant. "I'm sorry."

Those moments of kindness, set against a barrage of perfunctory bird-related lectures, confused me. Part of me fantasized that the invitation to Portland to pick up frozen rodents was actually a euphemism for lovemaking—I'd once believed a boyfriend's suggestion that we go watch the grunion run—but that morning, Jonathan seemed all business.

He met me at his back gate in jeans and a brown T-shirt printed with an image of a bird in flight. "The rats fly in at ten. If we pick them up by eleven and get them to the center by two, they'll hardly thaw, and we can stick them right in the center's big freezer. Is that what you're wearing?"

He looked at my seersucker dress and strappy sandals. "Guess I'll have to do the loading myself."

My cheeks burned. "I can go change . . ."

"Nah, you're fine. Dresses just always seem so uncomfortable to me."

Cody yipping at his heels, he led me down a flight of stone steps past a tangle of blackberry bushes to the bachelor pad they shared under his landlady's house. Coke cans and empty cereal boxes littered the kitchen counter. Photos covered the walls. A double futon spread with an orange-and-blue plaid blanket dominated the single room.

"This is gorgeous." I ran my hand over the soft wool and blushed again.

"That's the Buchanan tartan."

"What is?"

He nodded at the plaid blanket I'd been fondling. "And that's our castle." He pointed to a framed photo of a spired stone structure above the futon.

"You have a castle?" I shook my head, mystified. What was royalty doing in a studio apartment?

He reached for his camera on a high shelf and the sleeve of his shirt rode up to reveal one bicep. I hovered in the center of the room, unsure of whether to stand or sit. A backpack sat on his desk chair. Reclining on the futon might send a message I wasn't sure he'd appreciate.

I looked again at the castle. "I have an ancestor who was England's first pornographic poet." My family's claim to fame lacked dignity. The Second Earl of Rochester, the subject of a couple of books and a bad Johnny Depp film, had been a pandering, lascivious creature who—by his own account—liked to have sex with just about anything that moved. "I'll spare you a recitation of his verse."

Instead, I studied the black-and-white photographs thumbtacked to the walls. One showed a close-up of incense cones lined up in a sort of ceremonial circle. It reminded me of a gathering of monks, albeit monks intent on immolation. Another picture looked to be Jonathan standing in his tiny studio kitchen eating something out of a bowl; he'd burned the negative so the image appeared greenish and distorted like a scene from a fun-house mirror. I'd ditched high school in Los Angeles to go to the art museums, but I preferred installation art and the Impressionists. Photography meant Ansel Adams's landscapes of Yosemite—*not* incense cones.

I struggled for honest assessment, searching for terms that didn't exist in my vocabulary. "I've never seen anything like these before . . ."

He walked over to his desk and handed me a stack of glossy color photos. "They're . . . postmodern. These are from the raptor center. More traditional."

I flipped through the pictures, recognizing owls with their round faces and yellow eyes, plus a few birds I thought might be hawks.

"Falcons," he corrected me. "See how they're smaller than these red-tails? Also, they have pointed wings." He flipped to a photo of a big, ruddy bird, then shouldered his backpack. "Want a Coke?"

"It's eight thirty in the morning!"

He shrugged and dropped two cans of soda into his backpack along with a pair of yellow elbow-length leather gloves.

"So what exactly d'you do at the raptor center?"

As a child I'd visited the Exotic Animal Program at Moorpark College with my Girl Scout troop and watched caregivers feed the furred residents, but their lions and tigers and anteaters were healthy animals in training for movies and TV shows—not birds in need of Band-Aids.

"I do a little of everything." Jonathan led me out the door and back up the steps to his truck. "Feed the birds, medicate, fix perches, rescue injured or orphaned raptors, pick up frozen rats. You should volunteer."

"Actually, I've just started volunteering as a giant raccoon."

"A raccoon?" Jonathan paused by the dented passenger-side door. "I don't get it."

"This nature nonprofit for kids put out a call for volunteers. They needed someone to do environmental education in a raccoon suit. My name's Rocky; I have to talk in a Brooklyn accent."

These facts seemed to me unremarkable. My grandmother had owned a costume shop in Monterey all the years of my childhood, and I grew up prancing through her boyfriend's adjoining dance studio in hoopskirts and Chewbacca masks and tap shoes. After I'd abandoned my college babysitting gig, I found a job with a local acting troupe and spent weekends dressed like an elf, singing and dancing for the children of wealthy parents at holiday parties in Carmel. Public speaking as a teacher or a giant furry animal scares me not at all; give me a microphone, and I'll entertain, even when the audience is kindergartners and I'm speaking through a mammal mask's mesh eyehole.

"It'll be fun!" I told Jonathan.

He bunched up his brow. "A raccoon," he repeated and flung open the door. "Huh. Well . . . let's go pick up some rats."

The seating arrangement in his pickup confused me. We'd stack the rodent boxes in the plastic-lined bed—that was a no-brainer. But the cab had one long bench seat festooned with silver gum wrappers and a tangled trio of seatbelts. I'd always owned passenger cars, their boundaries clearly defined by a gearbox. Now I stood in the street, unsure. Obviously, Jonathan would sit in the driver's seat, but should I sit right next to him, where our knees and elbows would touch and he'd be in a position to judge the effectiveness of my Tom's of Maine deodorant, or should I sit in the seat farther over, beside the window?

He stuck the key in the ignition. "You getting in?"

I buckled myself into the far corner of the bench, breathed in spearmint and air freshener from the cardboard pine tree that dangled from the rearview mirror. Jonathan raised his unibrow. "Ready for an adventure?"

Men had asked me this question before. After the grunion run, the same boyfriend had taken me up to the Santa Monica Mountains to break bottles—"It helps diffuse my rage," he'd said. I'd driven through the Palos Verdes foothills with another man at midnight, the B-52s blasting out the window of his BMW, headlights off for maximum excitement on the winding roads.

"Do you have any B-52s?" I asked Jonathan.

"Nope. Sarah McLachlan. It's in the tape deck."

I didn't push play.

Jonathan drove up 30th Avenue past fir forests, a couple of snow-capped peaks peering up just beyond, then pulled onto the I-5. In my peripheral vision I studied him. When he clicked on his turn signal, his muscle rippled and the hawk tattooed on his bicep appeared to fly.

Skepticism tempered my admiration. I'd never known anyone with a tattoo, unless I counted my uncle Bob, who drove a big rig up and down Highway 101 and collected six-packs of Billy Beer from the 1970s. Tattoos had always struck me as a sign of unsavory character, an unwise decision made in a moment of drunkenness and destined to expand, spreading into a Rorschach blob by the time the remorseful recipient hit fifty.

Still, the longer I lived in Eugene, the more I saw inked patterns on the arms and legs and necks and backs of people my age and younger—people with nine-to-five jobs and 401Ks and Subarus. Piercings winked from nostrils, eyebrows, lips, tongues. Suddenly, my chic sundress felt square. I had no tattoo, and only one small silver hoop in each earlobe. My dress and sandals, even my calf muscles, seemed generic and forgettable. With my fingers I attempted to fluff up my bangs.

"Everything okay?" Jonathan looked at me.

"Fine." I clasped my fingers in my lap and gazed out the window, searching for something I could offer in the way of interesting conversation. "Hey, I'm interviewing that twenty-two-pound cat that lives in the lobby of the Bijou Cinemas, for a cat magazine."

His unibrow jumped. "Didn't realize the cat talked."

"Well . . . technically, I'm interviewing the cinema manager."

I didn't tell him that the manager kept calling and asking me out, or that I declined every time, thinking to keep myself available for the man beside me, now that I'd officially filed for divorce.

Stupid. Jonathan wasn't interested. He didn't ask me about the cat or about my increasing publications as a magazine writer. He turned on Sarah McLachlan and we listened to her whining as we drove past towns I'd not yet heard of—Coburg, Junction City, Brownsville, Corvallis. Cottony clouds drifted above sheep flocking placidly in emerald fields. Jonathan pointed out little blue-gray birds straddling telephone wires. "American kestrels—our smallest falcon. They eat mice and smaller birds. People call them 'sparrow hawks.'"

He nodded at a trio of dark V shapes on the horizon. "See how they dip from side to side as they glide? A tilting V equals turkey vulture. They're scavengers—they bury their heads into carrion at the side of the road. Their heads are featherless, so they don't get as messy from all the blood and guts.

Also, they pee down their legs to stay cool, and they throw up when they're nervous. People at the raptor center either love 'em or hate 'em."

My stomach lurched. I didn't love birds. They'd always seemed to me like little know-it-alls, showing off skills I could never hope to achieve and pooping in cement-like streaks on my car. My uncle's parrot, Stella, had genuinely terrified me in childhood with her button-lacerating beak and fierce claws. Raptors possessed similar sharp parts. Cats I could deal with; I'd been clawed and lived to tell the tale. Talons seemed a different story altogether.

"Peregrines nest on that bridge."

We approached Portland's sparkling skyline, far prettier than Los Angeles, with the Willamette River gleaming blue below. Jonathan pointed at a steel bridge spanning the water. "Rehabbers at Audubon keep tabs on the peregrines, make sure they're not harassed. It's interesting how birds adapt to urban environments. The falcons don't seem bothered by all the car traffic and the ships going by. There's even a pair of red-tailed hawks that nest on a high-rise in New York City—'Pale Male,' the little guy's called. Birders stand out in Central Park for days with their binoculars trained on the nest, hoping for a glimpse of him."

He drove through the city toward the airport and pulled into Delta's loading dock. Two coverall-clad men stood smoking near a tower of boxes. Jonathan jumped out. "I'm here to pick up some rats."

He addressed the older man, whose shaggy gray sideburns, worn with a matching pair of eyebrows, stopped just short of his neck. The man nodded. "Oh, you're the one." He jerked his chin at the box tower. "Strangest shipment I've ever seen. Tell me, son . . ." The guy leaned in close, cigarette punctuating his words. "What the hell do you do with six hundred pounds of frozen rats?"

Jonathan backed his truck up to the boxes and began lifting them onto the bed. "I work with birds. The rats are food for falcons, hawks, eagles, owls . . ."

"Why not serve 'em live?"

"Our birds are injured, and live prey fights back. They'd hurt themselves trying to chase prey around their enclosures."

The other man spoke now, nodding in the direction of the river. "We got some osprey living over there. I'm standing right here and one shows up with this fish in his claws. I swear to God an eagle—a big ol' sucker—comes out of nowhere and goddamn if he don't steal that fish. Osprey never knew what hit him."

"They do that."

I got out of the truck and stood there, not sure whether I should assist. My ex's Mexican-American parents, with a rigid definition of gender roles, had chastised me for helping to harvest lilies and mow down weeds on their ranch alongside the men. I recalled how Tony's father had demanded that I step away from the jackhammer and go bake a cake, and wondered now if I should make a Starbucks run for scones and lattes.

But Jonathan nodded at the giant stack of boxes on the dock. "Feel free to help."

The older man stepped back to make room. He glanced at my checkered sundress. "You work with those birds, too?"

"No . . . they scare me. I'm just along for the ride."

"Looks like one hell of a ride."

It was. I panted, sweating in the sudden sunshine, sandals pinching my feet as I staggered under the weight of the boxes. Jonathan's cheeks flushed, and his brow glistened. When we'd loaded all the rats, he drove the sluggish truck through the parking lot and stopped under the shade of a tree.

I looked around, confused. For an instant I thought I'd been wrong—maybe, weirdly turned on by his frozen cargo, he'd decided to initiate a make-out session. But then a white sedan pulled up, and he jumped out of the truck. "Here's the woman with the baby barred owl."

A middle-aged, wide-hipped woman got out of her car holding a cardboard pet carrier of the sort that I used to transport my cats to the vet. She handed Jonathan the box. "Here he is, and thanks for meeting me, sweetheart. He's had seventy-five ccs of EHS this morning and four dark mice." She pressed a round Tupperware container into his hand. "Here's four more for the ride home."

He leaned in the open window and placed the receptacle of dark, furry shapes on the dashboard. I grimaced, nausea coiling in my stomach. "Interesting lunch box, *sweetheart*."

"Hey, he's gotta eat." He walked around to my side of the truck and set the pet carrier on my lap.

"What . . . what're you doing? What if it gets out?"

The box felt impossibly light, as if it held only an apple. Still, I felt my shoulders tense toward my ears.

"You don't mind holding him, do you?"

The bird scrabbled and clacked, the sound belying its weight. How big was a baby owl? I imagined a giant bird bursting through the top of the pet carrier, latching onto my lips with its talons.

"You sure it can't get out?" I checked out the flimsy cardboard latches on either side of the handle.

"I'm sure." Jonathan thanked the woman and started his truck. "Let's go get some chickens."

"More raptor snacks?" Vegetarian for a decade, I recoiled.

"The rehabbing class practices bandaging them and gives them subcutaneous fluids. Then we euthanize them for our birds. Chickens stop laying after a couple of years, so farmers sometimes give them to us."

"Huh." I wasn't sure how to feel about this trade-off. Who determined that a hawk's life trumped that of an elderly chicken, that six hundred pounds of rats deserved less of an existence than, say, an owl? Then again, I fed my cats tuna and chicken, and I wouldn't turn up my nose at wild-caught salmon if Jonathan invited me out to dinner.

"How's the baby?" he asked.

I bent and peered into a breathing hole at the top of the box. "Okay, I think." I could make out something fluffy, one shining brown eye. "He's looking at me!"

"Shhh!" Jonathan put a finger to his lips. "The little guy's already traumatized—it doesn't need any more stress."

I shrank back in my seat. I felt as though I'd just gotten a spanking, and not in a good way. Jonathan could obviously tell that I was an imposter, an ignorant idiot from Los Angeles with no knowledge of wildlife etiquette. He'd never ask me to accompany him on such an adventure again, I was sure of it.

The thought filled me with sadness.

At a farm off the highway, he grabbed his leather gloves and stepped out of the truck to consult with a man in a business suit beside a black Miata. I rolled down the window to hear their discussion.

"So basically, the chickens are in a pen and you've got to get them into this wire cage." The man pointed to a small square cage beside a walk-in chicken coop full of red hens. "I'm getting ready to go to a wedding, so I can't help you."

"No problem." Jonathan pulled on the gloves and positioned the portable cage so its door faced the door of the walk-in pen. I watched as he unhooked the gate and stepped inside. Immediately, the flock rushed him and, in an onslaught of feathers and feet, flew the coop.

"Crap." Jonathan ran after one, grabbed for it, and missed.

Over by his car, the farmer laughed. "Elusive little bastards, aren't they?"

Chickens scattered across the clodded dirt field. Jonathan chased one and then another, long legs flying out from under him as he snatched at the air. I couldn't help it—I began to laugh. Once I started, I couldn't stop.

He returned to the truck to find me scarlet-faced, choking with merriment over the baby owl scrabbling in its box. His unibrow thundered down over his nose. "You could get out and help."

Instantly sober, I set the box on the seat and climbed out of the truck. I knew how to wrangle poultry. When I was a kid, my mother had kept a flock of Rhode Island Reds in her suburban backyard to save money and attempt a return to her Missouri farming roots; the hens were forever busting out of their enclosure. I tied my ponytail more firmly atop my head and assessed the situation.

"I'll flush them out from under this thicket." I knelt down beside a tangle of blackberries and peered at a trio of hens. "Then you can grab them."

With me functioning as herd dog, Jonathan managed to catch two chickens—one under each arm—and put them in the small cage. It took us an hour to round up the rest. His hair stood on end, festooned with bits of blackberry vine and feathers. Dirt streaked my legs, and something that looked suspiciously like chicken shit spattered my sundress. My hair pulled loose from my ponytail and stuck to my sweaty cheeks.

You think you know what's going to bring you joy—a carefully orchestrated life spent reading and writing and running in a tranquil setting, far away from loss and the complications of relationship. But then you discover a different life—one that includes the very stuff you were running from, but also an unexpected reward. That day, my veil of grief began to lift, and I remembered how much I craved adventure and a sense of purpose . . . even if it looked like frozen rodents, doomed chickens, and unrequited love.

In the truck Jonathan assessed me. "You've got dirt on your face."

"It'll wash."

"Let's take 99 back to Eugene. It's not as crazy as I-5. Calmer for the animals."

"Fine with me."

In his truck on the way home, we talked quietly, so as not to scare the baby owl. Farms stretched out on either side of us, and for a time we found ourselves cruising along at twenty miles an hour behind a red tractor. I busied myself counting red-tailed hawks. "There's another one!" I yelped, pointing. "That's five in about five minutes."

He nodded. "I should get these rats up to the center. Want to come? Faster than dropping you off at my place first."

"Okay." I knit my fingers together, stretched my arms above my head to flex my aching trapezius muscles. "I don't have to interact with any birds, right?"

"Nah. But I heard we might have a baby sparred owl in—be fun to get a look at it."

"A what?"

"Mix of barred and spotted. Barreds have been moving across the country, and they've displaced some of our Northern spotted owls. It's a problem, but the hybrid thing's kind of cool. Our center's got a resident hybrid prairie-peregrine falcon." He gave me a sideways look. "Sometimes disparate species hook up in spite of themselves, you know?"

I shrugged. "I know nothing about birds."

"You know about chickens."

Abruptly, he pulled the truck over to the roadside.

"Shit, I think a couple got out." He jumped out and walked to the back of the truck. I attempted to reposition my ponytail, craning my neck to catch a glimpse of my sweaty face in the rearview mirror.

I'd grown up in two worlds—that of my father and stepmother, which rewarded a sort of sterile urbanity, and that of my mother with her sprawling vegetable garden and a legion of rescued chickens and rabbits and cats . . . the antithesis of glamor. I knew which I preferred; I returned the rearview mirror to its original position and gave up trying to look good. I felt just fine.

"False alarm." Jonathan got back into the truck, but he made no move to start the engine.

I stretched my arms over my head again, enjoying the ache of muscles well worked. A seam in the sleeve of my sundress gave way. To cover my embarrassment, I began to babble. "Sometimes we couldn't get my mother's chickens in at night, so we'd soak bread in gin and make little pellets. The hens would eat them and climb up onto the fence to go to sleep, and then . . ."

And then I had to stop talking because Jonathan, his stubbly chin speckled with mud and his hair spiked with red feathers, leaned over the clacking baby owl in its pet carrier and kissed me.

4

Obligate Carnivores

"I could fall for you."

I pressed my fingers against my lips, bruised from the force of our collision. "*Really?*"

Jonathan set the owl in its pet carrier gently on the floor and pulled me to him as another tractor rumbled past. "Really."

Highway 99 is a slow affair to begin with, what with the two-lane country road and laconic pickups and the occasional cow and duck parade crossing perpendicular to traffic. Still, Jonathan eased his truck over to the side about twenty times on the way back to Eugene so we could make out, stretching the two-hour trip into three, frozen rats be damned.

"You're adorable." He plucked blackberry detritus from my hair.

"I am?"

I bore no resemblance to those tanned, buxom, bouffanted babes on my ex's DVDs. Still, slowly, I began to believe Jonathan. My convictions against romantic entanglement on the rebound wavered. Here was a man I could learn from, who would challenge me to be better than my sorry self . . . and he was hot. In a sexy tenor gone hoarse with farm dirt, he whispered sweet nothings into my ear about raptors who mate for life. Primeval longing stirred within me.

"At the Wild Wings raptor center in New York," he said, pulling away at last, "there's a wild female red-tail with a crush on a permanently injured male that staff tether to a stump in the courtyard. She brings him dead squirrels."

The anecdote struck me as a test of sorts. If I failed to see the romance in it, we were through. Fortunately, a shiver of delight skittered over my neck and arms. I gazed up at Jonathan. "I'd bring *you* a dead squirrel."

From its pet carrier the baby owl clacked its beak, the sound like the slow applause of tiny hands.

In between make-out sessions, I buckled myself snug beside Jonathan in the middle of the bench seat and asked questions, quickly, wanting to know everything about him before we got back to Eugene.

"What got you interested in raptors?"

He steered with one knee, twisting the silver bird ring on his finger, scouting for another private wayside. "I used to go fishing up in Canada with my dad, and he'd point out red-tailed hawks. When I moved here I went to a festival and found the raptor center's booth. The director had a golden eagle on her glove." His hazel eyes glowed down at me in the afternoon sunlight. "Falconer's eagle, 'til it got injured. I'd never seen anything like it. It looked so strong, and yet so delicate. I wanted that bird on my glove, wanted a relationship with it."

"What's a falconer?"

Apparently, even my ignorance was adorable, as Jonathan pulled over under an oak tree and kissed me again. His tongue held an exotic flavor, intoxicating. I considered disrobing right there on the highway. But he pulled away and started the truck again, taking up the conversation where we'd left off.

"A falconer's someone who hunts with a raptor—it's an ancient sport from Asia. People still practice it all over the world. I've always wanted to try it."

"So why don't you?"

It seemed to me that day that he could do anything, be anything he wanted. Here was a man unconstrained by a full-time job, with the leisure to rescue baby owls and take photos of incense cones. Why *not* hunt with an eagle?

"What would you hunt?"

"Ducks, mostly, maybe rabbits."

I winced, thinking of my beloved childhood pet, Frisky, with his velvet fur and his lop ears and his willingness to lie still in my little sister's doll carriage. "Rabbits?"

"Yeah, but falconry's a huge time commitment. You've got to hunt with your raptor every day. Sometimes the telemetry—that's like remote control for your bird—messes up and the raptor gets lost. You can't take a vacation, even for a day, without finding someone you trust to care for your falcon or hawk. It's like a baby."

"Only cuter."

We laughed together easily now, reveling in the warmth of the late-spring sun and our antibreeder self-righteousness. "Kids," I scoffed.

Jonathan reached into his backpack with one hand. "Give me an eagle any day." He handed me two warm cans of Coke to crack open. Aware of his eyes on me, I drank.

<hr/>

The Cascades Raptor Center sits at the base of Spencer Butte, a collection of elegant wood and wire structures and a few small buildings half hidden among maple and fir trees. Its director, Louise Shimmel, gave up a career in international banking and began rehabilitating wildlife in her backyard. Eventually, she moved to the city-owned acreage where—with staff and hundreds of volunteers—she established a rehabilitation and education facility that now attracts thousands of visitors eager to see bald eagles and peregrine falcons and great horned owls up close.

That first day, I had no idea what to expect from the place. Jonathan urged his truck along the winding mountain road and turned up a steep driveway. He took his arm from around my shoulders. "Better pick up the owl." His warm, dusty voice took on a professional edge.

I lifted the pet carrier onto my lap. The bird scrabbled inside. Jonathan pulled into a parking space outside a pair of blue-roofed structures and pointed at the taller building. "That's the visitors' center. We'll take this guy into the clinic so the director can examine him."

He jumped out of the truck and took the pet carrier from me. I stood on the driveway beside a lawn ringed with flowering bushes. Several walk-in cages stood just beyond; I could see birds on branch perches behind black hardware wire.

"Gotta get this little guy inside." Jonathan strode toward the smaller building. I remained standing next to a weathered picnic table, unsure of whether to follow.

"What'cha doing?"

"Is that a crow?" A big black bird called to me from a large cage. Bright strings of beads and little mirrors dangled from branch perches.

"The crow's next to her." Jonathan pointed out a smaller black bird with a similar playroom setup.

The crow titled her head and looked at me, then bent and rang a little bell with her beak. "Well . . . ha ha ha ha!"

"They talk?"

The larger bird with the wedge-shaped tail chimed in again. "What'cha doing?"

"That's Zach, the raven. Corvids mimic people."

"Are they raptors?"

"Nope. Director took them in as a general rehabber, before she started focusing on raptors." Jonathan turned. "People raise them illegally—give them the wrong food, and they get bone disease."

"What's the right food?"

"*Not* hamburgers. You coming into the clinic, or what?"

The clinic appeared to be a catchall name for a tiny space functioning as a raptor meal preparation station, computer lab, volunteer lunchroom, and coat closet. Dead quail stretched out on pie plates on the counter, their gleaming pink breasts sprinkled with green powder—a mixture, Jonathan told me, of algae and vitamins lost when prey was frozen and then thawed. A PC stood on a desk surrounded by a flood of leather gloves and soda cans and brochures and a half-consumed package of Oreos. The screen saver flashed photo after photo of raptors standing on Astroturf-covered perches or standing upright on people's gloved arms. Two small cages took up the far end of the clinic. In one a blue-gray bird—a kestrel?—chirped from a branch. The other cage stood empty.

"For the baby owl." Jonathan set the carrier on the desk and logged in on the computer. "He'll stay there until he's old enough to go outside. After he's learned to hunt, we'll take him back up to Portland and release him close to where people found him."

He tossed an empty applesauce container into the trash can, releasing a potpourri of garbage, cigarettes, and fish. Undaunted by the stench that nearly felled me, he reached for a syringe in a box beside a scattering of owl-decorated mugs. He filled it with something from a tube extracted from a dorm-size refrigerator, then picked up a phone on a file cabinet next to a couple of bundles wrapped in black plastic. "Owl's here."

He hung up and addressed me with stoic indifference, as if we hadn't just spent three hours exchanging our hopes and histories and saliva. "Director wants me to take him into the treatment room. You can stand outside and watch."

He pushed through a screen door into an even smaller room and placed the owl in its box on a stainless steel exam table. The treatment room reminded me of the vet's office—only instead of an empty space devoted solely to me and my cat or dog, there were large plastic pet carriers stacked on two counters, each covered with a sheet.

"What's in those?"

"Injured birds. Who's this?" Louise, her round, pleasant face framed by silvering shoulder-length hair, walked into the treatment room and gave me a swift assessment before turning to the cardboard carrier.

"Her name's Melissa." Jonathan set the box on a scale and penciled the weight on a printed sheet. "She's with me. Okay if she watches?"

"If she's quiet."

The discussion—conducted as if I weren't standing right there in my mud-and-chicken-shit-streaked sundress and ruined sandals—gave me a peculiar out-of-body feeling. I saw myself peering wide-eyed into the room as Jonathan lifted a ball of brownish fluff from the box and held it, one ankle in each hand, its back and head against his chest. A tiny yellow beak stuck out from the creature's amorphous face; it opened soundlessly. I squeaked in surprise, and the director glanced at me.

"Sorry."

Louise checked the owl's eyes and pressed her fingers gently into its downy chest.

"She's feeling its keel—that's the bone that runs down the middle of a bird's chest—to check its body condition. If the baby's emaciated, the keel will sort of stick out. The muscles around it shrink if a bird is starving."

Jonathan wedged his thumbs into the corners of the yellow beak. The owl struggled a moment, then stilled. Louise threaded a long tube down its throat and pushed the plunger to administer the clear liquid in the syringe. She shifted her position, blocking the owl from my view.

"She's giving him an electrolyte solution," Jonathan explained. "To rehydrate him. We'll give it to him several times over the next day or so."

That, I understood. For any run over six miles, I chugged a bottle of Gatorade. "Dehydration's awful." I turned to a whiteboard covered with a cryptic arrangement of letters and numbers. Under it, in a long plastic box, I glimpsed what appeared to be two black-and-white rabbits . . . dead.

I gripped the file cabinet, let my forehead drop briefly to the cool surface, then looked up. Two black plastic-wrapped bundles sat beside me. "GHO73?" I read the letters and numbers printed on masking tape affixed to one package.

Jonathan walked out of the treatment room. "Great horned owl 73. Electrocution case."

I backed into a closet full of leather gloves. "Those are dead birds?"

The director stuck her head out the door. "Jonathan, write down three ccs of EHS every four hours."

He printed some code on the whiteboard and beckoned me out the door. At his truck he pulled out a cigarette and lit it with a plastic lighter.

"You *smoke?*"

"Been trying to quit. Hold on—I'll give you a tour." He exhaled carefully away from me.

I had to tell him this wasn't for me. I didn't do smoking, and I didn't do death. It would be better—really, it would—to just take me home and we could get it on, then call it a day. He could go back to his plastic-wrapped owls, his rabbit corpses, his dead quail on plates, and I could zip into my raccoon costume and teach little kids about slugs and lichen and other living stuff.

Instead, I heard myself chirp, "Sure, I'd love a tour!"

"We'll start with the prey barn."

We walked under a canopy of newly leafed maple trees to a large shed. He opened the door, but I held back, stymied by the sharp smell of mouse urine. Twenty or so aquariums lined two walls of the room, each housing a bunch of mice who scampered on exercise wheels, gnawed on pellets, licked at the round metal ends of water bottles, and curled up with cage mates in piles of newspaper.

Jonathan explained that the center, to cut costs and provide birds with fresh food, raised its own prey animals. "Not rabbits and rats," he explained. "They need too much space. But we always have chicks and mice. We volunteers spend hours a day cleaning their cages, making sure the prey's comfortable."

I winced. My mother had once raised a litter of baby mice discovered in a thrift store couch cushion. I'd adored one in particular—a silky black-and-white creature who rode around in my sweatshirt pocket. Mom had been going through a church phase at the time; Sundays, we attended Unitarian services in the Ventura foothills. I begged to be absolved from the children's room with its esoteric pinecone art and Dixie cups of Kool-Aid. She allowed me to sit beside her among the adults, and so it was that one morning we stood up to belt out some Cat Stevens song and I took my hand out of my pocket and opened it to reveal my mouse. Its pink nose twitched up at my mother. She smothered such a torrent of laughter that nearly she wet her pants.

I told Jonathan this story, and he shut the door behind us and kissed me deeply. Now I recognized the smell and taste of tobacco. I had to admit that it wasn't entirely unpleasant.

Beside us a tower of cages housing baby chicks peeped beseechingly. I stuck my finger through a hole and stroked the yellow fluff on their backs. "It's like Easter in here."

"We euthanize them at seven or fourteen days old and pack them into bags in the freezer."

"*Not* like Easter. I need some fresh air."

I pushed out the door, hands pressed against my stomach.

Jonathan followed. "You sick?"

"No . . . it's just . . . why can't the raptors eat tofu? I mean, do you have to kill fluffy babies?"

His unibrow shot up. "Raptors are obligate carnivores. They have to eat meat, or they'll die. Tofu," he added, anticipating my argument, "isn't a protein most of them are willing to eat. Plus, it doesn't give them the nutrients they need."

I got that. During my first months in Eugene, I'd made vegetarian pet food by hand. The dogs scarfed it up, but the cats caterwauled at my millet-tofu surprise. Felines, like raptors, need meat to survive. Still, I found myself wondering again about the peculiar form of social Darwinism at work in this rehab joint. An owl's life mattered more than that of a lovely long-haired black-and-white mouse?

Jonathan steered me away from the prey barn and up the path toward several small enclosures, each obscured by black netting. "Let me show you the rehab mews. This is where we keep injured birds who've got a chance of returning to the wild. Visitors aren't usually allowed back here—we try to keep things quiet so these guys can heal."

The visiting privileges mollified me. He walked to a mew labeled R-3. Inside, I heard shuffling and clacking. "Screech owls. Whenever I feed them, they sit on the perch and chatter like the Three Stooges."

He looked around. "Go ahead, take a peek."

He opened the door a crack and moved a strip of shade cloth an inch out of the way. Inside, I saw a trio of fist-size tawny owls lined up on a branch, feathers sticking up comically on top of their heads. "This is what lives in my cedar. I had no idea they were so small. They're adorable. What's wrong with them?"

"Orphaned."

"How come?"

He closed the door. "Oh, someone cuts down a tree and there's a nest in it. Or a bird lays eggs in straw bales on a flatbed, and the driver discovers them when he stops for the night. The parents might get stuck in barbed wire or hit by cars, and then the babies languish. Gotta go check on the little barred now, and then I'll take you home. You can hang out on the lawn while you wait . . ."

He paused at the clinic and regarded me. "Or come back in."

I moved to the door and leaned against it, noncommittal, watching him attack bloodied, feathered pie plates in the sink with a scrub brush. A good sign, I thought—he washes dishes.

A young woman in black braids and cutoffs strode by me, spine straight and shoulders squared in the manner of someone who keeps regular dates with a yoga mat. She carried a pie pan full of quail. "These did *not* get algae," she snapped.

She slammed the plate down so that the little pink corpses bounced and upended a shaker of green powder. The kestrel chirped from the indoor cage and the woman lifted her head, walked over to an aquarium, and plucked a mealworm from sawdust with her bare fingers. She handed the writhing thing through the cage bars to the bird, who chirped again and gobbled it down.

This was the woman Jonathan should share his life with—this bold, fearless beauty with fierce, flashing eyes. "If you're not coming in," she told me, "shut the door. A bird could get out, and there're *flies*."

"Sorry." I closed it and found myself on the wrong side, back in the clinic. I felt awkward and enormous, baffled by what to do with my body. Jonathan walked into the treatment room with a plate full of skinned, cut-up something and invited me to follow.

"There're no birds out, right?"

"Nope. I'm just giving the baby owl some food."

I knelt and peeked through one side of the plastic pet carrier as he set the gruesome snack tray on newspaper inside. The fuzzy baby sat, dark eyes half-lidded, and clacked his beak at us. "It's fun to see them grow up." Jonathan's eyes met mine. "It's not all about death here, Melissa."

He stood up and draped the sheet over the carrier. We stepped out of the treatment room. The woman still stood there with her pie pan full of quail, glaring down at a clipboard. "Did Sam feed the osprey or not? Honestly, people, write your shit down." She tossed her head so that her braids whipped around, then jerked her chin at me. "New volunteer?"

I shook my head. "Just visiting."

She smirked at my sundress. "Thought so."

"That's Darcy." Outside, we walked toward Jonathan's truck. "Been volunteering a while. She's kind of a hard-ass."

"Yeah. Wait." I gripped his sleeve. "Who is *that*?"

He followed my eyes to a lower mew. "That's Juno. She's a great horned owl."

"Alive," I breathed. The screech owls were cute, the baby barred fluffy and precious. But this bird—two feet of black and brown and white feathers culminating in twin head tufts above a white V-shaped brow—compelled me to walk down the gravel path and press my face against the wire side of the enclosure. I gazed up at the creature on the Astroturf perch. "She's . . . stunning."

Suddenly, I understood Jonathan's desire to form a meaningful relationship with a bird. Juno looked magnificently feline. Later, I'd learn that the Chinese word for owl, *mao tou ying*, translates as "cat-headed hawk." And I'd never met a cat I hadn't wanted to possess, body and soul.

Other people talk about seeing their first Persian cat, their first poodle or tiger or boa constrictor, and feeling a shift—some conscious decision to invite the species into their world. After seeing a great horned owl inches from my eyes, my life would never be the same. But I didn't know that then.

Juno swiveled her head far around to look in my direction. A cough escaped me. She leaped in a rush of feathers to the ceiling of her enclosure and hung upside down by enormous talons, beak open and white chest heaving.

"She's scared of humans," Jonathan told me. "We'd better leave her alone."

Reluctantly, I followed him back to his truck. "Why don't you volunteer here? The people are great. You'd like them, and you'd learn a bunch about the birds." Down the hill he slowed to let a doe and two fawns cross the road. I watched them disappear into green underbrush. "What d'you think?"

What did I think? In spite of Juno, I thought he and his whole mouse-murdering, chick-slaughtering, raptor-wrapping squad were insane.

He reached up under his sun visor and handed me a photo. "Owl release."

In the picture he stood at the edge of a golden field, gloved arms outstretched, as a big, whitish owl sailed away from him into blue sky. Around him people stood with hands frozen in applause, smiles spread across their faces.

"A family found the owl stuck in a steel trap, and we worked with it for months 'til it could fly again." He replaced the picture under the visor.

"Makes it all worth it when you realize you've helped them return to the wild for a second chance."

He pulled up behind my car. The orange Isuzu looked garish—the car of some silly Los Angeles party girl concerned with appearance rather than substance. I felt like a different person from the woman who had parked there that morning—smarter, dirtier, more audacious . . . and ridiculously smitten with this man.

"So . . ." Jonathan dipped his head down and nuzzled my neck. "Do you want to volunteer?"

Sometimes love's obligations aren't immediately apparent. What's needed—what's, in fact, crucial—can take a while to reveal itself.

That afternoon, still ignorant, I leaned over and kissed Jonathan good-bye and hopped out of the truck.

"Thanks, but no," I told him. "I'll stick to being a raccoon."

5

Rehabilitation

BUT SOON, BECAUSE MY WAYWARD HEART LATCHED ONTO A RAPTOR rehabilitator, I—terrified of beaks and talons—found myself standing in a tiny room that stank of raw meat, cradling an injured and royally pissed-off great horned owl against my chest.

I'd lasted a few months in the slightly less gruesome role of didactic raccoon for the children's nature nonprofit. I liked the kids who gathered around my furry tail and listened to my stories of foraging for fish and garbage, but the costume's foam head, combined with the pollens from my field classroom beside the Willamette River, sent me into wild coughing fits that unsettled the students. During one of my talks, a boy ran away from me screaming, "Mommy, that raccoon has rabies!"

"Maybe this isn't the best costume for you." My supervisor handed me a cough drop. "You might be more comfortable as our spider."

I considered my options. Again, my new boyfriend invited me to volunteer at the raptor center. My divorce had become official, and we spent nights together at his studio or my bungalow. My own queen-size mattress felt forbidden, fraught with too many memories of my ex. Jonathan's and my lovemaking felt even more illicit conducted on the dog bed in the living room.

During the day, school and dog park and raptor obligations took up his time, so I agreed to sign up—"on a trial basis," I cautioned—to scrub bird poop off cages. "If we work the same shift," I reasoned, "we might at least see each other in the daytime, and not just at the park or in bed."

He kissed me, settling my head against his bare chest. "We say mutes, not poop," he murmured in my ear. "And not cages. Mews."

The raptor center had twenty-plus mews under canopies of trees. Volunteers had built the tall, wide structures from donated two-by-fours and hardware cloth. Long perches swathed in Astroturf stretched across each immaculate space, with tree stumps and water troughs and the occasional shrub springing up out of the gravel floors.

As a cleaner of mews, I'd be concerned with this base surface. Raptors were messy eaters. Much as a seafood aficionado might wrangle a crab into submission, leaving a macabre wake of claws and shell fragments, the birds ripped feathers, wings, tails, and feet from their prey with powerful beaks. Unable to digest these parts, they tossed them to the ground. I'd function as a busgirl of sorts, picking up the superfluous remnants of supper.

"What if the raptors attack me while I'm cleaning? Darcy told me the bald eagle could break my wrist with its grip." I touched the bandage on Jonathan's arm, where an injured owl had nailed him with a talon before he could get a good grip on her ankles in the treatment room.

He turned his truck up the steep driveway. "They're more afraid of you than you are of them. They won't hurt you."

I'd never been attacked by a bird, never viewed Hitchcock's avian bloodbath, never even been bitten by a dog. Still, I feared the unpredictability of raptors and their ability to do some serious damage to my body. In college, and for several years afterward, I'd worked with severely disabled people in group homes and schools; unable to speak and struggling with cognitive delays, my clients lashed out at their caregivers like wild creatures. I'd had my hair yanked, my arms wrenched, my head struck with bars of soap; once, a young man from the state hospital tried to strangle me as I drove him to the courthouse. I knew how vulnerable beings compelled by fear and anxiety could injure a caregiver, regardless of her good intentions, and I'd learned never to turn my back.

I assumed raptors would be as volatile.

Still, I resolved to trust Jonathan as far as I could, aware that if I kept freaking out about the birds' sharp parts, I'd lose him to Darcy—the acerbic volunteer with her braids and hirsute armpits and courage.

He parked and pointed to the larger building with a sloping blue metal roof. "The volunteer coordinator wants to meet you in there for an interview. Don't worry—she talks with all the volunteers before they start."

I stepped out of the truck, craned my neck for a glimpse of the great horned owl, Juno, in her mew. A brown shape perched in one corner, feather tufts lowered. She looked like a sleeping cat. In the enclosure closest to me, a little gray-and-blue bird chirped and bobbed behind wire. "Kestrel?" I tried.

"Yep. That's Toto. He's been here a while—he's a terrific ed bird."

An ed bird referred to a resident raptor who was calm enough to sit on a perch or gloved arm for an educational presentation at the center. The kestrel regarded me through one shining eye and chirped.

I chirped back. "Is he happy living here at the center?"

"You're assuming birds feel happiness." Darcy strode by in rubber boots and her cutoffs, brandishing a garden hose. "Thou shalt not anthropomorphize."

"Pardon me?" Jonathan shook his head slightly and extracted a cigarette from the ever-present pack in his pocket.

"I'll take one of those." Darcy reached for his lighter, flicked it expertly, and then walked off.

I frowned at this unexpected nicotine covenant.

"Oh, Melissa, don't worry about it." He turned to exhale away from me and Toto.

The kestrel turned his head to look at a songbird on a nearby feeder. I saw a flesh-covered patch where one eye had been.

"Cat caught." Jonathan pointed out the biographical signage in front of the kestrel's mew. "Raised by humans illegally. Vet couldn't save the eye. Outside every enclosure there's a natural and personal history of the birds. You can study them as you're cleaning."

From the sign I learned that kestrels like to perch on telephone wires and swoop down to open fields, snatching prey from the ground. Were I to nail up a nest box on my property, I might attract one. But the diagnosis of "cat caught" stopped me. I let my cats roam free, and for that privilege they occasionally gifted me with a dead vole or starling lying in state on the front porch. I'd never thought about them maiming some little kestrel. I wondered if Jonathan might help me build an enclosure so they could revel in the outdoors without committing murder or disfigurement.

I entwined my fingers in his. "So the birds here stay for life?"

"Not the ones in the rehab mews, but yeah, our raptors on display, for sure. They all have permanent injuries."

He walked up to the raven's mew and chortled. The bird trilled back, rattling a bell that dangled from a perch. "Also raised illegally by humans," he reminded me. "Look around—they've got missing eyes, bad wings, bum legs, developmental stuff. We've got two white-tailed kites 'cause they got stuck in a nest box during a California heat wave and the sun fried their brains. None of these birds can hunt in the wild . . . they'd starve. We keep them on display to educate and inspire visitors."

"D'you hand-feed them?"

"We put euthanized prey on their feeding platforms."

A limp brown mouse lay on the plywood next to Toto's mew door. Somehow, that rodent had to get from wherever it had been killed to the platform. I feared that such a transaction would now involve me.

I lowered my voice, seeing Darcy in the distance with her hose. "Can I use tongs to pick up the dead mice and rats?"

"Not unless you want to get laughed at. We've got gloves." He bent and kissed me, his breath fragrant with tobacco and spearmint gum. "Good luck in your interview. I've gotta go fix a perch in the eagles' mew."

"Watch your wrists."

We parted—he to perform his handyman duties, I to chat with the volunteer coordinator on a musty, sprung couch in the visitors' center.

"I just want to clean mews." I took in the woman's close-cropped orange hair, her faded sweatshirt and filthy sneakers, her blue jeans stained with spots of blood. She looked like an extra in a zombie film.

She regarded my skinny jeans, pink tie-dyed T-shirt, and sandals with equal horror. I looked ready to shop and lounge over a latte on the Santa Monica Promenade—not get down and dirty with birds of prey. "I don't want to pick up the raptors or prepare their food or kill anything," I began.

She squinted at me, and I got the impression of lying under a microscope like a feather, or a fecal sample. Jonathan had told me that some volunteers were tough older women who'd raised children to adulthood. Cutting up a euthanized rat paled in comparison to the terrors they'd endured as mothers.

The coordinator lowered herself into a folding chair and scowled over my application. Several parrots squawked from the director's apartment, separated from the visitors' center by a glass door. Louise lived on the property, immersed in the raptors and their welfare twenty-four, seven. Not only did she take in injured raptors and nurse them back to health; she also wrote grants and newsletters, oversaw fundraising projects, trained education birds, maintained an international listserv of rehabilitators, and fed orphaned baby owls at three in the morning. Reluctant to turn away a needy animal, she'd also acquired several cats and parrots who shared her living space.

The parrots' sausage-shape silhouettes bobbed and strutted behind the curtain. I recalled again my uncle's parrot, Stella, and shivered.

A parrot I recognized as an African gray, like the one from TV who could tell colors and shapes, began to climb the curtain; it hooked its tiny nails into the fabric and pulled itself upward. A fearful apparition with a naked plucked head peered out at me, then let out a resounding belch.

I choked back laughter.

"Read this and initial, all right?" The coordinator handed me a printed list of rules. Volunteering was a job: be on time, find a replacement if you have to miss a shift, don't gossip about fellow volunteers. The comfort and safety of the raptors—both permanent and those recovering with the goal of release—always take priority.

Up until that moment, I hadn't thought a whole lot about the responsibility of working in wildlife rehabilitation. Now I saw that I'd be directly accountable—amateur as I was—for these creatures' lives. Forget her rat, and Juno would go hungry. Miss a shift, and the chicks might go without water refills in the warm prey barn. Leave a mew door open, and a one-eyed kestrel could fly away forever.

It would be a relief, I thought as I initialed the paper, to care for something besides myself and my pets again. But birds of prey?

In a glass case beside the couch, three owl skeletons perched companionably. Their skinny, fragile bones jutted backward into wings. Cervical vertebrae—fourteen as opposed to our seven—snaked high up into skulls with bulging eye sockets. I could see the single bone atop the vertebrae that allowed an owl like Juno to pivot her head 270 degrees either way. Without feathers and skin the owls didn't look so formidable. They could've been a trio of buddies hanging out, waiting for a bus. I half expected one of them to pull out a pack of cigarettes.

"Can you commit to a four-hour shift every week?" The coordinator tightened her lips, pen poised over an owl-embossed day planner. "We run three shifts a day, seven days a week, every day of the year."

"Every day?"

She clucked her tongue against her teeth. "Raptors don't stop eating and needing fresh water and clean mews just because it's Christmas. Someone's gotta be here to care for them."

"They're like children."

The comparison seemed to me apt, but her scowl deepened. "No, they're wild animals. It's important that the public see them that way, as well. We won't want anyone trying to keep a raptor as a pet. That's a guaranteed disaster for everyone concerned."

I'd grown up around anthropomorphic animals in literature. Talking bunnies, squabbling duckies, irate hedgehogs—Beatrix Potter's images informed my understanding of animals, corroborated by E. B. White's eloquent spider and earnest pig and Orwell's *Animal Farm*. Still, I'd read that Beatrix boiled her deceased pets to study their bone structure. If she could remain unsentimental about the real thing as opposed to her literary creations, then I could, too.

The phone rang, and the coordinator paused, one hand on the cordless at her hip. Inside the apartment the director answered the call. The African gray chimed in from its position at the top of the curtain. "Hello, honey."

I bit my knuckles. A smile flickered across the coordinator's face, replaced by a deeper scowl.

"You'll be asked to help out with whatever's needed. Mostly, you'll clean mews, but we'll also ask you to repair perches, clean the gift shop, help with newsletter mailings. If there's no one else around, we might send you out to rescue an injured bird, all right?"

I pictured a siren mounted atop my orange Isuzu, me racing down the road with the theme song to *Knight Rider* blasting from the speakers as I came to the aid of a helpless, naked fledgling fallen from a tree. Then I remembered the talons.

"Um . . . all right."

"We'll expect you every Tuesday from noon to four." She shot me a piercing stare. "You know that's *not* Jonathan's shift . . ."

I knew. In the year after his fiancée left him and he lost his job and his house burned down, he'd begun to work Sunday mornings, reveling in the solitude of a shift no one else wanted. "I forget about everything else when I'm up here," he told me. "It's just me and the birds." From eight to noon he scrubbed mews, cleaned the prey barn, and did odd jobs around the center. He referred to the four hours, which often lengthened into eight, as his "church."

He preferred to worship alone, and so I signed up for a Tuesday afternoon shift instead.

"I'll be here noon to four, every week."

"Good." The woman shifted position, and I saw the pink rhinestone ribbon pinned to the collar of her T-shirt. Now her thin hair and gaunt cheekbones made more sense. I wondered if she, too, regarded the raptor center as some sort of bizarre sanctuary high above the mundane cruelties of the world.

She looked once more at my paperwork, at my sandals. "You know . . . you're gonna get filthy."

"I'm fine with that." More than fine. I looked forward to absolution from my computer, to the chance to get my hands dirty, to move about in nature the way I had as a girl in my mother's backyard.

"Well . . . let's go into the clinic and get you logged in."

She led me out of the visitors' center, down the stone steps, and across the driveway to the clinic. She paused beside a trio of hanging pots clustered with pink begonias. A hummingbird darted in to sip, its body a riot of pinks and greens so close that I could hear the vibration of wings. "Look." The coordinator tapped one dirty sneaker, and the bird flew off. "I'm concerned you might be afraid of the raptors, and that's not good. You'll be close to bald eagles, for instance, sometimes a foot away cleaning the mew. If you're distracted by fear, accidents could happen."

I shook my head. This blood-stained veteran was offering me an easy way out. But I couldn't accept it.

"I *have* to do this."

Her eyebrows lifted. Sudden pink circles stained her papery cheeks. "Oh. Sorry. I thought you were just Jon's girlfriend. I didn't realize the court had sent you to do community service. Usually, I'm told . . ."

"What? No!"

"So . . . you didn't commit a crime?"

"No."

How could I convey to her that the position meant so much more than retaining my charming new boyfriend? My whole sense of self-worth stood at stake. I'd fled from my grandmother's sickbed four days before her passing to buy a house in Oregon. Cancer had turned her comatose; I knew I'd likely never see her again, and I left my mother alone with her, too scared of illness and death to say good-bye. A dark shame slunk with me to the Northwest, beginning to retreat only after I agreed to commit to this volunteer position that scared the crap out of me.

"I don't mind getting close to the birds." I tossed my stubby ponytail in imitation of Darcy.

"Well . . . all right." The coordinator pushed open the clinic door. I unclipped my silver hoop earrings and slipped them into my pocket lest an errant beak or talon get stuck in them. It wouldn't do to go to the ER with an eagle tangled in my jewelry.

She dropped a stray bottle cap into the trash can, and again, the smell of fish and cigarettes hit me in the face. My eyes flew to the file cabinet. No plastic-wrapped bodies lay there today.

I turned my attention to the rescued baby barred owl, now sitting on a branch perch in one of the small indoor mews. He stood taller, still fluffy, with mild chocolate-brown eyes. I saw how his striated feather pattern different from the splotches on the pair of Northern spotted owls at the center—this guy sported bars instead of spots.

I walked toward him. He clacked his beak. Did he recognize me as his traveling companion on the long, romantic ride down from Portland?

No. I willed myself not to anthropomorphize. He was just a bird, and despite his fledgling status, he packed some seriously sharp heat.

The coordinator bent over the computer and typed in my name. "At our annual picnic we give a certificate for the most hours volunteered.

Clock in each time you come and go." She stretched a plastic bag over a small bucket and thrust it toward me. "You'll need this."

Jonathan walked in with an empty pie plate. On his fingertips, smudges of green vitamin powder and blood. "How's it going?" He moved to the sink and scrubbed briefly, then reached for an Oreo from the package on the desk. From his pocket he produced two latex gloves and a padlock key. "Ready to start?"

I thought of how he'd asked me that same question the night before, after we finished a bottle of mead and collapsed, hooting with laughter, on the dog bed.

"Yes, sir." I bit back a smile and pulled on the gloves. "Thanks for your help!" I called into the treatment room.

The volunteer coordinator stood hunched over a chart. Her shoulders twitched.

"It's my job."

"We'll start with the screech owls." Jonathan pushed out the door with a pan full of gray-feathered quail carcasses, some of them cut in two and trailing pinkish guts. "Those owls are so small that they only get half."

Western screech owls are as common as dogs in Eugene, adapting easily to suburbia with its ready supply of insects and songbirds. Jonathan imitated their call for me, a delicate sound like a bouncing ping-pong ball, but loud—the same call that floated down from the cedar over my bedroom. At night, now, I opened my window to hear it. Amazing that such a small bird could resonate like that; they stand only eight inches tall, about as heavy as an apple, with tiny feather tufts atop their heads to help them camouflage on branches. Screech owls prefer the ease of small prey, but I'd read that sometimes they catch animals larger than themselves, such as rabbits and ducks. I tried to picture one of the little birds flying with a mallard in its talons . . . impossible.

In the month since I'd first visited the raptor center, staff had released the three orphaned screech owls from the rehabilitation mew into the forest. The two birds in the mew in front of me, however, would never fly free.

"I know they're permanently injured," I said, unlocking the door and gripping my bucket in one hand, "but they could still scalp me, right?"

Jonathan stood outside the mew. "Go in, Melissa. They're fine. I promise I'll stay right here."

I pushed open the first of two doors. Every mew, he explained, had an entryway and double doors to prevent fly-offs.

"Fly-offs?"

"Sure."

"And then what happens?"

"Well . . . if we didn't catch it, the bird would eventually die. Our birds are too injured to hunt, remember?"

"Yikes. No pressure." I stood in the foyer next to a rake and a bleach bottle. "What're these for?"

"The bleach is for the water trough; there's a scrub brush in the corner. The rake's for after you pick up mouse tails, quail guts, whatever. You're supposed to smooth the gravel floor."

"Like a Zen rock garden." I closed the outer door and slipped into the main mew.

The owls remained on their perch, blinking at me through tiny yellow eyes. "So I'm just supposed to pick up the carnage . . ." I looked at the gravel littered with streaks of whitish mutes and feathered and furred bits.

"Yep."

I bent and plucked a bright yellow chick wing off the floor. "Oh . . . ew." Nothing in my life had prepared me for the sensation of picking up a disembodied rat tail. It hit the bottom of the bucket with a thud.

Above me the owls clacked their black beaks. "That means they're anxious. Move a little more slowly, love."

I sucked in a breath and let my right hand meander toward a scaly yellow chicken foot, placing it silently in the bucket. One of the birds burbled. I winced and glanced up. The larger owl was missing an eye. "What happened to him?"

"She's a she. In the raptor world females are larger than males."

Jonathan spoke in what I'd begun to refer to as his Barry White voice, deep and quiet so as not to scare the birds. Had I not been trying to extricate a long, sticky strand of mouse guts from the gravel, I might have gone weak in the knees. As it was, I bit down on my tongue and willed myself not to throw up. "She was raised illegally by people who had a cat, and it caught her. She can fly, but a one-eyed bird can't hunt."

"Like the kestrel." I straightened up muscle by muscle and studied the owl. Her solitary eye peered back at me. I remembered those moments in which my disabled students' wildness dissipated; unafraid for an instant, we met each other's gaze and rested in the comfort of connection.

Compassion sneaked up on me. I knew what it was like to see only half the world.

"Here, give me a quail." I opened the mew door a crack. "I think she's hungry."

Jon handed me two halves. I took the chilly carcasses between thumb and forefinger and set them on the plywood platform near the door.

"*Bon appétit.*" I grabbed my slaughterhouse bucket and tiptoed out of the mew.

Two months I worked to prove myself worthy of Jonathan on my Tuesday afternoon shifts. I discovered the pleasure of sitting quietly outside the great horned owl's mew to watch Juno swiveling her head and gazing at flies and kids and me from her high perch. I longed for a connection to her, but she'd come to the center a truly wild bird, not human habituated or imprinted like some of the others. When she heard my key click in the padlock and saw my pie plate of food, she flew to her ceiling and hung. I cleaned her mew swiftly, back hunched against the possibility of an attack, should my clumsy movements offend. My hand, as I picked up a rodent's hind leg, trembled. I left her rat or quail on the feeding platform in supplication and backed out of the mew; the instant she heard my key turn, she flew toward the food and tore in with that robust yellow beak.

Below us I could hear the city's cars and sirens and sometimes music from an outdoor concert. But here at the raptor center, peace prevailed. Volunteers reminded visitors to walk slowly, speak quietly so as not to scare volatile creatures. Sometimes I went four hours without speaking, simply moving from mew to mew with my bucket and hose. I could now understand why people spent twenty and thirty hours a week volunteering: Serving injured birds, we became part of something larger than ourselves—something that felt sacred. I went home at night covered in dirt and bird shit and scrubbed happily, murmuring prayers of gratitude in the shower.

—❦—

When Jonathan and I weren't volunteering, we courted. A collarless black cat followed him home on a walk with Cody, and we adopted it, naming him Iago after a trip down to Ashland for the Oregon Shakespeare Festival. On the long summer evenings, I sat in his studio with the windows thrown open and read his grad school papers on Foucault and looked at his newest photos while he made ratatouille and bread in his tiny kitchen. He spent nights at my house, helping me fix a broken water pipe and my screen door, then staying over to share a bottle of mead. We moved to my bedroom. I learned to make vegan cheesecake—a dessert his lactose-sensitive stomach could tolerate—and dairy-free lasagna. Eventually, he gave up his bachelor pad and moved in—the decision anticlimactic compared to the proposition that followed.

In bed one Sunday morning, he lifted Iago from his chest and turned off the alarm—his seven-thirty signal to get up and prepare for his shift at the raptor center. Our most recent rescue, a stunning long-haired black cat we'd named Alger Hiss, remained purring on my pillow while the tabbies yowled for food in the kitchen. "My favorite word in the world," I yawned, still half asleep, "is *meow*."

Jonathan let this pass, a more pressing topic on his mind. On Sunday he usually jumped out of bed and into the shower, barely pausing to dry his hair before pulling on his clothes and bolting out the door for a drive-thru hazelnut latte to fuel his shiftwork. But now he sat on the bed and looked at me with excitement in his eyes. His hair, cut short for summer, stood up like the one-eyed screech owl's feather tufts. "Hey, love." He spoke casually, his tone belying the significance of his next words. "Want to start volunteering with me Sundays?"

"What? Yes!" I leaped off the bed. Spooked, the dogs yelped and raced down the hall. Alger skittered under the dresser, hissing.

"I get to volunteer with you!" I threw my arms around Jonathan and kissed his stubbled cheek. "I thought you'd never ask!"

My sister, Katie, laughed when I told her. "God, sis, you act like he asked you to marry him."

"It's the same thing."

In asking me to share his shift, Jonathan had welcomed me into his sanctuary. Now we'd emerge together at noon—mute-covered and feather-festooned—an exhausted, exhilarated congregation of two. "He's made the ultimate commitment!"

My sister remained unconvinced. "I'm sorry—scrubbing poop and feeding dead stuff to birds is not the ultimate commitment. I'm married. I know."

How could she fathom, in her Orange County condo with her handsome triathlete husband, the joy of waking up early Sunday and heading out in grubby clothes for lattes at the coffee kiosk before the shift we now shared?

That first morning, we carried our steaming cups into the clinic, kissing over quail carcasses until Darcy glared at us. "Guys," she snapped, "get a room."

Still, she no longer referred to me as "Jon's girlfriend." I was Melissa, and if I was around, I could jolly well run to the prey barn and choose four brown mice for the barn owl who'd collided with a car and broken its leg. I didn't love the idea of playing God to small rodents, but teamwork necessitated some cooperation, and Juno and the others needed to eat or they'd expire.

At raptor centers across the world, volunteers and staff feed out hundreds of mice and rats and chicks and quail a day. Businesses such as the Gourmet Rodent ship caseloads of frozen bodies every day so that injured birds of prey can live. My delicate sensibilities, my little issues with death, weren't going to change this.

"I can't euthanize them, though," I told Darcy. "It's against my . . . um . . . religion."

She rolled her eyes on the way to the homemade euthanasia chamber in the bathroom. "Whatever."

With Jonathan as shift partner, I found myself more than a mere cleaner of mews. I threw myself into serving the live prey. Jonathan showed me how to refresh the barn, lifting the mice gently from the aquariums into a holding tank, then changing their sawdust bedding and food pellets and water. Sometimes I discovered half-inch pink babies, purple eye buds bulging, nestled under a cardboard box. Jonathan picked up each naked body in his fingertips and set it in an empty food bowl, returning the brood to a shredded-newspaper nest with their mother.

"They may be destined as dinner," he said, "but that's no reason they shouldn't have a good life while they're here."

I learned to clean the chick houses, too—to pull out the unwieldy metal trays under their cages and strip the foul newspaper, breath held against the sharp smell of urine. One volunteer brought her old copies of the *New York Times* to put down under the birds, and Jonathan and I stood and read articles to each other beside the peeping babies.

Volunteers on the shift after ours liked to get there early to sit on the carcass freezer and smoke and trade war stories, which grew to near legend, about treatment room disasters worthy of a *Times* front page. I caught fragments on my way out of the prey barn.

Once, Darcy reported, a volunteer leaned over a barn owl on the table to wrap its broken wing, and the bird reached up and embedded its talons into her cheek. It took three people to free her, unlocking the owl's hock joint and extracting the talons one by one. Another time, a woman bent down to a pet carrier to examine a hawk's eye and it bit her lip, holding on until another volunteer could get a thumb inside its beak to pry it off.

"At one center," I heard someone say, "an injured great blue heron poked a woman's eye out with its beak."

"You've just got to use common sense," Jonathan assured me. "Be aware of the bird's sharp parts at all times."

"Like you?" I looked at the Band-Aid on his finger where a feisty great horned owl with a punctured shoulder had bit him as he dosed it with electrolytes. "I'm *not* picking up a bird."

"Nothing's one hundred percent safe, love."

His rare admonition shamed me, and when he called from the treatment room one Sunday morning, I sprang to the door. "How can I help?"

"Is Louise around?" He peered into one of the pet carriers, brow furrowed. "The great horned's wound is bleeding a little, and I want to check it."

"She left for a meeting in Portland."

"Damn. Anyone else here?"

"Just you and me." I sucked in a breath. "What d'you need me to do?"

"Hold this owl so I can get a look."

"Isn't that the one who bit you?"

He met my eyes over the table and tossed me a pair of thick yellow gloves. "I'll talk you through it. You've gotta reach in—keep your face out of the carrier—and take the bird's ankles, then guide it out and hold it with its back against your chest. Make sure not to crush the wings; use your elbows to tuck them in, and *don't* let go of its legs."

"You've gotta be kidding."

I pulled on the gloves and peered through the carrier door. The bird looked as large as Juno—a foot and a half, with giant yellow feet and black talons. Despite the terror that iced my blood, I gasped at its beauty. At the sound it let loose a throaty hoot and clacked its beak and fluffed up its feathers. I could see the dried blood trailing down the inside of one wing. The yellow eyes gaped wide.

"Is it in pain?"

"Yep."

My hands shook in the bulky gloves. The owl swam in front of me. "So . . . I just . . . reach in and grab it?"

He turned away to prepare gauze and antiseptic cream. "Yep."

Cowardice compelled me to cover the carrier. I gripped my hands in the bulky gloves and tried to breathe. "It's just my body," I murmured. "Just my face. There's reconstructive surgery. . ."

Jonathan touched my shoulder. "I wouldn't ask you to do something unless I knew you could do it. Love, it's a great horned owl, your favorite. It *needs* you."

That got me.

I pulled back the sheet, slid back the latch on the door of the carrier, and swung it open. Head wrenched back and arms stuck out, I thrust my hands inside and took hold of the owl's legs, pulling them awkwardly to me and somehow getting the bird turned around so its back rested against my chest.

"It's light, but it's so strong!"

"Hollow bones," Jonathan reminded me.

The bird struggled to free itself, and I almost let go, almost fled from the room with its raw meat smell, its gauze pads streaked with blood, a swath of black plastic bags waiting on top of one cabinet in case someone didn't make it. Then I looked down at the owl's head—at the soft, striated feathers, the surprising white V lowered over scared, beautiful eyes—and redoubled my grip on its ankles. *May you be happy . . . may your body be happy.*

After my grandmother's diagnosis I'd begun listening to Buddhist lectures by Jack Kornfield, recorded at Spirit Rock Meditation Center near San Francisco. His hilarious anecdotes and his literary references in the midst of dharma talks on death and disappointment calmed me. He often spoke of lovingkindness meditation; I whispered his chant to the injured great horned now.

May you be free of danger. May your mind be happy. May you be at peace.

"Press your arms against its body . . . gently. It needs to be able to breathe." Jonathan lifted one wing and spread it out, wiping away dried blood. "Good. No infection. How's it look to you?"

"Fine," I squeaked.

"Are you still scared, love?" His voice softened, and his eyes moved from the owl to my face.

"Hell, yes, I'm scared."

But standing there with the injured owl in my arms, helping in a small way to work toward its recovery and release into the forest, I felt another emotion even more strongly—an unexpected and absolutely shocking joy.

6

Icon in the Closet

"Melissa. Tell Jonathan a hiker found a juvenile bald eagle beside the river with a broken wing," Laurin, the center's assistant director, said over the phone. "Louise went to pick it up. She may need his help."

I brought the phone into the room we'd adopted as our home office. Jonathan listened, then abandoned his thesis to dash up the road in time to witness the bird's unloading and medical exam.

Raptor center staff relied on community members—hikers, boaters, farmers, and the like—to alert them to injured birds. Then a trained volunteer would drive a half hour, two hours, even three, to pick up the patient in leather gloves and place it in a pet carrier headed for Spencer Butte. A whole slew of volunteers—veterinarians and city arborists and people from the electrical company with tall ladders on their trucks—helped to rescue and treat the raptors and put up nest boxes and replace fallen babies. In the case of the bald eagle, a pro bono vet had beat Jonathan to the center, offering to donate medical and massage services for as long as the recovery might take.

Over my dinnertime concoction of curried chickpeas and coconut rice, Jonathan described the eagle for me. "She's big, maybe twelve pounds. Still really dark, so she's a young one." He explained that it takes a bald about five years to grow the distinctive white head feathers.

On the floor around us, our four rescued cats ate their dinners, hissing if a dog nosed too close to the kibble bowl. Strays, all, abandoned or born to the streets. In the business of rehabbing one species, we'd found it almost impossible to say no to another.

I'd begun to feel the satisfaction of watching an exhausted, emaciated bird grow strong, struggling against my hands after a week of rehydrating fluids and twice-daily prey rations. Within a few weeks I no longer squeezed my eyes shut and prayed as I reached for an injured raptor in its carrier. I assessed the bird with a clinical eye, gauging how best to hold it to avoid further trauma to wing or leg or head, and held its legs firmly—a bit player in its recovery, but a player, nevertheless.

I passed Jonathan the basket of pita bread. "Why'd the eagle break her wing? Did she fly into a wind farm?" I told him about an article I'd read about an eagle that died after hitting one of the giant propellers used, more and more, to generate energy.

"Not sure. There's no gunshot wound. Maybe a car hit her. Either way, she'll never fly well enough to hunt. Louise is applying for a permit so she can be an education bird." His eyes shone as he forked up garbanzo beans. "I may get to work with her, as her trainer."

<hr />

A bald eagle, juvenile or otherwise, is a stunning creature. That Sunday morning, I stood outside the closet in the treatment room and peered over the makeshift plywood wall at the bird. She hunched on prehistoric yellow-scaled feet and blinked up at me through yellow eyes, one wing wrapped in bandages festooned with paw prints. "She's bigger than Cody!"

At the sound of my voice, the eagle shifted, restless on her newspaper. Jonathan dropped into his Barry White baritone. "Does she have enough water?"

"Yeah, but she pooped in it."

He slipped on an elbow-length glove and reached over the plywood, movements slow and careful, to retrieve the bowl. The eagle stood immobile, head lowered into a weary comma—a pause in her soaring adolescent trajectory.

"Why's she so calm?"

"She's hurting."

My hand gripped the front of my T-shirt, pressing against the sudden ache in my chest. Jonathan's own face clouded over with worry as he looked at the huddled pile of dark feathers. Center staff and volunteers could rehabilitate about half of the birds they took in. The other half died, their bodies wrapped and incinerated after the postmortem examination called a necropsy.

"Don't get attached to her," Darcy called from the bathroom as she euthanized mice.

"The director's named her Maya," Jonathan murmured in my ear. "Means 'Earth Mother.' Will you go get her food?"

"Of course."

Benjamin Franklin had argued against the bald eagle as our national bird. He thought they were cowards, stealing other birds' food and their nests. But my arms broke out in goose bumps at the sight of her, as I returned with a trout on a pie plate. "It's like there's an icon living in the closet."

Jonathan lowered the plate into the closet. We stood and looked down at her, breathing in the raw fish smell. His hand found mine. "She's going to survive," he said. "We'll make sure of that. I want a relationship with her."

Longtime volunteers could apply to be education team members if they committed to training one of the permanent raptors several times a week, teaching the bird to sit on a glove and a perch.

"We can talk raptor conservation 'til we're blue in the face," a cheerful red-haired volunteer named Jean had told me. "But it doesn't really click 'til people see them in the flesh and feathers."

Jean, ten years older than I, directed a transitional home for women who'd been incarcerated. She'd lately been driving up to the center every evening to handle a fledgling great horned owl who'd fallen from her nest and broken her radius and ulna irreparably. Oregon Fish and Wildlife gave the center a permit to keep her as an education bird. The staff allowed members to suggest names for the owl, and they chose Lorax, the Dr. Seuss character who "speaks for the trees, as the trees have no tongues."

The first time I saw Lorax, she stood atop the clinic desk—a bobbing two-foot column of tawny fluff with a white bib. Though the dark flight feathers on her wings had mostly grown in, her downy head had nubs instead of Juno's prodigious tufts, and her splayed toes seemed to me preternaturally large as she jumped to a perch and clung to the Astroturf, talons curved like fishhooks.

I regarded Juno with reverence. Lorax, however, made me giggle. "What's she doing?" I asked Jean as the fledgling bobbed her head in wild gyrations, pupils dilated so that only a ring of yellow glowed around black circles.

Jean held a bit of mouse up to Lorax's beak and she snatched it, swallowed it down. "She's triangulating. See the facial discs around her eyes?"

She pointed out the darker feathered circles on either side of the black beak. "They capture sound and focus it. Owls have lopsided ears, so if prey moves away, its noise decreases in one ear. She bobs her head to equalize the sound again, which puts the prey directly in front of her. Still with me?"

I shook my head. "She's tri ... um ... triangulating at me? Does she think I'm prey?"

"Nah. She's just gathering information about you."

Darcy had been listening from the treatment room doorway. Now she stepped out and flipped her braids. Lorax stared at her and backed away. "Try this." She took my arm and moved me across the clinic, away from Lorax. "You're an ear. Jean's the other ear. Close your eyes and point at me. Keep pointing as I move around."

She snapped her fingers in a steady rhythm, and I swiveled my index finger to follow the sound. "Okay, open your eyes."

I looked at Jean's pointing hand, at Darcy standing between us. "I'm the prey," she said. "Your hand is an ear. Jean's is another. Regardless of where I move, they create a triangle, capturing me like owls pinpoint rodents in complete darkness. "*That's* triangulation." She smirked and strode out of the clinic.

Jean looked at me, a smile playing on her lips. "Got it?"

"Got it."

She raised her arm to Lorax's feet, and the great horned stepped up. "For the next few weeks I'll have her on the glove constantly, so she bonds with me." She ducked her head to select a mealworm from the bowl on the desk, and Lorax ran her beak through Jean's hair, preening as if she were another owl.

Creatures crave connection—real connection, of the kind that requires presence, intuition, trust. Watching Jean with the great horned owl, I saw the possibility for an extraordinary connection, a chance to rediscover the the wild that existed within me—something I'd known as a child, when I'd bound outdoors barefoot each morning on my mother's third of an acre, just to feel the wet grass beneath my feet and listen to the world wake up. But how could someone like me, frozen with terror every time I had to pick up an injured bird, attain such an attachment?

Jonathan, Louise, and Laurin were the only rehabbers allowed to touch Maya. One clumsy move and the wing could relapse. But I changed her mute-streaked newspaper and refreshed her water dish while he held the eagle in his arms, gloves clasping her vibrant ankles.

"Oh . . . she's stunning." I paused in my cleaning to gaze at her, at the bright beak, the impossible yellow of her feet.

"She's a pretty one, for sure," he agreed.

Someone outside the world of raptor rehabilitation might have watched our treatment room tableaux and remarked on how we resembled a young couple fawning over their firstborn . . . until Maya bit the edge of Jonathan's glove and hung on.

"Wow, what a grip." He lowered her into the closet and slipped out of the glove, leaving it in her beak. He winked at me. "I like a feisty bird."

I wrapped my arms around his neck and kissed him until Darcy walked in with an armload of clean towels and suggested, once again, that we taking the mating ritual elsewhere and stop grossing out the eagle.

For a while Maya progressed. We cared for her in the closet a few weeks, and then the director moved her to a large wood-and-wire mew outside the clinic. She stood on a perch and peered through the windows at us while we washed dishes and prepped food plates. Jonathan drove up every day after school to hand her a trout.

"The director wants her to associate me with food," he explained. "So when it comes time to train her, we'll be bonded."

Through the hardware wire I watched him hold out the stinking rainbow-hued fish. Maya ruffled dark feathers as best she could with the pink bandage still affixed to one wing. He talked to her gently, words so quiet as he refreshed her water and picked trout detritus off her gravel floor that I couldn't catch them.

We'd been a team in the treatment room, working together toward Maya's recovery. Now, banned from the outdoor mew, I felt shut out. I saw Jonathan in the future—the eagle majestic on his gloved forearm—delivering talks on the lawn every weekend to a crowd of admiring spectators while I cleaned cages alone.

"Talking to a raptor builds rapport," he said one day after I complained about how he'd told Maya of his upcoming photo exhibition before me. "She's going to be a great ed bird."

Then the eagle developed a blood clot.

It happened the morning Jonathan asked me to feed a recovering barn owl in the treatment room. Whenever I held out the forceps loaded with mouse bits, the bird in its pet carrier hissed like the Sleestaks from the '70s TV show *Land of the Lost*. "It's okay, sweetie," I crooned, admiring the heart-shaped feathered discs around the owl's dark eyes. "Here's some mousie for you. Eat up . . . you've gotta grow strong so we can release you."

From the doorway Jonathan cleared his throat. "*Mousie?* It's not some toddler, my love."

"Thank God. Motherhood scares the hell out of me."

"Yeah, well, can you feed the four juvie screech owls in the big rehab mew?"

"Of course."

"Don't forget the ghost costume." He tossed a folded sheet onto the table and embraced me from behind, burying his face in my hair. "A costume. Isn't that right up your alley?"

I'd fed baby birds using a barn owl hand puppet while draped in a bedsheet. If young raptors saw food as coming from humans, they wouldn't get motivated to hunt. As human imprints they'd think of themselves and people as the same species. "An imprinted bird," Jonathan told me, "looks to people for food and companionship and, when the season's right, a mate. Pretty inconvenient if a bird we've released approaches a hiker for dinner followed by some amorous recreation."

I giggled and picked up the sheet with cutouts for eyeholes. "If the screech owls see me in this," I said, deadpan, "won't they imprint on ghosts?"

"Go." He kissed my forehead. "I have to get back to the eagle."

With eight thawed mice on a pie plate—brown, to mimic wild rodents—I donned the sheet and approached a large rehab enclosure covered in shade cloth. Instantly, the quartet of fluffy young screech owls scattered to the highest points of the mew and dangled from the black fabric. Jonathan had instructed me to distribute the mice on three stumps upended in gravel, then leave. I couldn't help pausing at the door to admire the owls through the holes in my sheet. Fuzzy and soft, with round yellow eyes, they looked like the stuffed Audubon toys on sale in the visitors' center.

"Melissa, will you be all right here for a few hours?" Jonathan appeared, merriment wiped from his face. I let myself out of the mew and pulled off the bedsheet. "What's wrong?"

"Contusion on Maya's wing. We removed the scab, and she won't stop bleeding."

He strode toward the parking lot, calling over one shoulder. "Louise is driving her to the vet. She needs me to hold the bird. There's no one else on shift . . ."

"I'll be alone here?"

I regretted finally watching Hitchcock's *The Birds* a month before. Would Jonathan return to find me lying among rat tails in some mew with my eyes pecked out?

"I'll be fine." I feigned a shrug of proficiency. "I hope Maya's okay."

Jonathan thrust the center's phone toward me. "We'll be in touch."

He hurried off and emerged from the clinic a moment later with the limp, bleeding eagle in his arms like a child. Drops fell to the asphalt as he slid into the back seat of the director's station wagon. She leaped in and raced downhill; I heard the screech of tires as they disappeared down the road.

Solitary, I expected to be scared. But after the first five minutes, in which I stood in front of Lorax's clinic mew and watched her triangulate adorably on a moth, I found myself unafraid. There was too much to do.

In the treatment room I cleaned up the bloody towels and gauze pads on the table and picked up a feather Maya had shed—the length of my forearm—and wedged it into the glove rack for Jonathan. I set out thawed rats on pie plates in the clinic and shook vitamin powder on their white bodies, then trotted around the center delivering them to hawks and falcons—a combination postal carrier and grim reaper.

The phone rang and I jumped for it, hoping for Jonathan, and recovered swiftly to tell the local farmer who'd called that, yes, I'd leave a message for the director about putting him on the wait list for two rehabilitated barn owls to hunt mice on his farm. Louise had left a sticky note on the computer monitor, imploring someone to clean leaves off the fiberglass tops of the resident screech owls' mew. I found a ladder and got to work. I talked to them as I troweled caked maple leaves and fir twigs off the roof.

"Don't worry, sweetie. I know it's loud, but it'll be over soon . . . then you can see the trees and the sky and the stars . . ."

I kept up a stream of steady, singsong chatter in time with my scraping. The owls clacked their beaks and let loose their burbling call. My cell phone buzzed, and I read a text from my sister.

Can you believe it? We're thinking of getting pregnant.

"Yikes."

At the sound of a thud, I looked up, expecting to see Jonathan with Maya, but it was Juno flying from perch to feeding platform in anticipation of her nightly rat. The center's owls ate in the evening to mimic their nocturnal feeding habits in the wild.

"It's still hours 'til your dinner, Juno."

She stood level with me on the ladder. We looked at each other a long moment. Though I'd never get her on the glove—her wildness made her off-limits as an ed bird—I felt a kinship with her, in part because she reminded me of one of my cats. But there was something else, as well. She was another maiden aunt, a comrade in my childlessness. Our organization had no breeding permit, and so the birds had no offspring.

Did Juno feel a need to have babies? Or, like me, did the idea of motherhood frighten her?

"What's my sister *thinking*?" I wondered out loud. Katie and her husband had sworn off kids as adamantly as we had. Had they heard the toll of a biological clock indiscernible to Jonathan and me?

I knew why he recoiled from the idea of parenting. He'd grown up with five siblings and a mom and dad in a little house next to a park. But at fifteen he learned that his father—with whom he'd spent weekends fishing in Canada—had a fast-spreading melanoma and only a few months to live.

"We all took care of him," he told me one night as we sat on the couch sharing family photo albums, cats on our laps and dogs at our feet. "When he got the diagnosis, he bought us a big house in the country. He died in the downstairs bedroom with all of us there."

"And your mom?" Tears had slipped down my face and—amazingly—his.

"Raised the three of us still in high school by herself. Took us to Europe, too, but I never went fishing again."

"Please . . ." I'd whispered. "Please stop smoking. I love you."

He nodded, wiped his eyes. "I'll try."

Jonathan had told me that losing his father when he was still a boy killed the desire to lock himself into a paternal position and expose his own mortality to someone more vulnerable than himself.

Myself, I felt terrified of taking responsibility for any young person. My own childhood had been happily humming along when my parents began to awaken my brother and sister and me each night with screaming matches embarrassingly incongruous with our chic suburban neighborhood. At eight years old I sensed it coming; even so, the afternoon my mother seat belted my siblings and me into her car and sped away, a few suitcases and book boxes tossed in the back, I found myself devastated by the divorce.

We moved into an apartment at the beach with a hard-faced, rough-voiced woman I learned to be my mother's girlfriend. A few weeks later, my father showed up with a posse of police cars and spirited us away to the safe, ugly house he'd purchased with *his* new girlfriend. With legal strongmen at his side, plus a homophobic social worker who insisted that living with lesbians would damage us for life, he persuaded the judge to award him full custody of my younger siblings and me.

For years I stood on my father's doorstep and watched my mother's VW bus pull away, her hand stuck out the window in a limp salute—the last I'd see of her for ten days, until she was allowed to pick us up for the weekend again. An image like that doesn't vanish; it burns itself into the skin like a sorrowful tattoo, marking the observer for life.

How could I have a child, knowing the anguish that separation might bring? It seemed to me the most wild and risk-taking thing that a person could do.

—◆—

By the time Jonathan and Louise returned from the hospital, I'd cleaned most of the mews, dusted the visitors' center, and watered the plants. I stood pouring seed into the bird feeders that dangled from the cherry tree when the station wagon crept up the driveway.

Slow was a good sign, slow so as not to frighten Maya.

Louise parked, got out, and headed for her apartment. She shut the door behind her without a word to me. Then Jonathan climbed out of the passenger seat. Blood streaked his T-shirt and shorts. For an instant I thought they'd been in a car wreck. I ran over.

"What happened? Where's the eagle?"

He wrapped his arms around his body, lips a rigid line. "Hemorrhaged in the car . . . kept applying pressure. No way to stop it."

He walked to the picnic table and sank to the bench, dropped his head into folded arms. "She's gone."

"Maya *died?*"

The back of his neck, newly shaved by a careless ten-dollar barber, shone naked and pink, badly in need of sunscreen. I could think of nothing to say, nothing to do but stand behind him, hands gripping his shoulders as the one-eyed kestrel chirped at us from his mew.

I'd gloated over not wanting kids, believing we'd spare ourselves the agony of falling in love with helpless creatures who might or might not be taken from us. How little I realized that, for the next several years, on behalf of both birds and children, we'd gamble our emotions again and again.

7

Detach with Love

A YEAR WENT BY. JONATHAN GRADUATED AND TOOK A TEMPORARY position at the Jordan Schnitzer Museum of Art on the University of Oregon campus, hoping janitorial work would lead somehow to a career in photography. I began teaching part-time at the journalism school. We met for picnic lunches in Pioneer Cemetery, across from the university's legendary track, and threw bread crusts to crows perched on mossy gravestones. Unattached to anyone but each other, we spent free days hiking coastal sand dunes and marveling at waterfalls and traversing the Alvord Desert with its juniper-studded plains and miles-long alkaline playa.

We read to each other on road trips: Kafka, the *New Yorker*, *The Unbearable Lightness of Being*. I stuck my head out the truck window and let the wind snarl my hair. My outstretched arm bobbed in the breeze, an ebullient kite. "Actually," I told Jonathan, "Kundera was wrong. I find the lightness of being absolutely bearable."

He nodded, one hand on the steering wheel, right arm stretched out on the seat behind me with his hand curled warm against my neck. Beholden to no one, we effervesced.

He decided to go ahead with the vasectomy after his third epididymitis infection in as many months. "Let's see . . ." He lay on the couch on yet another return from the ER doped up on painkillers, stomach churning from antibiotics. "I can walk around with giant swollen balls half the time and we can maybe birth an infant someday if we change our minds about children, or I can have a five-minute outpatient surgery and throw away our box of condoms."

I tossed him his cell. "Call your urologist."

I felt proud of our decision to sterilize. It felt so mature, so clean. The doctor told us thousands of men each day opt for vasectomy—a swift, nonthreatening surgery compared to the intense and risky ordeal of a woman having her tubes tied. Still, he faltered before doing the deed.

"Are you *sure* you want to do this?"

The doctor looked at us over his gleaming scalpel, and we nodded. In my most solitary moments over the past two decades, awake in the raw darkness of three o'clock in the morning, I'd looked into my soul to find not even a glimmer of longing to birth a child. Jonathan squeezed my hand. "Clip me," he said.

—◆—

In July, three years after we began dating, we found substitutes for our shifts at the raptor center and flew to New York for his family reunion in the tiny Adirondacks town of Old Forge. The place seemed expressly created for such gatherings, with its ice cream shops and 1950s-style motels and comic T-shirt venues. A newspaper devoted to reunion coverage ran homey text and photos of relatives stacked four and five feet deep. The streets smelled of tar and freshly baked waffle cones.

Our first morning there, we strolled along the main drag. Screams split the soupy summer air—cries of recognition from family members who hadn't seen each other in years. I turned to find two people hurtling across opposite sides of the street to embrace one another in bumper-to-bumper traffic.

I could count the members of my family on one hand, whereas Jonathan's cacophonous clan took over an entire motel. Old Forge buzzed with mosquitoes and kids. Young children staggered along searing sidewalks, trailing ice cream and popcorn kernels. Teens cast furtive glances at one another in anticipation of lakeside trysts once their parents had relaxed their restrictions over a third gin and tonic. Babies alternately squalled and slept in strollers. "Birth control," Jonathan joked.

I clapped my hand over his mouth and jerked my head at the family slogging along ahead of us, the two toddlers sticky with lollipops and the preteen in shades trying desperately to look like she had no connection to a pair of beleaguered parents in matching plaid shorts and sunburned noses. "You can't say that here. You'll get three months hard labor playing miniature golf with the under-ten set."

"Speaking of which, my sister asked if we want to go kayaking with her and the kids."

Jonathan's lovely older sister, Meg, had adopted two children from Korea with her husband shortly after the babies' births. Ferociously precocious, seven-year-old Nathan amused a table full of relatives at dinner with his plans to dredge up and restore the *Titanic*. He passed around the blueprints he'd sketched out on a napkin.

"But how will you afford the renovation?" Jonathan studied the plans and petitioned his nephew, who sat between his parents in brilliant buck-toothed glory.

"Oh, Uncle Jon." He sighed and shook his head in pity for our ignorance. "When your parents die you get all their money."

They were good for a laugh, these kids. Five-year-old Brynnli wore T-shirts printed with puppies, and cutoff shorts and sandals. When her ice cream fell onto the sidewalk, she didn't cry—she picked it up and mashed the chocolate scoop back on her cone and kept licking. Having once performed a similar action with a shrimp-wonton appetizer at a wedding reception, I admired her resourcefulness.

"You'd make a good raptor rehabilitator," I told her. "You've got a strong stomach."

"Thank you," she replied with gravity.

Outside the hardware store, posing for a picture beside a mammoth stuffed bear, I smiled up at Jonathan. "Kayaking with the kids sounds like fun."

We walked to Tickner's and rented kayaks to paddle on the cool, green waters of the Moose River. Nathan plastered himself beside me, so close that our sweaty arms touched. "I want to go with Aunt Melissa."

Aunt. The title caught in my throat. Like baby owls crowding around the bits of chicken on my forceps, the kids jockeyed for position.

I gave Nathan the thumbs-up. "I'll share a kayak with you."

Brynnli attached herself to Jonathan, hands locked around his arm. "Dibs on Uncle Jon."

Meg and her husband looked at each other, hope barely contained in their eyes. "Would that be okay?"

Jonathan glanced at me for confirmation. I shrugged. "It's only an hour."

Meg beamed as if we'd just awarded her a night in a four-star hotel with a gourmet dinner and massage. "Oh, thank you!"

She and her husband got into a kayak and paddled off to commune among the lily pads. Nathan clambered into a boat, nearly overturning it, and I climbed in after him. Jonathan helped Brynnli into their kayak. Then we stared at each other.

I hadn't babysat in a decade. I'd never kayaked, and Jonathan had been out on the river only once. What were we supposed to do now?

Nathan gripped his paddle. "Let's race!"

We spent an hour racing and splashing and singing, and then fishing Brynnli out of the river when she leaned too far over to try to catch a frog. The commotion startled a great blue heron, who sprung up from behind a low-hanging tree and sailed into the air over our heads. Brynnli gasped. "That is a beautiful bird."

Suddenly, longing walloped me. I'd babysat only boy ruffians as a teenager—not by design, but because that's what friends of my parents had birthed. I knew nothing about little girls. I thought they were all made of sugar and spice and prissy little ruffles and toy Sleeping Beauty cell phones. I never dreamed that one of them might be willing to step away from a game of fashion show and paddle a river or help prep food for injured birds. Brynnli was rocking my boat.

She pursed up her lips at the salmon-hued bandanna I pulled off my head to blot the river water from her black ponytails. "Aunt Melissa?" Disapproval furrowed her brow. "Pink stinks."

"You're right. I don't even like this bandanna."

I resisted the urge to throw myself down at her dirty white sandals in worship and instead let loose a barrage of questions. What did she think of school? Did she like boys? What was her position on Barbie? What did she want to be when she grew up?

She replied with gravity to all of my inquiries. "Fun." "Yuck." "Double-yuck." "A veterinarian."

I wanted this child.

The realization pissed me off. Having listened again to Jack Korn-field's audio lectures, I grasped the idea of how inner peace emerged from a cessation of desire. I'd finally achieved a balance between work and vol-unteering and romance. Jonathan and I had sold my little bungalow and bought a house on a third of an acre surrounded by oaks and maples, firs and cherry trees; we had a vegetable garden and backyard potlucks with friends, and we had lots of exuberant sex. Why want anything else?

At the end of the hour, Jonathan and I returned the kids to their parents. They sang out a chorus of gratitude. "Thank you, Aunt Melissa. Thank you, Uncle Jon."

I reached for Brynnli's little hand to help her out of the boat. "You're so heavy!" I laughed and swung her to the dock. She stood on the sun-warmed golden planks for a moment, her hand still in mine. Then she shook herself like an owl fluffing its feathers and ran for her mother, leav-ing my palm damp and empty.

I joked as Jonathan and I strolled toward our motel. "That's the beauty of being an aunt and uncle—you can have fun with the kids and then give them back." But the quip sounded hollow, an exhausted cliché, and he didn't laugh. Instead, he pulled me into a shabby cafe off the main drag, and we sat down at a table under a red-and-white umbrella.

"You know . . ." He handed me a ketchup-stained menu. "I wouldn't mind having a daughter if we could adopt one like Brynnli."

His words shocked me. To protect my blossoming heart, I plunged into the role of devil's advocate. "Do we really need something else to care for? We've already got all our pets and the raptor center. Plus, we're not even married . . ."

I shot him a pointed scowl. Here among hundreds of happy couples—the only unmarried woman in his family unless you counted his teenage cousins—I found myself longing for legitimacy. My role as "girlfriend" felt lightweight, contrary to my conviction that here across from me, navi-gating a pile of greasy French fries and a watery Coke, sat my soul mate.

"I'm still working out my feelings about marriage," he said.

I pushed my own plate away.

"I refuse to even *think* of adopting a kid unless we're married."

No response.

"I mean, a child needs stability, parents who're gonna stick together. Anyhow, why the hell are we even talking about this? You got a vasectomy. We don't want children."

Across the street I glimpsed Brynnli and her mother window-shopping, hands clasped. Meg pointed to something in a shop full of stuffed animals, and Brynnli doubled over with laughter. I pressed my palms to my chest and prayed for cessation.

On the lawn behind the motel that evening, I sat with Jonathan's mother and sisters as their children tumbled around us. Their eyes went to the great horned owl I'd had tattooed on my ankle earlier that summer. No one else in the family sported body art except for Meg's ex-Navy husband with a panther on his forearm. I felt weird and ostentatious—the rebel faux-aunt who might or might not have a red Harley parked outside her motel room.

"Why'd you do it?" One of the teenage nieces stretched out on the grass to get a closer look at the black-and-brown bird perched on a fir branch across my pale skin. "I mean, it's cool and all, but *ouch*."

"Rite of passage." I mumbled something about how the tattoo commemorated my transition from L.A. urbanite to Oregon environmentalist. "I just love great horned owls."

But what I loved even more was Jonathan, so when he'd announced his plan to have the trio of black ravens from the Ravenswood wine bottle tattooed on his chest in admiration for the species, I'd stuck out my leg and said to the leather-clad ink artist who called herself Miss Joy: "I'd like to be in severe pain for two hours, as well, please."

Love hurt. That fact seemed to me nonnegotiable. In spite of the longing I felt when Brynnli ran across the lawn and up to Meg, accosting her with a bear hug complete with snarls and growls, I folded my arms across my chest and refused to entertain the possibility of motherhood any longer.

"Tell us about Lorax." Meg wrapped her arms around her daughter. "Aunt Melissa works with a great horned owl, honey."

"Oh, I don't work with her. I just feed her and clean her mew. She's like a big brown-and-white cat, tall rather than long."

Brynnli looked up, interested.

"Lorax was hilarious as a baby," I told her, "bobbing her head all over the place and chasing down mealworms with her big feet. Now she's more dignified, super calm around people. Still triangulates like crazy, though—she looks like one of those bobblehead dolls you see on people's dashboards. She's bonded with her trainer; Jean can hold her toes and put balm on the bottoms of her feet, and Lorax lets her."

One of the girls held up a hand. "Why don't you help train her?"

I shifted on the grass, looked away. "Oh . . . I don't really have time," I said vaguely.

In truth, what I lacked was courage. When I walked into the raptor cages with my bucket and hose, I cringed and glanced over hunched shoulders, ever anticipating an attack. Another volunteer had recently been footed in the arm by one of the ferruginous hawks, talons sunk deep into flesh. For weeks she couldn't lift anything heavier than a plate of mice.

I adored the idea of bonding with Lorax, of learning what it meant to trust each other, but such a relationship seemed beyond my ability.

⚊ ⌣ ⚊

The next week, back at home, I paused in cleaning mouse aquariums to skim an advice column in the newspaper. The columnist—one of those snarky, straight-talking hipsters who strikes terror into the souls of journalism's gentler Abbys and Anns—had responded to a reader's question about whether to start a family. Basically, she wrote, if your life is so full of love that you have extra to offer a kid, then by all means, consider breeding or adoption.

Otherwise, don't bother.

I had love enough for Jonathan, for a few stray dogs and cats, for a flock of injured birds. I didn't realize then that the heart is marvelously accommodating; it expands and accepts as needed.

"Detach with love." I muttered a writer friend's twelve-step homily as I strutted around the raptor center with my gruesome pie plates and dropped prey onto feeding platforms. Then I accidentally let an injured bird go, and my lofty goals of detachment crashed to the ground.

It happens to almost every raptor caretaker—you unlatch a pet carrier in a treatment room and an edgy little kestrel bolts out, or you get a bit cavalier and forget to reposition the shade cloth you've ducked under in a rehab mew, so a falcon makes a dash for it. In my case, I walked into one of the recovery mews, and a Cooper's hawk nursing a broken leg shot out from the darkness before I could pull the black fabric closed behind me.

"Crap!"

I sprang up but caught only air.

The bird took off at a ragged clip for the hillside separating the center from the Ridgeline Trail below. I managed to observe, as I scurried after the brown-and-white blur, that the director's car wasn't in the parking lot. I hollered for Jonathan.

"Come quick, and bring gloves!"

He bounded from the clinic. "What and where?"

"Injured Cooper's. That way!"

I pointed down the hillside to a tangle of blackberries. The hawk perched on a low fir branch, breast heaving and white-feathered legs trembling like a Victorian streetwalker's pantaloons. One yellow foot dangled, wrapped in a pink bandage.

"The director's gonna kill me!" I yanked on oversize leather gloves. "We've gotta catch it!"

A year before, another volunteer had accidentally released one of the center's permanent residents—a kestrel used in educational presentations—because of a malfunctioning clip on a glove. In spite of posting "Lost Raptor" signs all over Eugene, staff received no leads. They conceded grimly that the kestrel had vanished. The bird had one eye; it could never survive in the wild. The volunteer, who'd previously enjoyed a reputation for stoic steady-handedness, didn't stop crying for days. It was as though she'd lost someone's child.

Jonathan shouldered a long-handled net and waded down into the lethal mixture of thorn-tipped vines and poison oak. "Calm down, love. No one's gonna fire you."

"But the bird's injured. It'll die of starvation."

"Shhh. I've got to concentrate."

He tripped, and all six-feet-two of him went down. The hawk flew up and landed in a higher branch. "Injured, my ass." He got up, arms blackberry shredded, and crept toward the tree. The bird's eyes glowed like orange glass beads, fixated on a patch of blue sky above the fir tops. I cringed at the thought of its long, slow decline.

Bloody, but goaded on by the ferocity of his Scottish ancestors, Jonathan crept up behind the hawk—William Wallace with a bird net. Gracefully, he swung it up and over, trapping the Cooper's.

"Oh, thank God." I clasped my gloved hands to my chest as he climbed the hill. Stupid with relief, I giggled. "A bird in the net is worth two in the bush."

"Shhh. Everything's fine." Back on the lawn, Jonathan reached into the tangled mesh and clasped the bird in a firm hold. "Wouldn't Brynnli and Nathan love to see this." His own chest heaved from exertion. "Well, let's get him back to the mew and leave him alone. Poor guy—we'll check on him every half hour, make sure he's okay."

The hawk had gone nearly comatose with fear. I shoved my hands into my jeans pockets, resisting the urge to stroke the tiny brown and black feathers on his head—a gesture that would comfort me rather than him. At his mew I opened the door and removed a pair of pink quail legs from his feeding platform. I fetched fresh water as Jonathan deposited the hawk back on his perch. "We'll keep his little adventure between us." He closed the mew door and dropped the net over my head, pulling me to him. "It'll be our secret."

His lighthearted recovery from the fly-off surprised me. I knew the Cooper's could have died. Really skillful wildlife rehabbers don't pin their hopes on one animal's survival. They try not to fall in love with injured creatures, entangling themselves in emotion. They stay detached. I sensed the wisdom in this and resolved to renew my efforts at dispassion.

That day, I fed motherless baby screech owls without crooning to them and paused only a moment in my shift work to check on the Cooper's hawk, who sat on his perch and plucked feathers from half a quail as if freedom hadn't, for a moment, offered him another possibility. Jonathan and I ministered to birds in the treatment room and then hiked to the top of Spencer Butte for a picnic dinner. On the sun-warmed boulders, we ate sandwiches and looked down from our lofty perch at the weighted world below, refusing to admit a change of heart.

8

Meow

IN AUGUST A SUNBURNED CROWD EXCRETED BEER AND SWEAT AROUND the folding tables where Jonathan sat with Louise at the county fair. At one side the tethered screech owl perched in the cavity of a sawed-off stump, gazing at visitors through one yellow eye. On the other side a kestrel chirped on a short pedestal covered with Astroturf. The laminated posters of owl and hawk species taped to the tarp behind the table did nothing to block the searing sun. Stacks of literature, usually at risk of wind dispersal in the center's education booths, sat static in the still, close air.

The director wore a wet kerchief around her neck. Diamonds of sweat glistened in Jonathan's unibrow. He picked up a spray bottle and misted the crow in her cage beside the donation jar; the bird opened her black beak wide to take in the water. From my vantage point behind the table, I could see her tongue bobbing. Raptors typically get all the water they need from their carnivorous diet—even so, Jonathan misted the golden eagle, as well. Messiah ruffed his bronze feathers in a small but dramatic earthquake of bird. The crowd inhaled a communal gasp at the display from a creature the size of the open-mouthed toddler standing in front of the T-perch.

"That's called a rouse," Jonathan addressed the onlookers. "It's a grooming method—birds do it to tidy their feathers."

A rotund man in undershirt and overalls pushed to the front and jabbed a finger toward Messiah. His voice exploded over the blaring midway music and the screech and smash of bumper cars. "I shoot birds like that," he said.

Louise pushed out of her chair and stood up to face him.

Jonathan had told me of the controversies that surface when raptor rehabilitators venture out into the world at large with its various demographics and political agendas. That morning before the fair, he'd described the previous year's event for me while we drank coffee on our lopsided porch under a fifty-foot cedar shared with squirrels, raccoons, and wild turkeys. "There're always a few people who think rehabbing raptors is nuts. One woman chastised us for saving owls 'cause she saw a great horned take her daughter's new kitten."

"They do that?" I pictured mellow Lorax triangulating on some obtuse ball of feline fluff and snatching it up in her talons. "I had no idea."

Terrified of disseminating incorrect information to visitors, especially in front of the director, I never signed up for education booths like the one at the fair. "I just clean cages," I said when Darcy pointed out holes in the weekend schedule. "You experts can staff the booths."

Still, I resented Jonathan's all-day commitment on a summer Saturday. "Can't you skip the booth and drive over to Fall Creek with me? It's gonna be scorching, and it'd be so much fun to swim."

"You know I can't cancel the day of an event."

"Well, do you have to sign up for *all* of them? I mean, you don't even do photography right now."

"Summers get really busy at the center. I want to help out."

Despite our idyllic setting I scowled into my cup. After the family reunion Jonathan had spent most of Eugene's precious sunny weekends staffing booths at outdoor festivals. Public outreach was a critical component of the center's work, he explained. "Not everyone takes the time to drive up to visit. If we're going to educate people about raptors, we need to come to them. They need to see the birds up close and talk one-on-one with staff and volunteers."

I understood that. And I knew that Maya's death had shaken him; his involvement in the center seemed doubly important now, therapeutic after the loss of a bird with whom he'd begun to bond.

"Love, what's wrong?" Jonathan looked at me with equal parts irritation and concern.

I stared up into the cedar, searching for camouflaged creatures, avoiding his eyes.

"It's just that we can't go to the coast or the mountains or anything because you're always volunteering."

"I committed to the county fair booth months ago. You can come, too . . ."

"Will Lorax be there?"

"She's not trained to ride in the car yet."

"Then no."

His shoulders slumped. I saw that I'd become *that* kind of girlfriend—a shackle, a time suck, the proverbial ball and chain. He dropped his head to stare at a brown-and-orange moth on the cement steps, its once-lively body overrun with scavenging ants.

I put down my cup and rescued the moth, placing it on a leaf of the Japanese maple we'd planted. "How about this?" I tried to sound airy and devil-may-care, though Satan himself poked at me with his damned pitchfork. "I'll jog over to the fairgrounds at four, and we can walk the midway and get an elephant ear. Your favorite, right?"

"Yeah." He pulled on his volunteer T-shirt—royal blue and silk-screened with the image of a hawk flying over an eye-popping yellow sun—pecked me on the cheek, and headed for his truck.

I prided myself on having a life away from the center, unlike other volunteers who spent thirty and forty hours a week there, joking about the spouses they left at home as "raptor widows." I trained for marathons. I taught at the journalism school, wrote for magazines and newspapers, and started a memoir. I saw friends at the dog park, went out for coffee with other writers, went to the movies. But I missed my boyfriend.

"If you can't beat him, join him." My running partner, Kat, chuckled as we jogged the Ridgeline Trail below the center. "Aren't you gaga for that great horned owl you're always telling me to come see? Learn to put her on your arm, or whatever it is you do, and go with Jonathan to festivals. You guys can be bird nerds together."

I sidestepped a branch of poison oak. "Maybe."

Jonathan had taken me to Wild Wings, the wildlife rehabilitation center in Honeoye Falls, New York. We'd seen how the director's family members pitched in to help with cleaning and fundraising and staffing the cozy little gift shop. While I didn't relish spending all my free time in service of the raptor center, I could give more than my agreed-upon four hours. Then, maybe, Jonathan would be willing to take a day off now and then so that we could have an adventure.

I swiped my sleeve across my sweaty face. "I'll go over to the fair this afternoon and see if I can help, and maybe tear him away from the booth for a ride on the Ferris wheel. It'd be sort of a date."

Kat had two children and a husband who worked full-time. She tossed her ponytail, diamond earrings sparkling in a sunbeam that shot out between Douglas firs. "Hey, take it where you can get it," she told me. "Nothing's perfect."

—◆—

But at four o'clock I jogged over, and Jonathan couldn't leave his station. The man in the undershirt and overalls said what he said about shooting eagles, and the director sprang up from her chair, so fast that Messiah spread his six-foot wings and opened his beak. I leaped away to the far side of the table.

"It's illegal to shoot a raptor." Louise's eyes flashed fire at the man who towered over her. She told him about the Migratory Bird Treaty Act and the Bald and Golden Eagle Act.

He appeared unimpressed. "They eat my sheep, lady, they're fair game," the man shot back, his cheeks turning purple.

Jonathan stood up, poised to intervene. His face wore an expression I recognized as diplomatic, nonconfrontational. It was the same blank, pleasant look he turned on me whenever I asked him if he'd had time to work out his feelings about getting married.

"Let's just relax," he said now, "try to see both sides of the issue."

I knew that golden eagles, while capable of eating livestock, preferred rabbits and prairie dogs—small animals that wouldn't put up a fight. "It's highly unlikely that an eagle would take your sheep . . ." I began.

The man stared at me. Jonathan and Louise stared at me, as well. I shrugged, the color in my own sweaty face deepening. "I'm just saying no one—not even an eagle—wants to work that hard for a meal."

"*Whatever*," the man spat before he moved off, muttering about his Second Amendment rights.

Louise sank back into her folding chair and reached for the spray bottle to mist the crow. "Well," the corvid called, head cocked. "Ha ha ha ha!"

I sidled up to Jonathan and put my lips to his ear. "Can you take a break?"

"Better not."

He turned to check on Messiah. "He looks calm."

The eagle stood with one yellow foot balled into a fist—a raptor's indication of relaxation. "Can you believe that guy?"

"No." I knew you couldn't just blow an eagle out of the sky. For centuries farmers around the world have struggled to grow crops and raise livestock threatened by weeds and insects and disease and predators. But shooting one's adversaries, like smothering them with poisons, appeared to be falling out of favor. These days, though the sight of slugs feasting on my hard-won tomatoes made me want to pulverize the audacious invertebrates between two rocks, I bought a case of Pabst Blue Ribbon, poured it into bowls, and let them die a happy death.

I wondered what the man with the sheep would say if he knew of the local vineyard owners who actually requested rehabilitated owls and hawks to patrol their fields, keeping voles and other rodents at bay.

Louise began to chat with a group of preteens in 4-H shirts. In spite of their training in dispassionate animal husbandry, they couldn't help hopping up and down and crooning baby talk to the one-eyed screech owl in her hollowed-out log.

"He's such a cute little guy. Can we pet him?"

I shook my head. "She could take your finger off with her beak."

The director gave me a warning look. "Don't exaggerate."

Chagrined, I turned to the smallest of the 4-H kids. Despite the heat she wore a long, striped stocking cap with earflaps—a junior Holden Caulfield. "Have you ever been up to the raptor center?" I asked her.

She shook her head and presented me with a wistful smile missing several teeth. "I'd love to work there like you."

Jonathan leaned over to speak in my ear, one hand on my arm. "I need to stay here another hour, love, then load the birds and take them back to the center. Want me to pick up Thai food on the way home?"

His palm felt hot, cloying. "No, thanks."

I walked away, refusing the comfort of yellow curry and spring rolls, and stalked past booths of prize-winning pigs and rabbits and quilts and photos and pies to my bicycle. Everyone needed a passion. I got that. I had writing and running and traveling; Jonathan claimed raptors.

Could they be mine, too?

On my jog home I ran around the Adidas Amazon Trail to a soundtrack of cawing crows and explosions of twittering songbirds. A larger bird caught my eye; it rose from the creek and sailed over the mulched path into the ash grove. I whipped off my sunglasses and stared at the brown, black, and red feathers.

Another jogger ran by me. "What is it?"

I pointed up into a branch. "Red-shouldered hawk! It's got something in its talons . . ."

The man ran on. But I stayed for a long time, watching the hawk.

That afternoon, gratitude filled me as I jogged home. Not only could I identify a red-shouldered hawk in the middle of the city; I'd held one in my arms at the raptor center as Jonathan poured life-giving fluids down its throat. I wanted to know what he knew. I wanted to help.

At home I sat down to e-mail Louise. She'd put out a call for volunteers to staff a booth at the Fifth Street Public Market—a chic shopping area near the river—the following weekend.

"I'd like to volunteer at the booth next Saturday," I typed.

Wildlife rehabilitation centers exist across the world. Google the term along with the name of almost any city, and some place will pop up. Tiny, rickety buildings and ultramodern facilities alike house people working around the clock to save animals' lives. Their staff members seldom do what they do for the paycheck. Between running a nonprofit and caring for animals with continuous feeding and cleaning needs, they and volunteers end up donating endless hours and dollars to help vulnerable species.

"I'm proud of you." When Jonathan learned that I'd signed up to help staff an education table, he kissed me deeply. "Messiah will be there."

"Yikes. He scares me."

"Louise will be there, so you won't have to get near him. But Melissa, he won't hurt you."

"Aren't you coming?"

He shook his head. He had business, he said, at a nearby art festival. "Gotta go see this metalsmith guy."

Frustration tightened my lips. I'd assumed that if I signed up to volunteer, he'd sign up as well. "Why? Are you taking up metalsmithing?"

"Um . . ." He reached for Cody and plucked at an errant whisker, smoothing it back into place. "I'm studying his business model in case I want to start selling my photos."

"Oh." I pushed out the door, let it close harder than usual, and stuck my head back in to apologize. "Marley raided the compost pile again. I wouldn't let him in the house, if I were you."

Jonathan looked up from his cell phone, unibrow raised. "Got it."

———

"Raptors are hawks, eagles, falcons, owls, kites, osprey, vultures." I rehearsed the litany as I bicycled over to the Fifth Street Public Market in my volunteer T-shirt and the blue jeans I'd hacked into cutoffs. I locked my bike near the fancy kitchen store and found my way to a brick courtyard. The center's folding table stood there. Bricks weighed down stacks of literature on how to build nest boxes and the steps to take should one find an injured raptor. Two empty folding chairs waited. I perched on one and rehearsed facts under my breath.

"The center has over thirty resident birds with permanent injuries. They act as ambassadors for their species . . ."

My spiel sounded wooden, the snake-oil testimony of a sham environmentalist. For a moment I thought longingly of my fake-furred raccoon costume. Then Louise stepped into the courtyard, the golden eagle on her glove.

Eagles tend to shock people because of their size. Goldens have the added attraction of bronze feathers and strong, curving black beaks. They appear mostly in the western United States, in landscapes ranging from tundra to desert to conifer forest. Four decades ago, golden eagles—so large that their body parts can touch two electrical lines and create a fatal circuit—inspired people to design raptor-friendly power poles across the states. Worldwide, they're revered, a national symbol in several countries.

Messiah sat on the director's glove like royalty, regarding the people around him through serene amber eyes. A feathered pied piper, he'd attracted a bevy of followers—unsuspecting shoppers who'd looked up from cashmere sweaters and racks of copper pots to find a two-foot raptor staring at them.

"You haven't put the perch together!" Louise stopped beside a fountain and cocked her head toward the white-painted pieces of wood lying beside the table.

"Sorry." I fumbled the T-perch into place.

"Give him room, please." She walked toward the perch and backed Messiah up to the Astroturf rung. He stepped onto it with yellow feet the size of my hand. She unwound the nylon leash and clipped the loose end to the carabiner on the perch stand.

"What are those bracelets around its legs?" A little blond girl in a ladybug dress tugged on my sleeve. She pointed at the wide leather straps encircling the eagle's feathered ankles. Louise remained silent, examining the bottom of one of Messiah's feet. I attempted an answer. "Um . . . those are jesses?"

The upward inflection at the end of my sentence humiliated me, but I found myself unable to muster up any authority in front of the child. "They have a slit in one end for round metal swivels? The handler threads the swivels through and then clips them to her glove . . . uh . . . so the bird doesn't fly away?"

As if on cue, the little girl's mother dropped her keys, and so I didn't get to explain that along with telemetry, falconers tie bells onto a raptor's legs above the jesses so they can detect the bird's position when it's hunting out of sight. Spooked by the clatter of metal on pavement, Messiah cried out and leaped from his perch. Wings flapped; I felt the air from them hit my face. In one smooth movement the director caught up his leash and reeled it in so that the eagle came to rest on her gloved wrist.

"Good catch!" I cried.

Around us, onlookers let loose a patter of applause.

Louise pursed her lips, concentrating on Messiah. "Everyone please stand back."

The crowd moved respectfully to the courtyard's perimeter. The eagle preened in a patch of sunlight that bronzed his brown feathers becomingly. I stepped backward and addressed the crowd like a circus barker. "An eagle's grip is so strong he can break a handler's wrist?"

"Shhh!" Louise replaced Messiah on his perch. The eagle sat seemingly unruffled by his flight, but Louise's cheeks flushed and she turned her back to the crowd and addressed me in a low voice. "Don't teach people to be afraid of the birds. A golden eagle wouldn't deliberately hurt a human."

"I'm sorry."

Five minutes, and I'd flunked my first education booth. Louise would tell Jonathan, and he, with his infinite diplomacy, would suggest that I stick to cleaning mews and doling out dead stuff to the raptors.

"Goodness, I thought that eagle would fly straight into the jewelry store." The mother with the little girl walked over to the table and stood in front of Messiah, jingling her keys again.

Louise frowned at the woman's manicured hand gripping a Coach keychain. "The birds don't like loud noises."

The child's eyes went to the Tupperware container beside my backpack. "What's in there?"

I looked at the director. Were we allowed to discuss prey with the public?

She picked up the box. Opaque plastic partially obscured the white rodent within. "This is a rat. The eagle's food."

The child shrank backward. "Ew! That's gross."

I thought of Jonathan's fierce little niece, Brynnli. She wouldn't recoil; she'd ask if she could pick up the rat and feed it to the bird.

I missed her.

At the mention of Messiah's meal, displeasure furrowed the mother's blond brow. "Can't you feed him vegetables?"

The director massaged her temples. "Raptors have to eat meat, or they'll die."

"Well . . ." The woman put her hands on her hips and considered this. "What about tempeh?"

"You don't see a lot of soybeans running around in the forest." The words flew from my mouth before I could stop them.

"Hmm!" The woman shot me an aggrieved look, caught up her little girl's hand, and walked off.

I gazed, stricken, at Louise, steeling myself for her wrath. But she busied herself straightening piles of literature, a twitch at the corners of her lips. "Can you please talk with them?" She nodded at a group of people with cameras approaching us. "I need to go use the restroom."

"You're . . . you're leaving me alone with the eagle? What if he tries to fly away again?"

She nudged her leather glove toward my elbow. "Put on the glove and take his leash. He'll fly straight to your arm."

"Oh . . . okay."

I watched her walk off and plastered a cheerful smile on my face to hide my terror.

"How old is the eagle?" a goateed man wanted to know.

"Ah . . . I'm not sure." I closed my eyes, pictured the websites I'd browsed that morning. "The Oregon Zoo's website mentions a golden eagle that lived to sixty-eight years in captivity. In the wild their lifespan's a lot shorter—fifteen to twenty years. They collide with cars, die by poisoning or electrocution." I thought of the irate sheep farmer at the county fair. "And gunshot," I added.

A silver-haired woman in a T-shirt silkscreened with owls approached, reading the eagle's name tag stuck to the perch. "What does Messiah eat at your center? I understand he can't hunt."

I paused an instant before risking offense. "We feed him rabbits, fish, quail . . . oh, and rats, of course."

"He's in beautiful shape. Obviously well cared for."

Now I really looked at the eagle. He held his head high, eyes clear and alert. His chest swelled over feathered feet. In spite of his injury, he looked capable of the 120-mile-an-hour dive executed by his wild counterparts. My own chin lifted with pride. "We do take excellent care of the birds."

The woman reached into her handbag and inserted a ten-dollar bill into the donation jar. "Thank you for your good work. This should buy him a rat or two. By the way, I volunteer at a raptor center in St. Paul, Minnesota."

"Thank you!"

"Oh, honey, keep on smiling. This work can be hard."

I nodded, thanked her again. After she and the others left, I reached into my backpack for a five-dollar bill. I'd been saving it for a mocha and a chocolate-dipped biscotti at the cafe across the courtyard. Instead, I dropped the money into the donation jar. Messiah looked up at the faint jingle of coins beneath my offering. His eye met mine. "You're worth it," I said.

~ ~

That fall, Jonathan and I spent Thanksgiving in Southern California with my mothers and got permission to tour the Ojai Raptor Center near their house. It's almost always closed to the public, but bird nerdism merits special privileges. Kim Stroud, ORC's director, described for us how she'd started a rehabilitation operation in her backyard and found funding through grants and donations to help over fifteen hundred birds a year.

"We've got a great horned owl about that size." I studied the bird in her mew. "Her name is Lorax."

"Glove-trained?"

"Yeah. Her handler's a pro, like him." I cocked a thumb toward Jonathan.

He shrugged off the compliment. "Laurin asked if we could volunteer on Christmas."

"Oh . . . I hoped we could go snowshoeing."

"I can see if there's someone else to cover the shift . . ."

I sighed. O. Henry's Della had cut off her beautiful hair to buy her husband a chain for his prized watch one December 25. My own sacrifice, despite my affection for the birds, felt no less significant.

Beside us Kim nodded. "I'll be working Christmas, too."

~ ~

"Not everyone gets to spend their holiday tube-feeding sick hawks and cleaning eagle mews."

103

Jonathan's smile glowed electric on Christmas afternoon as we changed soggy newspaper under the chick cages in the prey barn. I snorted, overly warm in the orange glow of heaters after freezing in the mews. My hand slipped, and I overturned a swath of disgusting paper onto my hiking boot.

"You know, love," I began, unable to contain my dismay. "Some people go snowshoeing or ice-skating on Christmas Day, or they cuddle up on the couch with hot buttered rum and *It's a Wonderful Life*."

"It is, isn't it?" He helped me peel the paper from my shoe and kissed me over the foul garbage can.

"Ugh. It stinks."

I missed my mother and her partner, who were likely in their kitchen cooking turkey, mashed potatoes, and stuffing with my younger siblings. I missed the stockings we made for each other, the midmorning brunch and gift exchange.

"I want my family," I told Jonathan.

"I know. I do, too." But his words sounded automatic, preoccupied. I abandoned him in the prey barn and returned unmerrily to mew cleaning.

At home that evening we exchanged gifts on the couch in front of the fireplace. The cats draped themselves around us, languishing in the warmth. I gave Jonathan tickets to the Broadway touring production of *The Producers*, ensuring at least a half day with him in Portland at the show. He handed me an eight-inch square box. "Hope you like it."

He reached down for Cody and lifted him onto his lap, offered him a strip of red-and-green rawhide from one of eight miniature pet stockings hanging from the mantel.

Jonathan's gifts to me tended toward bird identification books and binoculars. I studied the package and suspected an Audubon whistle or maybe a superior magnifying glass so I could study up close the tiny mouse skulls embedded in the two-inch gray pellets I'd picked up in Lorax's mew. Instead, I unwrapped his comic-strip paper and found a page-a-day calendar, the companion to the rather morbidly titled book *1,000 Places to See Before You Die*.

I looked up at him. "Are we going on a trip?"

"Maybe you should take the calendar out of the box." Jonathan bent over Cody, examining the inside of his dog's ear. "I think he has mites."

I slipped the calendar out. Blue sticky notes marked three pages, printed with his neat black script. I turned to the first page, which bore a description of something called the Castle Trail in Scotland. *If you say yes on this day . . .*

I looked up, confused. "Oh my God, are we going to visit your castle?"

"Flip to the next page." He plucked at his unibrow.

I turned to the next note, this one affixed to March 2, my birthday, with a page about the Prague Castle District. *Then we will go . . .*

"Are we going to Prague?" I bounced up and down on the couch. "To visit your cousin?"

The unibrow looked to be in danger of total destruction. "Flip . . . to the last . . . sticky note. *Please.*"

"All right, all right." I turned the page and burst inelegantly into tears.

There are as many ways to propose marriage as there are suitors to propose it. I'd heard of men proposing to women in hot air balloons, women proposing to men at the end of marathons, people proposing simultaneously to each other underwater through scuba masks. But none seemed to me as romantic as the proposal that lay before me now.

Jonathan had razor-bladed out an inch square from the calendar pages and tucked a scrap of black velvet into the recess. In it sat a silver ring dotted with tiny sapphires and diamonds. He fished out the band.

"Marry me?"

He turned the ring over so I could see the inscription inside.

It read, "Meow."

9

Distressed Baby Great Horned Owl

A PURPLE-HAIRED MINISTER MARRIED JONATHAN AND ME AT THE RAPTOR center two days after my birthday, on the lush spring lawn with birds on the gloves of education team members and Lorax as ring bearer. Jean tied our silver rings around the owl's tawny feathered leg with a loose blue ribbon; she stood beside us under the windmill, and the owl triangulated on insects alighting on the daffodils and crocuses.

"She looks like she's doing Steve Martin's King Tut dance," someone said, and people laughed. The scene must have looked bizarre to the handful of friends and family members shivering on folding chairs on a bright, chilly day in early March. Jonathan wore kneesocks and a kilt in the blue-and-orange version of his clan's tartan. I wore a short lace skirt with knee-high brown boots. In wool sweaters we stood under maples on ground still spongy with rain as the minister, nose ring gleaming, conducted the ceremony beside the head-bobbing owl.

"I promise to love and care for you and treat you as my best friend, always," I told Jonathan. The screech owls burbled from their mew below. Songbirds trilled from the cherry tree. Blue sky flung itself over us like a canopy. Raised on Disney, I half expected the warblers to drape a crown of wildflowers over my head. But Lorax killed the mood. Fractious, she hooted her throaty call, then ripped our rings off her ribbon and flung them into a patch of mud.

The audience, previously reverent and misty-eyed, erupted into laughter as we bent to retrieve the silver bands.

"What'cha doing?" From her mew the raven repeated her litany like a dubious priest.

My new mother-in-law beamed in her long, elegant skirt and clasped my mother's arm. "This is the strangest wedding I've ever attended."

Jonathan slipped the muddy ring onto my finger. I giggled, giddy with the perfect imperfection of it all. I'd grown up believing a wedding was supposed to be an orchestrated affair of interminable vows and linen tablecloths and champagne flutes and awkward first dances. In rebellion to all that, my first wedding had been a slapdash affair, buffet on the cheap and a friend's Zydeco band after Tony vowed into a karaoke microphone to help me clean out the cat boxes.

My marriage to Jonathan held none of the expected formality, and none of the trepidation that marked my first doomed celebration a decade before. I kissed him over and over as the minister pronounced us married, held onto him with my face pressed into his neck until my younger brother tapped my shoulder and said above the applause, "Hey, sis, how 'bout a hug?"

"Sorry . . . of course."

He held a basket of birdseed balls as party favors; they bore ribbons printed with Raymond Carver's "Late Fragment," a love poem that ran through my mind so often when I looked at Jonathan.

My mother, who wrote for a traditional wedding magazine, likely hid her horror when she saw that I'd forgotten my daffodil bouquet. My homemade carrot cake slumped lopsided under its mound of fresh flowers, and one of the raptors in attendance hacked up a pellet in front of my new father-in-law. But I married my beloved in a ceremony no one would ever forget, with a great horned owl more charismatic than any maid of honor.

Our guests crowded around Lorax with Jean on the lawn, and piled into the visitors' center for sparkling cider and slices of cake. They pressed their fingers into Audubon stuffed toy raptors to hear their various calls while the trio of owl skeletons looked on from the glass case, bachelors checking out my curly-haired sister-in-law and Sandy—our sassy vulture trainer with fairy tattoos and long, pink acrylic nails.

"I want this T-shirt!" My running partner, Kat, held up a green shirt from the stacks lining one wall. "*Carpe praedam.*" She read the words under the silkscreen of an owl with talons outstretched, descending on a mouse. "'Seize the prey.' I love it!"

Guests crowded around the cash register in the visitors' center, delighted with the idea of a witty T-shirt as a wedding souvenir.

"So, honey." Jonathan's mother sidestepped the frenzy and put an arm around my shoulders. "When are you and Jon going to have a baby? Of course, he'll have to give up smoking—that's not a good idea around a child."

I put down my fork. Did she guess that I'd been thinking about Brynnli again?

My sister had lately described her own attempts at starting a family; she wanted a baby, and she wanted it now. I'd resisted the urge to point out the fact of our deplorable genes; if she wanted to take a chance on passing down our father's temper and his chin, fine, but—confused by my feelings about a new niece or nephew—I bluffed.

"Jonathan and I aren't having a baby," I told my mother-in-law, just as I'd told my sister. "We're going to be child-free."

"Child . . . free?" My mother-in-law searched her internal lexicon for the term. Finding none, she gave a hesitant laugh. "Well . . . never say never."

Jonathan approached with the assistant director, Laurin. Mischief sparkled in her kind brown eyes. "We have a gift for you both." She handed us each a pair of leather gloves. "But you have to walk down to the lawn to get it. Jean, will you put Lorax back in her mew? She might get spooked."

Jonathan and I traded a mystified look and followed her out of the visitors' center. "Everyone come on," Laurin called over her shoulder. "Believe me, you'll want to see this."

The crowd filed down the cement steps, cake plates in hand. Laurin looked toward the clinic and raised her hand. "Now you two stand right there," she directed Jonathan and me, "and everyone else can stand in a half circle a little away. Close your eyes . . ."

Laughing, Jonathan and I shut our eyes. Around us, friends and family gasped at whatever it was that approached us.

"Surprise!"

I opened my eyes to find a juvenile red-tailed hawk in her arms—a small male, maybe a foot tall. The bird wore a tiny leather hood, making him look like a feathered aviator. I recognized him as the patient from recovery mew five, injured as a fledgling. We'd been taking him mice and cleaning his mew for months, waiting for him to grow out his flight feathers before we released him.

"He's ready to fly now!" Over the hawk's head Laurin addressed our guests. "Only thing is, he's still missing tail feathers, so we had to imp him."

"Imp?" my mother repeated.

Laurin had a reputation as a feather-magician of sorts. She explained so that our family and friends could understand. "Imping means we glued feathers from a deceased hawk into this guy's hollow feather shafts. They'll fall out after his first molt." She grinned. "Problem is, we only had feathers from an adult red-tail, so we're sending this juvie out into the world with mature plumage. He's going to be mighty attractive to the ladies."

A runner friend of mine, resplendent in a blue polyester leisure suit, cracked up. "This sure beats watching Jonathan remove Melissa's garter belt with his teeth."

I'd read of bird releases at other raptor center weddings, but I hadn't dreamed we might get to experience one ourselves. "I like this gift so much better than registering for silverware," I whispered to Jonathan.

"Me, too." He accepted the hawk from Laurin and passed it to me, leaning close to my ear. "I want you to release him, love."

The hawk felt heavy in my arms, too vulnerable for a return to the wild. I gripped his ankles in my gloved hands and pressed him to my chest.

"Don't hug him so tightly." He put a hand on my arm. "He's pretty scared."

"What's the hood for? Does it come off?" my mother's partner wondered.

Guests crowded around to see the bird. White feathers streaked his breast, contrasting with his dark wings. The hawk's hooked beak protruded from the headgear, bright yellow in the sun.

"The hood keeps the bird calm. He's gonna be anxious when he sees all of us." Jonathan reached over to tug on the tiny leather cords, loosening the hood. "I'll take this off and Melissa can let the bird go."

For so many people involved in wildlife rehabilitation, witnessing a creature's release represents a reward for dealing with the pain and death inherent in the work. About half of the birds we took in at the center didn't make it, each expiration a small, cruel blow to the psyche. We'd spent months as a team nurturing this red-tailed hawk, examining every inch of its body, rejoicing in its health. Our wedding guests, eyes shining with anticipation, caught some of our excitement. To watch a bird that arrived damaged make a full recovery and fly up toward the sky reminds us of our own resilience, of our own ability to change.

Jonathan and I had met in the dog park—damaged beings fraught with loss and heartbreak. Today, we stood together in our weird wedding finery, whole and mostly healed.

"One . . . two . . . now!" he said.

I tossed the hawk into the air, felt his buoyancy become my own. Guests around me rose up a little higher on their toes, the sight of his flight a reminder of the wildness within. The hawk executed a confused U-turn and hurtled toward us, sailing over our heads. He righted himself and flew to a fir tree, settling on a low limb. We applauded, some of us longing to bear ourselves aloft, to join him.

"He'll stay there a while and get his bearings," Laurin told us, "then take off and find new territory. We'll keep an eye out for him a couple of days to make sure he's successful."

"How do you know he can hunt?" my mother wondered.

"He graduated from Mouse University. For weeks we've been training him on live prey in our flight cage. Raptors have to prove that they can catch live mice before we release them."

"Mouse University." My mother's partner folded me into an embrace. "Lissa, this place is stranger than it needs to be. I love it."

We returned to the visitors' center for more cake and cider. Jonathan described for guests our upcoming honeymoon to Europe. I half listened, thinking about the hawk in the fir tree. I could still feel him in my arms—a weighty, needy pressure against my chest, astonishing in its sweetness.

We headed for upstate New York before our honeymoon to Europe, for a second wedding reception attended by those in Jonathan's family who couldn't fly out to Oregon. Once again, his niece, Brynnli, captivated us. Fueled by bakery frosting on the giant layer cake weighing down one end of the buffet table, she and her brother and Jonathan and I played hide-and-seek and tag and foosball and air hockey, finally settling down at dusk in the yard to listen to a great horned owl in the forest.

Brynnli shivered. "It sounds spooky."

"A little. You know, I've never heard Lorax hoot."

She looked up. "Lorax like the Dr. Seuss book?"

"That's right. I'd love to introduce you to her."

She cuddled against me. I looked down at her glossy, black hair, at her small grubby hands constructing a daisy chain in the moonlight. Jonathan reached to touch my shoulder, met my eyes. We stared at each other a long moment. We couldn't possibly want a child, could we?

The question followed us to Venice. After a day of milling around through the crowds with Jonathan, Rick Steves's cerulean guidebook in hand, we bailed on Piazza San Marco and wandered down the canal to stroll quiet neighborhoods tucked into narrow streets. "No raptors here," I observed. "Just a hell of a lot of pigeons."

A bell rang, compelling us toward a courtyard. Children filed out of a school in white shirts and blue pants and skirts, scampering to parents who stood on the perimeter with arms outstretched or weighed down with bags of produce.

Jonathan took my hand as a little girl skipped past us to an angular, mustached man on a bike. She hopped onto the handlebars, and they took off laughing and chattering down the alley. "Wow. They look like something out of *Cinema Paradiso*."

My husband remained silent, eyes following the bicycle until it disappeared.

Children appeared everywhere in Vienna. They monopolized the interactive Beethoven display at Haus der Musik, shoveled in Sacher torte at bakery counters, pointed and giggled at the musicians dressed as Mozart on every corner. I hummed arias, trying not to hear their high-pitched voices and overtired squalling.

In Prague we toured the largest ancient castle in the world with its garden display of tethered falconry birds—hawks, a peregrine falcon, an enormous Eurasian eagle-owl with orange eyes and feather tufts twice the size of those on Lorax. We saw few kids, and yet the possibility of them remained ever-present. Jonathan's cousin, an elegant entrepreneur, lived there with his lovely Czech wife. They took us to a neighborhood pub redolent with cigarette smoke and drunken laughter.

"Are you two having children?" I asked my new cousin as we ordered another round of beer.

She widened her eyes. "You are teasing me, right? Why . . ." She waved a delicate hand at the comely crowd shouting political debates over their pitchers and platters of pricey meats. "Why would I give this up?"

She'd asked a rhetorical question; I knew that. Still, I answered.

"I have no idea."

My last morning in Prague, the last day of our honeymoon, I woke early and crept from our room with my camera to walk the streets. Here was the astrological clock with the animated figures that appeared in the film version of *The Unbearable Lightness of Being*. Here was the statue that protesters had blindfolded, a scathing comment on Russian invasion. I wandered the streets where once thousands of young people with courage and vision had jangled their keys, demanding regime change, insisting on a new doctrine.

How liberating to be able to change one's mind, I thought, to challenge ideology and embrace new ideas, even if ridding oneself of the old ones seemed initially impossible, absolutely terrifying.

⁓

I returned to Jonathan. We flew home to our house and our pets, to our jobs and our raptor duties. Several months after our honeymoon, a hiker out with her dog discovered a baby great horned owl in the bushes and brought it in a box to the center.

"Bet its sibling pushed it out." Darcy readied a pet carrier in the treatment room with newspaper and a rolled-up towel.

I raised my brows. "They do that?"

"Oh, yeah. They compete for food and space. You've seen how one baby tries to get most of the food when we're hand-feeding a bunch. Survival of the bossiest."

"We need to find the nest right away," Laurin told us. "We've got about forty-eight hours before the parents stop looking for it. If it's not back in the nest by then, we'll have to raise it here."

Jonathan reached for his truck key and tossed me my stocking cap. "We'll go."

"How d'you find an owl in the wild?" We headed out toward the tiny town of Lorane and the trail where the baby had been found.

"Sometimes they'll come if you call them at dusk, but not usually. That's why we have this." He handed me an Audubon CD of bird calls. "Track seven, on a loop until we find them."

I read the title: "Distressed Baby Great Horned Owl."

"I'll carry the laptop; you get the binoculars and look for signs of the parents."

"Um . . . what sort of signs?"

He unwrapped a stick of gum, in effort to avoid lighting the cigarettes he knew I loathed. "Look for white streaks on bushes and trunks, pellets, bits of fur and feathers under the trees, anything that looks like it might be a nest."

We parked and headed into the forest. Jonathan opened his laptop and slid in the CD. Suddenly, sorrowful bird cries filled the air. I'd never heard anything like them—piteous, gut-wrenching shrieks. I gripped the binoculars. "That baby sounds so bereft."

"It is."

Back at the raptor center, a gray ball of fluff huddled in one corner of a pet carrier, propped up on its towel roll. What must it feel like to lose your home, lose your mother, find yourself alone and abruptly orphaned?

I clutched the sleeve of Jonathan's coat. "We've gotta find the parents."

"All we can do is try." He hit repeat on track seven, and we searched trees and fragments of open blue sky for the bulky shapes of owls.

"Let's just listen a while." He sat on the duff and patted the spot beside him. I leaned my head on his shoulder. My ears ached from straining to catch a twig snap or any faint hoot.

At four thirty the forest began to darken. "We'll hike out slowly and play the track again. Great horneds start hunting at dusk."

We walked single file, the distressed baby's cries ringing in our ears all the way back to the truck. "Can we try again tomorrow?"

Jonathan nodded. "I'll call in sick."

At the center we cared for the owl, fed him bits of skinned mouse while we stood to one side of the pet carrier, our faces invisible. The baby jerked his beak toward the forceps, silent and hungry. Sated, it hunkered down once more.

The next morning, we headed back to the trail with Scott, a city arborist. He worked pro bono on cases like this, climbing hundred-foot trees to replace baby raptors or search for them.

"So you say the bird was found here . . ." Scott peered up into the branches of a fir. "It's possible that the nest's up there." He pointed out a dark spot near the top of the tree. "Could be an owl or squirrel nest, could be just branches. Won't know 'til I go up."

Jonathan and I watched as he looped ropes over a high limb and buckled himself into a harness. He put on gloves and began pulling ropes, ascending into the tree with a camera poised to take photos of whatever he found.

Down below, Jonathan opened up his laptop and pushed play again. Screams filled the air. He leaned his chin on my head. "We're gonna find the parents today. I know it, love."

But after an hour of treetop exploration, Scott lowered himself and pulled off his helmet. "No mutes, no prey residue." He showed us pictures of the abandoned nest he found. "No feathers, either. The baby didn't come from this tree."

We split up, each of us taking a different path. Jonathan walked down the main trail, holding the laptop out in front of him. With "Distressed Baby Great Horned Owl" cranked full volume, he craned his head upward. I climbed to the top of a small hill and practiced my owl call. It's a nasal sound, I'd learned, producing a vibrating tone in and around the nose and lips. Do it well enough, and you can call curious owls to a nearby tree branch.

I didn't do it well enough.

"Nothing," the men conceded when we met at the truck hours later. The parents, we decided, had vanished.

"What's this mean for the baby?" Scott leaned against Jonathan's truck, upended a bottle of water and drank.

Jonathan cracked open a Coke. "We'll raise it, hand-feed it until it moves to a rehab mew, and then give it euthanized mice and chicks. It may be that Lorax can act as its foster mother, teaching it to be an owl. In a few months we'll put it in our flight cage and train it on live prey. If it can learn to hunt mice, we'll come back and release it here."

Scott examined a scratch where a limb had scraped his forearm. "What's its chance of survival?"

"Good. The bird's not injured, just scared, so it should be fine."

"You guys do a heck of a job." Scott shook our hands, then got in his truck and drove off.

We headed back to the center without talking. We returned the CD and gloves to the clinic, and Jonathan walked off with a rat for the other golden eagle, Amazon, whom he'd begun to train. The evening shift left, and Louise disappeared into her house. Alone, I slipped into the treatment room.

I'd been trained well. I knew better than to do what I did, but I couldn't help it. I tiptoed over to the baby owl's carrier and lifted one side of the sheet that covered it, then bent and peered through one airhole.

It slumped listless, despondent as a child after its mother has vanished.

"It's okay," I whispered.

But it wasn't. Young creatures need someone to parent them.

I knew then. I replaced the sheet and vacated the treatment room, clocked out on the computer, and went to sit on a log outside Lorax's mew. From her feeding platform she swiveled her head to look down at me, ear tufts lowered and one foot curled calmly. What a gift, I thought, to be able to teach an orphaned owl how to function in the world. I zipped up my coat and dropped my head into my hands.

"Everything okay?" Jonathan crunched down the path and crouched next to me. "I thought you were cleaning the visitors' center. The light's still on in there."

"I have something to tell you."

No man thrills to this sentence. "Okay . . ."

The sun had set; in the mew near us, the screech owls began their nightly chorus. A pair of wild barred owls had lately appeared; they hooted from the trees. Loki, the center's ancient resident barred, called back. Jonathan covered his hand with mine. "What is it, Melissa?"

I held my breath. No going back once the words were out.

"I think . . . I think we should adopt an orphan."

He closed his eyes. Though I longed to bury my fingers in his hair, I kept my hands folded, waiting. He sat for a long time without speaking. Then he opened his eyes and smiled.

"I thought I'd done something horribly wrong." He leaned over and kissed me deeply, the way he had that fateful afternoon when we'd picked up a load of frozen rats and the chickens and the baby barred that now flew free. "Wife," he said, "I agree."

10

"If We Have to Eat Roadkill"

Maybe there's some genetic predisposition for wanting to help orphaned and abandoned creatures, even if doing so sometimes proves detrimental to one's own mental and physical well-being. If such a gene exists, people who adopt a dozen kids have it; likewise those who run wildlife rehabilitation centers. Donald Kerr, founder of Oregon's Birds of Prey Center, certainly has it.

A biology major and self-proclaimed "desert rat," he founded the center, part of the High Desert Museum, south of Bend. It's smaller than the one in Eugene, with the same mission to display permanently injured raptors for educational purposes. Visitors can see bald eagles, a golden eagle, a great horned owl, and—in a delightful bit of oddity—a porcupine and a badger.

The morning of our trip to the museum, Jonathan and I drove over the pass along the McKenzie River with a couple of barred owls in pet carriers, special delivery to a rehabber near Bend.

"It's a three-hour drive each way," he'd cautioned me.

"A road trip with you? I'm in."

I wrapped my arms around him, then slapped together a couple of peanut butter sandwiches and called a neighbor to let out our dogs. In the truck I looked over at him and beamed. "We'll have lots of time to talk about the adoption."

—◦—

We began the process of procuring a child mired in spectacular ignorance. Jonathan's mother had adopted his oldest brother and sister in the early

1960s. In that era secrecy was still the norm; people seldom discussed adoption, and Jonathan was ten before he realized his oldest siblings weren't genetically related.

My aunt—a quintessential '60s flower child—had a kid just before my birth and put her up for adoption, but this was not a topic of conversation, either. The only adopted kids Jonathan and I knew were his niece and nephew from Korea, and so we called up an international agency in our city and begged for assistance.

We wanted a girl just like our niece Brynnli, I told the receptionist on the phone, only younger—a toddler spitfire who would despise pink and become an instant fearless accomplice on all our adventures.

"Ideally," I instructed, "she should be three years old. That way, she's out of diapers, but she can still fit in a backpack while we do our shift at the raptor center."

"Come on down!" The woman described the agency's monthly meeting for prospective parents. She had a chirpy voice like the cheery hostess of some prime-time TV program: "Choose Your Child!"

She put our names on the list for the October meeting. "That first night, we won't need a check," she said, "but be prepared to write one within the month!"

Jonathan and I hadn't considered the financial factor of adoption. In the world of raptor care, rehabilitators regularly offer up birds to centers with facilities best suited to the creatures' needs, free of charge. Should a raptor prove nonreleasable but calm around people, a director could apply to the state's Fish and Wildlife Department to keep the bird for educational purposes, *gratis*.

Because of this, we thought we'd simply declare our willingness to offer an orphan a good, safe home, and no money would need to change hands.

We were wrong.

But that day in Bend, we walked around the High Desert Museum blissfully unaware of adoption politics. Hand in hand, we checked out two Northern spotted owls—Polka and Dot—in the limbs of a large tree encased in an indoor atrium.

"Ugh." A couple of men in jeans and raincoats turned away and headed outside. "*Spotted* owls."

I looked after them, surprised. I'd seen bumper stickers that read, "I love spotted owls . . . fried," and the controversy confused me. Visitors to our center—realizing we had two of the few spotteds in captivity—made a beeline for their mew. But I'd heard only exclamations of admiration, never disgust.

"In a nutshell," Jonathan said, "these owls can only live in old-growth forests. Oregon legislation to protect them put loggers and mill workers out of jobs. It changed the state's economy."

A willowy woman with a jaunty black ponytail, silver owl earrings dangling from her lobes, pushed through the double doors leading to a small auditorium. She wore a blue collared shirt imprinted with the center's name. Her smile broadened as she caught sight of Jonathan's green fleece jacket with our center's logo.

"Oh, you're from Eugene?" She flashed a mouthful of startling white teeth. "Awesome. We're just about to do a presentation." She propped open the doors. "Come on in."

We sat down in folding chairs beside a scattering of families and couples. The ponytailed woman disappeared for a moment, then returned with a great horned owl on her gloved left arm.

"It's smaller than Lorax," I whispered to Jonathan.

"He's male. Shhh . . . I want to hear her."

The woman spoke about owls' lopsided ears, the eyes that are more like long tubes fastened in the skull by bony rings. "They're only able to look straight ahead," she said. "But they have binocular vision and lots of light-sensitive rod cells, so they can see clearly at night." During her talk the great horned sat unmoving on her glove except for his head, which swiveled toward a fly on a window, the whimper of a baby in a stroller. At one point the owl leaned over and picked up a strand of her ponytail in his beak.

"He's preening her," Jonathan whispered.

They reminded me of Jean and Lorax, connected by trust as well as by leather jesses and glove. I watched with envy as the young woman strode about the room in her khaki pants and sturdy boots, showing off the handsome creature.

"Maybe I could handle Lorax if she were that small," I whispered to Jonathan when she disappeared and another, older woman walked out with a bald eagle.

"I've had her out for ed programs. She's not heavy—that male's only about half a pound lighter than Lorax," he whispered back. "Why not give it a try? Didn't Jean offer to train you?"

"Yeah. But maybe she was joking." I jabbed my right thumbnail into my left palm, trying to gauge the pain of an accidentally embedded talon. Jonathan looked down at my hands. Comprehending my experiment, he put an arm around my shoulders.

"You're a goofball. It's not that dangerous. I've only been footed a couple times."

I thought of the inch-long scar under his rib, another between thumb and forefinger on his hand. "Did it hurt?"

"Of course. But it's worth it. I get to have a relationship with a *raptor*. How many of us can say that?"

The presentation over, he walked off to get another look at the spotted owls. I approached the ponytailed volunteer who'd returned with the great horned on her glove. "Thanks," I told her. "That was really well done."

"Awesome." The owl, spooked by a squeak from the baby stroller, stretched out his wings. The woman turned her wrist slightly so that the bird tightened his grip on her black leather glove and returned to his at-ease position. "Do you handle raptors?" she asked me.

"No. I just clean mews."

"Oh. Well, that's important, too." Her shoulders twitched in a dismissive shrug. "I mean, everyone poops, right? I'd better get this bird over to the treatment room. His beak needs coping."

"Everyone poops," I sighed as she disappeared into a door marked "Staff Only." In a million years I'd never have her confidence or her long legs.

Jonathan walked in from the outside mews, brow furrowed. "Sad story about the guy who founded this place . . ."

"Donald M. Kerr?" I read his name on the wall beside us.

He nodded. "One of his great horned owls scratched him with mouse blood on its talons, and it got into his bloodstream. Now he's got encephalitis."

"What's that?"

"Some sort of blood disease."

"Holy moly . . . is he gonna die?"

"Not sure. He's in a wheelchair, and he can't talk. Didn't want to come out and ask the staff about his prognosis . . ."

I shivered and zipped up my coat against the desert's September chill. Jonathan fell silent, hands plunged into the pockets of his fleece. We walked around the outside of the museum, looking at the replica of a pioneer homestead, a stable, a covered wagon. I thought about Kerr—the picture I'd seen of him showed two great horneds on his glove and an expression of quiet adoration on his face.

He'd given up his own health and well-being to help injured raptors. Had his intimate relationships with beautiful, powerful birds proved worthy of the sacrifice?

<hr />

"Osprey!"

Back on the highway, I pointed out the window at the M-shaped black-and-white bird flying up ahead of us. "Has a fish, I think."

Suddenly, a larger raptor barreled toward the osprey. Jonathan yelped, "Bald eagle!"

"Hang onto the wheel!"

Right in front of us, the birds tumbled together in the sky.

Something struck the road. I whipped around to look out the window. "What the hell was that?"

Jonathan glanced in the rearview mirror and broke into the laugh he reserved for particularly absurd surprises. "The fish!"

Happier now, we chattered about the osprey's trick of turning a newly caught fish around in its talons midair to a head-first position, so it's streamlined with the bird's body. Their feet have barbed pads and fishhook-like talons, perfect for gripping trout and salmon and the like. We spoke of the nesting platforms alongside the river in Eugene, of the times we'd both almost driven off the road to catch a glimpse of the birds within. Osprey like to nest in flat- or dead-topped trees near water; when these are scarce, employees from electrical and transportation companies sometimes erect platforms on power poles. Pairs of the nearly two-foot-tall birds may build their bulky stick nests there, returning year after year to raise babies.

Our talk turned from fledgling osprey to baby humans and our potential adoption.

"Our first agency meeting is this week." Jonathan guided the truck past the lava fields near Clear Lake. The vine maples had begun to turn; they spread like bursts of leafy flame against fields of black rock. "You excited?"

I reached to massage his neck. "I can't quite believe it. This time next year, we may have a little daughter from Korea."

<hr>

"Not gonna happen."

A petite woman with a swingy blond bob laid down the law on orientation night. "I'm Marissa." She offered a firm handshake coupled with scrutinizing sapphire eyes. "I'm one of the social workers here. First-time parents?"

Jonathan and I nodded.

"Thought so. They're always on time."

Marissa looked to be our age. She wore an embroidered felt jacket with blue jeans, a blue velvet cloche, and a chunky silver necklace on which hung a ceramic dove. I pictured her exchanging a handful of oddly shaped coins for the pieces of her outfit at exotic little bazaars overseas while searching the streets for orphans.

We stood in a stark, chilly meeting room in the adoption agency's office. Jonathan picked up a brochure from the table and looked down at the photos of gorgeous black and Asian children embraced by beatific adults. "Why *can't* we adopt from Korea?" he asked.

Marissa cocked her head. "I didn't say you can't adopt from Korea—you just can't have a girl. Korea adopts boys to first-timers."

I bit my lip and glanced at my husband. He frowned. A smell like wet feathers rose off his peacoat. "Why's that?"

"The country's got more boys than girls. Most adoptive families want a girl, so if you go with Korea as new parents, it's almost a given that your first kid will be a boy. Girls go to those who've already adopted at least once."

A couple in Oregon Ducks gear walked in. "This where we get a kid?" The man, big and burly, towered over the social worker.

Marissa nodded, her expression neutral. "It is."

The room began to fill. A woman with curly brown hair sat down beside me and shook my hand and Jonathan's. "What country?"

"Korea, we thought . . . but I guess they won't give first-timers a girl."

"I've heard that." She shrugged off her fleece jacket. "It's a seller's market, for sure."

I cringed at the idea of reducing the joyful process of family creation to stark economics, but as the spaces around the table filled and Marissa began talking us through the agency's brochure, I realized we really were looking at the most basic rules of supply and demand. Right then, millions of children in Asian and African countries needed permanent homes, and millions of adults in North America and Europe hoped to provide them with one. Government officials overseas could pretty much name their price. While Jonathan and I had an ever-growing desire to help an orphaned child, we didn't have the money.

Marissa folded her hands on the table and addressed the three couples and two single women who sat around her. "You can expect to spend upwards of thirty thousand dollars on your adoption."

"Thirty thousand?" I stared at her. "Who on earth can afford that?"

Across from me, the husband and wife in their green-and-yellow Oregon Ducks sweatshirts and stocking caps smiled knowingly. "We're taking out a second mortgage." The woman looked into my eyes, and her dimples deepened. "The Lord told us to help a little Chinese orphan, so that's what we're doing."

I wondered if the Lord might front Jonathan and me a zero-interest loan. I worked as an adjunct instructor and a freelance writer—two precarious jobs that could give way to poverty at any time. Jonathan collected a modest salary from the art museum for his new job as a gallery preparator.

"Maybe we could hold a fundraiser." Only half joking, I considered the idea. "How many bake sales d'you think we'd need to earn a daughter?"

Again, Marissa reminded me that if we hoped for a girl, we'd have to adopt from another part of the world. "Here are the countries we work with." She handed out another brochure and directed our attention to a world map above a chart detailing each country's requirement for adoptive parents.

My eyes went to South Korea. "Boys to first-time families." I read the stats out loud. "Couples must be married for at least three years. Single adoptive parents need not apply."

"Wait a minute . . ." The curly-haired woman beside me leaned forward and petitioned the social worker. "You mean if I want to adopt a Korean kid with cerebral palsy, the government won't let me?"

"I'm afraid not." For an instant Marissa's snapping blue eyes shone with sympathy. I looked down and saw that the woman beside me wore a brace on her leg.

"You have to understand that most countries are pretty conservative," Marissa continued. "They're looking to place their kids in households they can understand—namely, what looks to them like wealthy, two-parent heterosexual homes. Haiti would be a good bet for a single woman."

As a group, we looked down at Haiti's criteria. "Single women accepted." But now Jonathan had a question. "Hey, what about single men?"

I elbowed him. "Something you're not telling me?"

The couples around us laughed. Even the woman next to me smiled, but Marissa remained serious. "Countries overseas won't adopt to single men or same-sex couples."

"You're *serious?*" My same-sex coupled friends did a fine job of child-rearing. Ditto single moms and single dads. I raised my hand. "What'll these countries say when they find out I have two mothers?"

Marissa considered this. "*I* believe a child should have as many grandmothers as possible."

"Hmm." I read the mission statement printed on the front page of the brochure. "Dedicated to providing every child with a forever family."

But—I added privately—*you'd better adhere to our definition of family.*

Marissa shrugged off her jacket and talked us through the rest of the countries' criteria. She explained that families adopting from China were almost guaranteed a girl because of the government's one-child policy and the elevated status of boys in that country.

We'd wanted a daughter just like Brynnli; still, China and Korea were next-door neighbors. I circled the larger country on the map in my brochure and nudged Jonathan. He looked down, caught my meaning, and nodded.

Now I saw in my head a little Chinese girl skipping across the raptor center's lawn in cutoff shorts and a "*Carpe praedam*" T-shirt, ponytails flapping as she giggled and threw her arms around me like the toddler in the promotional DVD Marissa showed us.

"Don't get attached to an image of the child you want to adopt." She turned off the television. "No cutting out magazine photos and putting them on the refrigerator; no choosing names. You'll set yourself up for disappointment."

I wondered if the young woman next to me had a clear picture of the child she hoped would be hers. At the break she stood up and walked to the reception area. A binder labeled "Waiting Children" sat on the counter. I looked over her shoulder as she flipped to a section marked "Haiti" and stopped to study a photo of a skinny, grinning boy with a brace on one leg.

"Is that the child you're thinking of adopting?"

The woman looked up at me, startled, then smiled so that two shy dimples crept in her cheeks. "Yes." In spite of the cold, she wore a sleeveless dress and her face looked flushed. "He's got a developmental delay, as well as CP. I think I could be a good mother to someone like him."

I envied her conviction and her selflessness. I'd helped to raise my younger brother with Down syndrome for over a decade, an experience that differed little from my friends' experiences with their nondisabled little brothers. I adored Tim, but I saw how my mother and Annie, both nearing retirement age, chauffeured him to Special Olympics events all over the county and escorted him on weekend dates with his girlfriend, who also has Down syndrome.

Eighteen years of parenting I could handle. Any more than that, and Jonathan and I might as well scrap our plans of adopting a child and commit to a falcon.

We returned to the office room, and Marissa passed around a bowl of M&M's, maybe to sweeten the blow of her concluding statement. "We'll need a check for three hundred fifty dollars and a whole stack of paperwork within a month," she told us. "Personal data sheet, financial statement, medical reports, criminal records check, employment verification form, certified birth certificates, marriage certificate, and something called an I-600A so you can take your child out of the birth country."

Jonathan and I understood paperwork. On the raptor center's filing cabinet, I'd seen stacks of mandatory application forms for adopting a permanently injured raptor. Oregon's Department of Fish and Wildlife required a thorough description of the bird, plus veterinarian reports on the nature of its injury and why it would make a good education bird instead of being euthanized.

"But thirty thousand dollars?" I fumed in the truck on the way home. "I thought this would be so easy. Find an orphan, give it a home. But it's stupid and complicated."

"It *is* kind of crazy. We've gotta stay focused." Jonathan wove his fingers through mine. "There'll be sacrifices. We'll make them together. Even if we have to eat roadkill."

I stared at him. "What are you *talking* about?"

His lips twitched. "Don't you know that some raptor centers are so poor that volunteers pick up roadkill to feed to their birds?"

He let loose his delighted laugh, which lifted my mood and made me think tonight might be a fine evening for a bottle of wine before bed.

"My love?" I preened his hair with my fingers and reached to kiss his neck. "I'm so glad we're in this together."

11

Owl with a Foot Fetish

UNWILLING TO WRITE A CHECK TO THE ADOPTION AGENCY, BUT RELUC-
tant to spend our money in case we did decide to commit to a little Chinese girl, Jonathan and I ate dinner at home and replaced evenings at the
cinema with visits to the raptor center so that he could help to train one
of the Northern spotted owls. He'd worked little with Amazon since the
death of the bald eagle he'd been scheduled to train, but Louise had asked
him to help her with Chenoa.

"Visitors connect better with the birds when they see them outside
the mews," he told me, "and we want them to see the spotteds, in particular, since they're endangered."

While he trained I helped out with another shift's feeding and cleaning and sat outside Lorax's mew, wondering what it would feel like to
walk around with her on my arm. She sat on her perch and triangulated
at me, feather tufts poised like my tabby cat's ears. Once, she opened her
beak wide and hacked up a large gray pellet.

"For me?" I laughed. "Oh, you shouldn't have."

Jonathan walked down from Chenoa's mew and kneaded my shoulders. "You're so in love. Just ask if you can work with her. She's not gonna
hurt you."

I thought of encephalitis, of wheelchairs, and shook my head.

We left Lorax fixating on the rubber duck in her water trough and
walked back up the path to the clinic.

"Careful!" Jean held up a warning hand as we opened the door. "Loose
bird!"

Occasionally, volunteers allowed one of the smaller permanent residents to stretch its wings in the clinic. I expected the one-eyed kestrel on the paper-towel holder or a screech owl on the computer monitor. Instead, I looked down to find—mounted on a portable ground perch—a foot-high owl with a round, tuftless head and bright white feathers speckled with black spots. He looked like a cue ball with a beak.

"Kids, meet Archimedes." Jean stretched her gloved hand toward the bird, poised to grab him if he spooked. The creature's enormous feathered feet remained gripping the wood-and-Astroturf block.

I remained by the door. "Named for the Greek mathematician? Um . . . his talons are twice as big as Lorax's."

"A snowy owl?" Jonathan's brow shot up. "Is he permanent? How'd we get him?"

Our center had a policy of taking in resident birds native to Oregon. Even I, thanks to our Audubon book at home, knew that the big white owls lived mainly in Canada, Alaska, and Eurasia.

Jean ran a hand through her auburn hair. "Snowies are a gray area. They come down to the lower forty-eight every three or four years to hunt when the lemming population in the Arctic dries up. This guy's an imprint, though, part of a captive breeding program back east. They couldn't find a female for him . . ."

"So we got him." Jonathan bent down to get a closer look. Archimedes clacked his black beak but remained standing on the perch.

I stood silent, staring. At a center where birds came in varying shades of black and tan and brown and white, and sometimes dull red, I'd never seen such an owl. He seemed to glow, lit from within. And he appeared to have a mustache—fluffy feathers cascaded from either side of his beak. He squinted up at me out of slanted yellow eyes that looked too small in his fluffy head and peered at my footwear, a pair of new white running shoes.

Suddenly, he opened his beak and emitted a sound like squeaking bicycle brakes. He scuttled over and jumped on top of my sneakers, spread his vast wings and let out a series of dog-like woofs.

Black talons squeezed my toes. I fought the urge to shriek.

"*Jonathan.* What . . . what's he *doing*?"

Jean knelt and reeled in the nylon leash clipped to the leather jesses around the bird's ankles. Archimedes stepped panting onto her gloved wrist. "Remember, he's a human imprint."

"So why'd he jump on my feet?" I wailed.

Jean grinned at me. "Darlin', he's trying to have sex with your shoes."

"Oh . . . that's disgusting."

She laughed, flushed with excitement over the bird. "Harry Potter's made snowies a big deal. This owl's gonna be a rock star."

Jonathan nodded, and I saw a look of longing in his eyes. "So . . . who's training him?"

"The director's asked me to work with him. He might've been trained at some point—hard to tell. For a while it'll be just him and me. Then, if I can get him solid on the glove, we can share. Better put him back in his mew now."

She touched her glove to Archimedes' legs and he stepped up, but as she took his jesses and stood, he leaped off her arm and hung upside down, twisting and writhing at the end of his straps.

Piercing shrieks filled the clinic. From the treatment room a recovering kestrel screamed. Jean sank to the linoleum, abruptly mournful.

"Here we go again." She put her free hand on the owl's smooth white back and guided him—still screaming—to the ground, untangling the jesses from his huge, struggling feet. "If he used to be glove-trained, he isn't now."

"How come he doesn't fly back to your arm like the other birds?" I asked. If a UPS truck rumbled up the driveway while Jonathan stood with Chenoa on the lawn, the spotted would sometimes fly off the glove in a defensive move called a bate. But if Jonathan stood immobile with his arm out, Chenoa flew right back to his glove.

"Snowies are ground nesters," Jean explained. "If they get scared, they fly downward toward what they think is a safe spot and end up hanging. It's not safe . . . he could asphyxiate and die."

She put him in one of the clinic mews and unclipped his jesses, pausing to prod gently around his keel for undigested food.

"What's he feel like?"

"Like putting your hand inside a down comforter. Want to touch him?"

"No, thanks." I took a bag of mice from the freezer and set them in the sink to thaw for the nocturnal birds' dinner. Their brown forms bobbed about in the warm water, thirty tiny, macabre swimmers.

"I'm off to work with Amazon." Jonathan set a rat on a pie pan and headed up to the golden eagle's mew.

I began to wash plates and syringes and coffee mugs. Jean spoke over the running water. "I really think," she said in her meditative drawl, "that you'd make a good bird handler. What d'you say? My offer's still good—I could teach you to work with Lorax, and maybe someday you could help with Archimedes."

I turned off the water. The new owl looked like a droll little snowman, albeit a snowman with a foot fetish. Though I knew better, I suspected him of a damned good sense of humor.

"Maybe," I allowed.

She handed Archimedes a mouse. He took it in his obsidian beak and held it a moment before throwing his head back and swallowing it whole.

"He looks like my college roommate doing a shot of Jägermeister."

Jean wet a towel and bent to scrub splattered mutes off the floor. "He's just gotta get solid on the glove. He's so exotic, visitors are gonna love him."

"Oh, yeah. He's amazing."

If the ardor in my voice surprised her, she didn't let on. I certainly wasn't telling anyone just then that I'd fallen madly in love with a foot-fetishistic snowy owl who sported a fluffy mustache.

—◆—

"If we adopt a little girl from China, she'll be as exotic as Archimedes," I told Jonathan on the way to the dog park. "That's okay for an owl, but what if we're putting her in a difficult position? I mean, I've seen a few adopted kids in town, but what if she feels like she sticks out too much? Eugene's pretty white . . ."

Jonathan pulled up to Morse Family Farm and opened the back of his truck. Three dogs came tumbling out. He grabbed their leashes and hurtled down the gravel path. "My sister lives in a mostly Anglo part of New York," he called over his shoulder. "Nathan and Brynnli seem fine."

I remained unconvinced. Growing up in the 1980s, I'd felt as if my siblings and I were the only kids in the world with lesbian moms. We didn't march in the Gay Pride parade or join PFLAG. We had no idea that young adults with same-sex parents had begun to organize across the country into political and support groups. I thought we were weird, an anomalous family that had nothing in common with the families of my friends. Lonely, I wandered through junior high and high school longing for comrades who grew up watching *Victor Victoria* and knew that a "bear" didn't always refer to a backcountry quadruped.

I recoiled at the thought of my daughter experiencing a similar isolation.

Jonathan and I slogged around the muddy perimeter of the park, waving to acquaintances, petting their dogs. "Wonder how Selena's doing." My first friend in Eugene had finally given up on local canine-friendly bachelors; she met a man online and moved overseas to marry him.

"Isn't that your running partner?" Jonathan pointed across the field to where Kat and her children pushed through the gate with their black Newfoundland.

My friend waved, and we walked to where she stood near the kiddie pool. "This is the first thing he does." She shook her head at her dog, who'd collapsed with a splash into the blue plastic tub. "Then it takes me half a day to wash him. Kids, go run with Boris."

Jonathan and I watched as her kids—ten and twelve—scampered off in full rain gear with the dog. Kat sighed and stretched her arms over her head. "How's the adoption coming? Did you commit to China?"

"I've gotta go rescue Cody." Jonathan excused himself to disentangle his sheltie's fluffy tail from a blackberry bush near the fence.

I turned to Kat. "We haven't written any checks yet."

My friend was, in a word, blunt. And while I enjoyed that characteristic for its lack of ambiguity, sometimes she pissed me off. When I'd told her on one of our training runs that Jonathan and I had made the mental switch from a Korean daughter to a girl from China, she'd snorted.

"Why don't you adopt locally?" she'd called over her shoulder on the trail.

"Nah," I'd panted. "We want a kid like Jonathan's niece. Besides, these girls are abandoned. We want to rescue one of them."

She'd turned then to jog backwards, shaking her head at me. "Have you ever thought that if Americans didn't adopt these children, the Chinese might change their policy?"

This was not a possibility I'd considered. Unwilling to navigate a slippery cognitive dissonance, I'd scoffed at her suggestion and invoked the one word I hoped would justify Jonathan's and my potential five-figure expenditure. "Kat, they're *Communists*."

Now she zipped up her parka and attempted again to put in her unsolicited two cents. "There are teens in this county who're pregnant, looking for adoptive parents. Why not help one of them?"

I bent down to scratch Kawliga behind the ears and tossed a sodden tennis ball for Marley. "They usually have infants. Jon and I don't like babies."

"I'd be careful who you say that to."

I turned away. "I've gotta go get a poop bag. Marley's squatting."

She followed me, worrying the debate like a hunk of rawhide. "It's just so trendy to adopt an Asian baby, Melissa. First Meg Ryan does it, then Angelina . . . it's like you're all Paris Hilton buying a Chihuahua."

My daughter," I sputtered, yanking a plastic bag from the dispenser, "will *not* be a lapdog."

"I'm glad to hear that. You guys already have three dogs."

My chest tightened with rage. I liked Kat. She'd once left a pan of enchiladas, along with homemade corn tortillas, on my doorstep when Jonathan landed in the hospital with a raging foot infection. Still, people should encourage their friends to follow their heart, I believed, no matter how imprudent they found that muscular organ. "Can't you just support me?"

"I'll try. Just promise me you'll honor your kid's birth country. Otherwise, she'll write a memoir about how you denied her heritage and expose you on *Oprah*."

In the middle of penning a memoir involving my own mother, I fell silent and stalked off to scoop up dog feces.

"So, honey, why China?"

My mom flew up from California the following week. She rode down the airport escalator in her demure dark slacks and blouse and carried a black leather bag; even so, sharp-eyed passengers who looked past her austere attire could still spot in her pink cheeks and merry blue eyes the granddaughter of vaudevillian comics.

"I mean, what does that country have that we don't have, besides sweet-and-sour pork?"

Still stinging from Kat's commentary, I stiffened as she hugged me. Over the clank and rattle of the baggage carousel, I repeated our reasoning. The phrase felt so tired it barely had the energy to leave my lips. "We want a little girl like Jonathan's niece, and we want to help a Chinese orphan."

My mother reached for her suitcase—distinguishable in a sea of black rolling bags only by a tiny silver *Star Trek* communicator pin. "Sorry—this is all pretty new to me."

I wondered if she ever thought about the baby her younger sister had given up the year before my birth. Had attitudes been different then, my cousin and I might have grown up together in our grandmother's costume shop. As it was, my aunt had no idea where her daughter lived, and no way to find her.

"If we do end up adopting, we're going to name the girl Lydia." I rolled my mother's suitcase across the carpet toward the sliding glass doors. "We'd keep her Chinese name as her middle name, of course."

Lydia was the name of my great-grandmother, a woman I'd adored for her bawdy humor and her vibrant stories of a life spent in show business.

"That's funny. Your great-grandma hated her name. After she left the farm to join the circus, she changed it to Mary."

She moved ahead to examine a trio of large framed children's portraits mounted on easels beside Wings Bar and Grille. "Oregon foster kids." I glanced at the text on a fourth easel. "Looking for families."

My mother studied the photo of a little blond girl holding a daisy. "Foster parenting's gotta be so hard . . . one day you're a family; the next day you're split up."

"Sort of like how we grew up."

After our parents' divorce my siblings and I had bounced between our mother's bohemian beach duplex and our father's chic two-story near Los Angeles. We'd just get settled in one house with its particular rhythms and rules, then find ourselves shuttled to the other one ninety miles away. In such shifting surroundings I felt forever foreign.

"Jonathan and I are *not* becoming foster parents."

"Well, someone's gotta love them."

I couldn't help smiling. On Friday nights when we were kids, my mother would give my sister and me a dollar to spend in Pic 'N' Save—a discount store down the street from her house, full of weird remaindered stuff. Always on these shopping excursions, my mom bought the inevitable one-eyed, ratty stuffed animal lying bereft on the dirty linoleum.

She'd place the duck or rabbit or snake on the dashboard of her VW bus, a symbol of her fondness for hard-luck cases. "Someone's gotta love them," she reasoned.

I heaved her bag into the back of the car. "The little girls in China are needy, too," I told her. "You know about the country's one-child policy, right?"

She got into the car and reapplied her lipstick and fluffed her hair, the better to confound Eugene's collective gaydar. "I know a little."

"Couples are allowed one kid, and they all want boys to carry on the family name and take care of them when they get old. So what d'you think happens to the little girls?"

"I have no idea."

I recounted what Marissa had told us. "It's illegal to give up your kid for adoption in China, so parents abandon their girl babies at birth in parks and under bridges. If people find a baby, they stick her in an orphanage until people like Jonathan and me come to get her."

"Oh, honey . . ." We passed an osprey nest on a platform beside the West Eugene Wetlands, and so I heard the urgency in her voice rather than witnessing it on her face. "You go get one of those little girls out of there."

⌒⌒

The next morning, I took her to see Archimedes. Staff had moved him to a large outdoor mew with a stump and a couple of long wooden perches.

He gleamed white under cloud-covered skies. Hearing our feet on the gravel path, he shot to his stump and honked a greeting.

"Snowies are the heaviest owl in North America," I told her. "Did you know that in France there's Paleolithic cave art showing two snowies and their chicks? S'posed to be the oldest depiction of a bird species . . ."

"He's beautiful." My mother crouched down and studied the big feathered feet splayed out like the paws of a lynx. "What's his story?"

"Human imprint. He can actually fly just fine."

Archimedes had spent the past few days swooping in giant circles around his mew, landing with a splash in his water trough. He performed for us now, white wings spread wide, executing dizzying revolutions. This time, he dropped to the gravel and emitted a call that sounded like squeaking bike brakes with his beak stretched so wide that we could see the pink inside of his mouth.

"Gorgeous," I said.

"Odd," my mother countered. "How come he's here?"

"He was born in captivity, so he's . . . developmentally delayed." I struggled to put my sparse knowledge of imprinting into terms she could understand. "He doesn't recognize other snowies as his species. If we let him out, he might fly down and accost someone's tennis shoes. Also, he thinks food comes from people. Imagine this." I jerked my thumb toward the hiking trail just visible below his mew. "You're enjoying a peaceful hike up Spencer Butte when, suddenly, a four-pound white owl flies toward you. What d'you do?"

My mother considered this. "I'd probably grab a branch to protect myself."

"Exactly. And some people might fire a gun. An imprinted bird in the wild is doomed."

"Poor guy. Do you think he misses Alaska?"

Archimedes had never seen the Arctic, but I wondered, as his yellow eyes shifted from the snowberry bushes near his mew to the sky just visible through the fir branches, whether some part of him longed instinctively for the bright open tundra.

"It's sad that he's all alone. The other birds here live in pairs."

"Most of them . . ."

Long ago, staff had committed to housing species in pairs whenever possible, so we had two red-tailed hawks, two great horned owls, and the like. "But the Northern goshawk's by herself," I said, "and the sharp-shinned hawk and our great gray owl don't have cage mates."

The goshawk and great gray were rare; hence, their solitary status. But the little sharp-shinned hawk, like others of her species, was hyper—suited only to solo captivity, especially compared to languorous Lorax and the placid spotted owls.

A breeze rose, permeated with the chilling hint of a wet Northwest winter. My mother turned and walked up the path. "I'm going in search of caffeine."

I remained standing beside the mew. A snowy owl in the wild might live ten years. In captivity, safe from predators and with a daily meal and health care, Archimedes could live thirty. Good for us at the center; already, visitors headed straight for his mew after paying admission and learning just how many rodents his wild counterparts eradicated: sixteen hundred lemmings annually. But if he couldn't stay glove-trained and had to remain caged his whole life with sparse sensory stimulation and little contact with humans—whom, for better or worse, he'd formed a bond with—would his situation be good for him?

━ ⌣ ━

My mother flew home, promising upon her return to help paint the room full of dog beds that would become our child's nursery. My little sister called that afternoon. "Sis, I'm pregnant."

I sat on the window seat among fragments of spilled cat kibble and gripped the handle of my coffee mug. "*Pregnant?*"

My little sister, my *Sesame Street* and candy store compatriot, carrying not her beloved pom-poms, but a *child?*

And me, Aunt Melissa.

We already had an Aunt Melissa, a charismatic mess of a woman spinning in my memory in a loose-fitting robe to old Beatles albums, scent of pot in the air of her living room, where her cockatiels were free to fly about. She lived in snowy owl territory now—so no more phone calls or birthday cards, no giggly girlish shopping trips with her nieces.

I promised better for my niece or nephew to be. "Congratulations, Mama!"

"I hope it's a boy." Katie let loose her perennial laugh, and I saw in my mind her head thrown back, tawny curls bouncing, eyes like flakes of cobalt paint. "I'd love to be mother to a boy."

"Maybe Jon and I should scrap our adoption plans and get pregnant." I stared into my coffee cup, trying to discern the right choice. A cat hair, long and black, drifted down and landed in the dregs. It told me nothing. "God," I said. "I wish I could just lay an egg and be done with it."

Jonathan appeared at the back door, flushed and sweaty from his uphill bike commute. "Gotta go." I hung up the phone and stood to kiss him. "Katie's gonna have a baby."

He registered my plaintive tone and sat down beside me. "I've been thinking. Maybe we shouldn't be so concerned with money. I mean, the thirty thousand includes a trip to China—it doesn't all go to agencies and the government. We get to go on a fascinating adventure."

"How much does it cost to reverse a vasectomy? Is it cheaper than thirty grand?"

His brow furrowed. "We wanted to help an orphan, remember?"

"I know." I sighed and slumped down on the window seat. "I'm confused. I need to go to the zoo."

"The *zoo*?"

"Yeah. Jack Kornfield tells this story about the author Rilke, who'd been working as a secretary for Rodin, the sculptor. When Rilke confessed to having writer's block, the artist sent him to the zoo to observe the animals. That's where Rilke's poem 'The Panther' comes from."

Physically, writing isn't a wild act. The mind, however—especially after hours and hours alone at it—goes a little feral. I've found myself howling with a delight so dramatic that my cats scurry behind the couch, and weeping in a fetal position between my dogs over some remembered loss now present on the page. I wondered about the state of Rilke's brain as he wrote the final stanza of "The Panther," translated by Stephen Mitchell:

> Only at times, the curtain of the pupils
> lifts, quietly—. An image enters in,

rushes down through the tensed, arrested muscles,
plunges into the heart and is gone.

Watching wildlife with mindful deliberation conjures images of ourselves as we once were, eye to eye around a cave fire, gloriously and ferociously tangible. Aldous Huxley once advised a young writer to get a couple of cats so he could better craft psychological novels. "Primitive people, like children and animals," he wrote, "are simply civilized people with the lid off, so to speak—the heavy elaborate lid of manners, conventions, traditions of thought and feeling beneath which each one of us passes his or her existence. "

I left my own cats sleeping on the bed and headed for Portland, hoping a visit to the zoo would grant clarity.

The "Wild Life Live!" show at the Oregon Zoo features raptors in a twenty-minute comic presentation designed to teach visitors about birds of prey and showcase their flying skills. "*Their* birds," Darcy told me, "don't just sit on the glove. They fly off it and over the audience's head to land on a perch."

"How do you train a raptor to do that?" Jonathan and I walked through the Pacific Northwest exhibit with its black bears and bobcats and bald eagles, ending up on the wide, damp lawn beside the flight-show stage.

"Positive reinforcement in the form of food, I'll bet." Jonathan tore an elephant ear in half and passed me a hunk of deep-fried dough dripping with butter and cinnamon sugar. "Trainers here can *buy* imprinted or baby birds. They're easier to train."

"I don't get it. Archimedes is an imprint, and Jean can't get him to stop hanging upside down."

"Archimedes," Jonathan said, as visitors enticed by music from the loudspeakers sat down on a low wall around us, "is a snowy owl. I've done some research—they're a pain in the ass to train. That flying to the ground thing is a real problem."

The Oregon Zoo's free-flight show didn't feature any snowy owls, but red-tailed hawks and golden eagles soared over our heads in an arc between handlers up on stage and tall perches mounted on the lawn behind a gasping, clapping audience.

The song "What a Wonderful World" came on over the loudspeaker. Suddenly, a bald eagle sailed above us and came to rest on a handler's glove. Goose bumps rose on my arms. The handler, around my age and height, stood calmly telling jokes to an audience of hundreds while the three-foot bird sat on her leather-clad arm. I knew without a doubt that if my vaudevillian great-grandmother had been given the opportunity to perform with some big bird, she would have jumped at the chance, talons be damned.

After the show we stood up and walked toward another handler who had a Eurasian eagle-owl on her glove. "So beautiful." I studied the black and brown and white feathers, the extraordinary orange eyes.

"*Bubo bubo.*" The handler told us the bird's Latin name.

"The bird so nice they named it twice." Jonathan quipped as the audience chuckled.

"This species is an alpha predator." The handler turned her wrist slightly so that the owl focused on her, rather than triangulating on a nearby baby stroller. "It has no natural predators. In the wild they're killed by electrocution, car collisions, and gunshot. I've heard of one that's almost sixty years old, living in another zoo."

Jonathan nudged me. "Look."

A family stood in line near us, waiting to hand a dollar to a turkey vulture. The bird had been trained to accept donations and put them in a box. Two Anglo parents smiled down at a little Chinese girl in ponytails and an owl–silk-screened T-shirt. We watched as she held out the bill in her tiny hand, unflinching at the touch of the bird's beak. "Vulture!" she cried.

Up until now the idea of a Chinese daughter had been just that—an idea. That afternoon, I looked at the little girl at the zoo and thought of how she could have spent years languishing in some orphanage, abandoned and alone. Somewhere, a little girl lay in a crib waiting for us.

Jonathan laced his fingers through mine and led me past the orangutan house, where a red ape sat high up, gazing out at the forest beyond the zoo. "Let's go home," he said, "and send in the check and application for our daughter."

12

Lost Girls

·

We mailed in our check and embraced solemnly outside the South Hills post office, crows cawing at us from the trees. "Oh my God," I whispered into Jonathan's ear. "We're adopting a child!"

He rested his chin on my head for a moment, looked toward a dread-locked man with a baby on his back and several large boxes in his arms. A toddler trailed behind him. "I think that guy used to volunteer at the center." Then, "I'm gonna be a dad. *Dad* . . . I like that better than *Daddy*."

"Funny—I prefer *Mommy* to *Mom*."

We grinned at each other, giddy, and drove up to the raptor center to share the news. "Her name will be Lydia," we told our friends. "We're going to go pick her up from China."

"When?" they asked.

"No idea. We could wait a year."

"In the meantime, go to the movies," said the volunteer coordinator, who had two adult children, as she scrubbed out the mini-refrigerator with its cargo of sodas and yogurt cups and someone's leftover rat. "Go out to dinner, 'cause you won't get to do those things once you're parents."

"Have sex." Darcy, with a new peregrine tattoo covering her wrist, put her hands on her hips and looked down her pierced nose at us. "I hear that goes out the window, too."

Jean winked at me. "Learn to train Lorax."

"I may not have time." I ran my fingers through my rain-damp bangs and rebraided my hair, stuffing a stocking cap on top of my head. "We've gotta sit through a bunch of classes, and there's tons of paperwork."

"No problem. Just remember, the offer's always there."

Two days later, Jonathan and I received a hefty packet from the adoption agency. We stopped at the post office on our way out of town, heading for Bonney Butte three hours north in the Mount Hood wilderness, near the Columbia River. We were going to observe volunteers from HawkWatch International as they caught and banded raptors on the birds' southern migration along the Pacific flyway. Some people spent the entire months of September and October helping out.

"The birds come from as far away as the Arctic," Jonathan told me, "heading for Central America for the winter. The HawkWatch folks hang out in a bird blind all day, waiting for raptors to fly by. It's supposed to be pretty exciting to see."

"Bird blind?" Vaguely, I remembered sharing pizza and beer years before with a running group in a rickety shack near the West Eugene Wetlands, our raucous singing scaring away the waterfowl.

Jonathan nodded. "That's right—it's a camouflaged structure that hides us from wildlife, with holes for cameras and binoculars. There's a good one out at the Malheur Wildlife Refuge, where I went with a group of photography students once. We saw all sorts of pelicans. Today, we'll see mostly hawks."

"You sure know how to show a girl a good time. First frozen rats, and now migrating hawks."

"I try." He draped an arm around my shoulders and jerked his chin at the manila envelope on the car seat between us. "So what'd the agency send us? Do we dare look?"

I tore it open and pulled out a list of medical and physical conditions that our Lydia might present at birth or soon after. A cover letter instructed us to discuss each one thoroughly, in terms of what medical care it might require and how such a child would fit into our present life-style, then check off those we'd be willing to accept.

I'd heard of wildlife rehabilitators who operated, out of necessity, with such a checklist—more according to species than disability, though. Native birds and mammals got superior treatment; nonnatives such as European starlings got hand-fed only if inundated volunteers had time.

"Sometimes we have to toss food into a starling's or invasive tree squirrel's cage and hope it survives." We'd once met a rehabber on a trail, and she'd described the pecking order. "We do our best, but we can't save 'em all."

The same went for children. Jonathan and I decided our agency's checklist functioned as a sort of litmus test for potential adoptive parents. Think you're ready to take on a child? How about a seven-year-old with schizophrenia and open sores?

I read the potential issues out loud. "What's FTT?" Jonathan asked.

"Failure to thrive. Means the kid's not gaining weight properly. Lack of nutrition, and other stuff, too."

"What's micrognathia?"

I read the definition in smaller font. "That's when the baby is born without a chin. Do you have a pen?

"Glove compartment."

"Might as well get started."

Our center accepted all birds of prey; Archimedes, with his species' status as a sometime-visitor to Oregon, served as a case in point. No one who worked in our treatment room—privy, as we were, to the secret of how nurturing works its magic to transform a limp and huddled nature into something glorious—could leave any checklist blank.

Still, Jonathan and I left many boxes unmarked on our agency's list. Guilt jabbed at me as we chose which characteristics we'd be willing to accept in a kid and nixed those that didn't jive with our lifestyle. Would my parents have chosen *me*, had they known I'd be prone to chronic insomnia and anxiety and occasional outbreaks of hives?

I thought not.

My sister had described her amniocentesis and the doctor's vigilant search for Down syndrome genes; biological parents could, in effect, operate under a checklist as well. But mostly, what you birthed was what you got, whether it had eleven fingers, Grandpa's honker, or a birthmark the approximate size and shape of Florida. Our list felt like an unwarranted luxury.

"So it's yes on missing hands, no on club feet?" I looked over at Jonathan. "We do a lot of hiking, so . . . ugh." I threw down the packet. "This is just so weird."

"It's like applying to be a falconer. There's a ton of paperwork and hoops to jump through, then you apprentice with a seasoned falconer for years and trap your own kestrel or hawk. Finally, you work with your bird until the board says you can hunt alone. It takes almost ten years to become a master falconer."

I studied my husband's hawk-like profile. When we met he'd talked of becoming a falconer—a passion that demanded chunks of time daily and made vacationing impossible unless you toted your raptor along with your snorkel gear. A photography career and marriage had won out over his dream of hunting with hawks; a wife doesn't demand as many training hours or live rabbits. But a child would require an infinite amount of time.

"You sure you want to do this?"

"Of course I do." He massaged my neck. "It'll be fun. My sisters and brothers with kids seem happy . . ."

Satisfied, I picked up the list again. "We like to go backpacking, so a child with a missing leg might not be a good fit. But I'm fine with a missing hand."

"Even a one-armed kid would be fine with me." He glanced over at the paper. "What's the difference between cleft lip and cleft palate?"

"No idea. I think they're both correctable with surgery, but what if it leaves a scar?"

"Would that be a problem?"

We weren't strangers to scars. A car accident at eighteen had left Jonathan with a fused spine and pale railroads snaking across his back. Sometimes I ran a finger along them, wondering about the steel rods within that sent airport TSA agents into a tizzy and caused him, in more self-deprecating moments, to refer to himself as a cyborg.

Doctors had suggested he'd never walk again, but his mother presided over his physical therapy and enrolled in community college herself so she could play chauffeur and help him navigate the school's hallways. Propelled by her fortitude and his own, he busted out of his body cast and threw away his crutches in under a year. Now he could backpack through the Three Sisters wilderness ten miles at a time.

"How's a birthmark a disability?" he asked me.

My fingers went to my cheeks. "If it's on a girl's face, I guess it could cause self-esteem issues. What's your position on partial blindness?"

"Hey, it's better than total blindness."

I thumbed past the checklist to another form. "The agency wants another check so the social worker can write an adoption study. Guess how much?"

"No idea."

"Eighteen hundred dollars."

"Eighteen *hundred*?"

For an instant I wondered again why we didn't just return to the urologist, demand a vasectomy reversal, and get pregnant. "It'd be so much easier . . ."

Jonathan pulled onto Highway 35 and headed toward the Butte. "It might be, love, but then we'd be denying a good home to a blind Chinese orphan with one arm, a cleft palate, and a giant facial birthmark."

Watching the HawkWatch volunteers do what they do at Bonney Butte is, in a word, remarkable. To learn more about the raptors that travel south along the migration route each fall, volunteers donate weeks to sit in a dim bird blind, peering through a crack in the makeshift plywood wall to spot small black dots that grow into red-tailed and Cooper's hawks, sharp-shinneds, golden eagles, American kestrels, and merlins. Using a pigeon as a lure, they entice raptors soaring by on updrafts to fly down; the birds get tangled in a net, and volunteers race out barehanded to catch them. In the blind these men and women swiftly weigh and measure the raptors, band them, and then send them back out to their migration route.

When the HawkWatch people learned that Jonathan and I worked at the raptor center in Eugene, they allowed us to watch from the blind. I gazed through the crack at snow-capped Mount Hood framed by pine trees under a mutable September sky. A pigeon strutted about on the ground under the net.

"It's wearing a coat?" I squinted at the plump gray-and-white bird.

"Flak jacket." The bearded man next to me wrote down something in pencil on a chart. "Keeps it safe from talons." He peered out and pointed. "Hawk!"

A large red-tail, white streaks on its breast, flew into the net. A woman darted out and disentangled it, then gathered up its feet and wings, its back against her chest so the bearded man could band it.

"No gloves?" I whispered to Jonathan. "Are they crazy?"

"She's got it in an ice cream cone hold." Jonathan demonstrated with his hands. "You hold the bird upright with its wings tucked in and its feet down. Then, when you're ready to release it, you just open your hand. Less traumatizing than other holds."

The woman disappeared, then returned to the blind without the hawk. "Aren't you afraid that you might get footed and get some disease?" I whispered to her.

She shot me a quizzical look. "No."

I felt like an idiot.

We remained in the blind for an hour, thrilled by how a tiny black speck approaching in the sky—more an idea of a bird than anything—grew within a minute into a beautiful raptor in somebody's hands. I caught sight of a sharp-shinned hawk before anyone else saw it, and Jonathan got to practice his ice cream cone hold on a Cooper's after volunteers banded it. "Thank you," he said to the couple who stood on a rocky outcropping talking to visitors about the raptors, all of us glowing with cold and excitement against the panoramic backdrop of Oregon's stateliest mountains.

As we drove away from the Butte, we looked across the expanse of forest. Far to the south, I saw the tilting outline of a turkey vulture on a thermal headed for California. For an instant I longed for the scrubby mountains and arid hiking trails of my old hometown, for the vultures that hung out in the eucalyptus trees all winter, spreading their wings to dry under the reliable sun. But Oregon, wild Oregon, had captured me for good.

"I can't wait to share all this with Lydia." I ran my fingers through Jonathan's hair, rested my head on his shoulder as he drove.

"Maybe this time next year she'll be with us."

"Did you see that beautiful camping spot near the Butte? Let's make a plan to drive up and volunteer here a couple days. She can help us band birds."

—◦—

Back at home, we embarked on a crusade to learn all about the country from which our little daughter would migrate. I knew nothing about China beyond reading *The Joy Luck Club* and a smattering of Taoist literature—the latter only because an Eastern philosophy professor at U.C. Santa Cruz had insisted that we add to his pile of esoteric reading material Benjamin Hoff's mercifully comprehensible *The Tao of Pooh*.

Now I scoured the library for Lonely Planet guidebooks and Chinese movies. In the documentary section I discovered a National Geographic film. Titled *China's Lost Girls*, it attempted to deconstruct, in under an hour, that country's history and culture as it pertained to adopting out children.

That night, I made popcorn while Jonathan mixed chocolate martinis. We sat on the couch with the cats and turned on the documentary.

Commentator Lisa Ling, earnest in a pink sweater and skinny blue jeans, narrated the plight of girls in the country, framed by her travels with American families flying overseas to pick up their adopted babies. She explained that over a quarter of the children adopted into the United States that year hailed from China. Most were female.

"Girls are often abandoned, aborted, or hidden." Ling's sunny voice dimmed. "Sometimes they're even killed."

Over images of squalling babies in car seats and cribs at a Chinese orphanage, she described how over one hundred thousand baby girls in that country are discarded each year. I looked closely at the orphans but saw no club feet, no missing arms, not even a cleft lip.

For a moment the camera focused on a round-faced little girl in a fuzzy blue sweater. The child clutched a puppy-dog chew toy, and my throat emitted a longing squeak. "I want that baby," I told Jonathan.

He reached for my hand. "I know you do."

The director had interspersed short interviews with school-age adopted Chinese girls throughout the narrative, in the style of Nora

Ephron's *When Harry Met Sally*. One child, around ten years old, told her story to the filmmaker.

"My real biological mother left me in a basket with my sister, saying that we were twins, and she waited to make sure that we were safe, and then my mom right now, Betsy, she came to get me in China."

I cringed at the distinctions between "real biological mother" and "my mom right now." I recalled my father's long-ago insistence that we call our stepmother "Mom" and my staunch refusal to bestow a maternal moniker upon another woman. But Lydia would have more than one mother—I couldn't deny that.

In a voice-over across images of smoldering ash heaps and desolate country roads, Ling posed a question: "How could a mother give away her baby girl?" She answered it through interviews in rural towns, with women forced under threat of government fines and draconian husbands to surrender their daughters.

Some of the orphans had been discovered wrapped up warmly, notes pinned to their blankets with biographical information and maternal wishes for a happy life. I recalled what Kat had suggested to me that day in the dog park. Did our willingness to rescue a Chinese girl perpetuate her abandonment? Would Jonathan and I, in traveling overseas to make Lydia our own, be complicit in causing her birth mother a lifetime of grief? Or would many of these children be abandoned anyway, left to languish in orphanages or worse? I just didn't know.

I recalled how my own mother's shoulders had slumped as she dropped us off at our father's house every other Sunday evening after spending the weekend with us. Often, my stepmother stood at the door, calling out promises of cookie-baking and Disney movies. How did my mom feel thirty years later, I wondered, having been forced to surrender her children again and again to another woman?

National Geographic had gained permission to film a ceremony—known in adoption circles as "Gotcha Day"—in which Chinese foster parents presented adoptive parents with their new babies. To us the scene looked like chaos. As government officials read off each name, tears flowed from the hordes of adoptive mothers and from the screaming, red-faced children.

Jonathan put down his martini glass. "Those kids look terrified."

Most of the babies were maybe a year old, wrapped in red blankets. When the names of the new parents were called, the women who'd raised these children from birth merely handed them to pale strangers convulsed with weeping.

I tried to imagine whether, put into their position, I'd become so overwrought with emotion that I, too, would traumatize a sobbing toddler with a torrent of squeezy-huggy kisses. Maybe the behavior was akin to what my friends reported about the birthing process—mild-mannered women who'd never let the f-bomb fall from their lips suddenly found themselves prostrate on a hospital bed, letting loose an arsenal of "assholes."

When the film ended we turned off the TV and dumped the leftover popcorn in the front yard for the squirrels. We didn't talk about what we'd seen and heard—just let the dogs out, fed the cats, and went to bed.

That night, I slept little. At last I dreamed of little girls wrapped in red blankets, flying in a steady stream above my head until my hands, ring finger banded with silver, reached to pluck one from the sky.

———

Jean had agreed to cover our Sunday shift for us while we went to Bonney Butte, if we worked for her Tuesday night at the raptor center. "I'd like you to go in and sit with Lorax after you give her a quail," she told me, "if you have time. That's what I usually do."

I trotted around the center feeding the other nocturnal birds, and stuck my head into the treatment room where Jonathan and Louise were bandaging a red-tailed hawk's wing. "Jean's asked me to hang out with Lorax for a few. I'll be in her mew if anyone needs me."

Louise looked up. "You're not going to handle her."

"God, no. Her talons are huge."

I walked down to the great horned owls' mew and fit my key in the padlock. Lovely Juno, the first raptor to capture my attention, had passed away. Lorax's new cage mate, a skittish female unsuited to the demands of working as an education bird, shot away from me and landed on a high corner perch.

"It's okay, little girl." I placed her quail on one feeding platform, then crept to the other platform near Lorax's favorite perch. She blinked at me from her branch.

Jean had told me to talk to her. "Good afternoon." My sudden formality felt silly. "As you probably know, Jean's down south visiting her daughter . . ."

Lorax triangulated on my gold padlock key, head bobbing. "Wish I could dance like you," I murmured. My muscles relaxed incrementally, and I sank to the edge of the plastic chair. "So . . . um . . . how's it going?"

Without a directive to clean the mew and get out, I had time to admire the striated brown and black feathers outlining the white. Again, I jabbed one fingernail into my palm, gauging the potential pain of getting footed by one of those lustrous talons.

Despite my fear I could begin to envision myself as a bird handler, walking about the center with Lorax on my glove, pausing to answer visitors' questions and delivering educational presentations in the woodsy pavilion. Watching the bare-handed HawkWatch volunteers had reminded me that I'd once been a girl to take chances—walking across the top of the monkey bars at school, swimming far out into the ocean on Manhattan Beach, riding my bicycle down the Pacific Coast Highway from Monterey to Ventura past belching tour buses.

"What's a little mouse blood between friends?" I quipped.

Lorax shifted her talons on her perch and clacked her beak at my laughter. I fought the urge to duck out of the mew. "Sorry . . . I'll whisper. Um . . . Jonathan—he's that tall guy who sometimes brings your food—he and I are adopting a little girl." At a loss for topics of conversation beyond dead quail and the squeaky duck toy floating in the owls' water trough, I babbled about what was first and foremost on my mind.

"Her name will be Lydia, and she's from China. As soon as we get her, we'll bring her to the center and I'll introduce you. She'll have black hair and black eyes, and she'll be sort of feisty, like our niece, Brynnli. We're going to hike and camp all over Oregon with her, and when she's old enough, she can volunteer here."

A yellow jacket appeared near the quail, and Lorax swiveled her head to stare. The insect rushed her head, and she gave a startled hoot.

I stood up to help and accidentally stepped on a second plastic duck lying by my foot. Both owls, spooked by the squeak, jumped from their perches and slammed into the wire ceiling; they hung upside down and panted, huge pupils fixated on me.

"Sorry . . ." I murmured again and backed out of the mew.

Jean had told me about the time it takes to establish rapport with a raptor. "Weeks, sometimes months. You've got to prove yourself trustworthy before you ever ask a bird to stand on your glove."

"We'll try again tomorrow." I headed up to the clinic with the offending duck in my pocket.

Before the flight show at the zoo, before watching volunteers at Bonney Butte, I would have conceded to ineptitude and fear. Now, however, I had too many role models. I longed to become as confident, as courageous as the women who thought nothing of using one arm as a raptor perch, of banding a bird with bare hands and showing it to an appreciative public before releasing it to the sky.

A dog-eared paperback lay on the computer monitor in the clinic—*Don't Shoot the Dog*. An animal trainer at Sea World had written it, and the education team had adopted it as their bird handler's bible. I'd heard that the author preached positive reinforcement for behavior modification. As a teacher for the developmentally disabled, I understood how to train students to read flashcards by offering a reward of M&M's. But how did one train an owl?

"Can I borrow this?" Laurin walked in with a vulture on her arm, preparing to check its weight and medicate its feet.

"Really?" She peered into my face. Satisfied, she nodded.

"Please do."

———

I read the whole book, bought my own copy, hung out in Lorax's mew whenever I could. She and the other great horned stopped flying away from me whenever I opened the door, and we sat quietly an hour at a time. "She likes you," Jean assured me. "There's a handler training session coming up soon. I want you to take it."

"I will," I said, "unless we get a kid right away."

At home I gathered paperwork for the adoption agency and resisted the urge to cut out a photo of a little Chinese girl in pigtails from their magazine and affix it to the refrigerator. In early January Jonathan went to work and I sat down to check my e-mail. At the top, a post from Kat.

Thought you might want to see this. Sorry.

She'd pasted someone's blog post below her message, headed by a troubling title: "Planning to Adopt from China? If You're Fat or Ugly, Don't Bother."

I chuckled, thinking the blogger had written a post in the satirical style of the faux newspaper *The Onion*. But Kat despised satire. And why had she written "Sorry"?

I read on and realized the blogger, in spite of the irreverent headline, was serious. The Chinese government, reporting that adoption applications exceeded the number of available babies, had come up with new restrictions designed to provide their kids with what they considered the best possible homes. Now adoptive parents had to have a net worth of over eighty thousand dollars and a body mass index of less than forty. They couldn't have a facial deformity, and they couldn't take anxiety medication or use a wheelchair.

None of this applied to Jonathan and me, but as I read on, the full implication of Kat's apology hit me. China also mandated that adoptive parents, if either had a divorce, must be married for at least five years.

Jonathan and I had been married for one.

I closed the computer and called him at work. "We need to talk."

"I'm in a meeting. Whatever's wrong, love, we'll fix it."

But we couldn't fix it. That morning, I spent an hour on the phone with the grimly apologetic director of our agency's Chinese program. She assured me that the blogger's news was true.

"Can't we get grandfathered in?" I pleaded with the woman. "We've turned in our paperwork and written our checks . . ."

"I'm afraid not." Her voice iced around the edges. "You've had a divorce, my dear."

"It was a starter marriage. I had to buy my own ring!"

She clucked her tongue. "The Chinese government's not going to understand that. We'll transfer you and your husband over to our Vietnam program."

"Vietnam?"

"Yes, Vietnam. They have plenty of boys available for adoption."

"But no girls?"

I knew the answer before I asked.

"Vietnam's adopting boys to first-time parents. You can adopt a girl later. I have to hang up now—I have several other calls."

I upended my oatmeal into the compost bucket and slumped at the kitchen table. Jonathan called and got the whole story. "So what'd the adoption lady say?"

He'd never judged, never faulted me for my imprudent marriage and divorce. Even so, I could barely speak the verdict for the guilt that threatened to throttle me.

"Oh, love," I said, "We've lost our Lydia."

13

Hazed

AFTER THE CHINESE GOVERNMENT FORBADE US TO ADOPT ONE OF THEIR little girls, my guts felt raw and ravaged. My arms dangled empty and useless, as unsure of their purpose as when I'd flailed around as an amateur actress on my high school stage.

A few weeks later, my sister had a miscarriage.

"Oh, Lissa . . . I bled for two weeks."

Katie's voice, over the phone, sounded faint, anemic. "Finally I called Mom, and she drove down and rushed me to the hospital."

"That's horrific. I'll fly down."

"No, you know how I get. I just want to be alone." She fought back tears. "I've been telling myself the miscarriage isn't my fault, it's just fate, but . . . but what if I'm not able to carry a baby to term?"

I thought of Lydia, of guilt, of resignation.

"Of course you'll conceive again."

In my role of big sister, I dispelled comfort in the only terms I knew. "You just laid a bad egg."

Then the tears came, so clamorous with sorrow that I held the phone away from my ear. "But Lissa . . . I wanted *this* baby."

I made a fist and pressed it hard into my stomach. "I know, sis. I'm sorry."

—◦—

The next week, Kat drove up to the raptor center to pick up pellets for her daughter's school project on owls. She ducked through raindrops and ran up the steps to the visitors' center. On the couch she cradled the grayish pellets in her hand. "Awesome," she said. "My kid's gonna love dissecting these."

"Great."

Her hand went to my knee despite my filthy, mute-splattered blue jeans. "How *are* you?"

I blinked at her. My head felt stuffed, my eyelids heavy. "How am I? Honestly . . . getting kicked out of China makes me feel like I've just had a miscarriage."

Kat clucked her tongue. "Oh, sweetie . . . I'd be very, very careful comparing your adoption issue with a miscarriage." Her cold, clipped syllables chastised me for forcing an analogy where there was, apparently, none. "You did not have a dead baby inside you. You didn't bleed for two weeks straight."

I looked away, toward the vase of daffodils on the desk beside the cash register. Someone had cut the flowers before last night's frost. They gleamed with yellow promise, and I fixed their image in my mind to recall in the chill darkness of five o'clock, before Jonathan returned home from work and we could forget ourselves in pizza-making and pet-tending and marathon episodes of *Arrested Development*.

Kat was wrong, I thought. I *did* have a dead baby inside me. My whole being had danced around the surety of a little Chinese daughter, and now she was gone.

I stood up and rearranged the scattered toy vultures and hawks and owls so that they sat more sociably on the shelf together. "You know," I began, "I'd love to be able to talk freely with you about the challenges of this adoption without feeling judged."

"Well, I'm sorry." Her cell phone rang, a disco beat. "The kids."

She ducked outside onto the covered porch. I watched her gesticulating as she spoke, long fingers splayed as if filibustering. The director's African gray parrot climbed up the curtain over the door to the apartment and peered at me. "Hello, honey," it said.

"Hello," I muttered, impervious to its charms.

Kat returned to the couch. "That was the kids. A fight over whose turn it is to make dinner."

I shrugged. "I have to go clean mews."

"Oh, dear. *Look.*" Kat stopped me on my way out the door. "I'm just fearful for the family animosity you'll run into if you compare yourself and your sister. Believe me, things will be easier with time and distance, when both of you have babies in your arms."

She contemplated the three barn owl skeletons in the glass case behind us as if asking some committee for wise council. "Didn't you say your sister's started volunteering for the Ovarian Cancer Society?"

"Yeah. She thinks it might distract her."

"Why don't you do something like that, take your mind off stuff. Hey, you could help me lead my daughter's Girl Scout troop . . ."

Girl Scouts. Constant reminders of the daughter I might never have, all of them squealing and sewing their oilcloth sit-upons and singing about making new friends but keeping the old. I had a photo of myself from the 1970s, solemn in my chocolate-hued beanie with my right index and middle fingers held aloft, reciting the Girl Scout oath. My mother had been leader of our Brownie troop before she left my father, and in the back of my head, I'd allowed that the position sounded like fun . . . provided I had a little Brownie of my own.

But Vietnam was assigning us a boy.

I moved to the door. Outside, I saw Darcy striding through the rain with the diurnal birds' pie plates, in her daisy-pattern rubber boots and Jonathan's yellow slicker from the coat closet. I bristled.

"I already volunteer four hours a week at the raptor center, plus some."

Kat settled the owl pellets into a glass jar and dropped it into her purse. "Well . . . maybe you should take another shift."

I let us out the door, too exhausted to argue. "Yeah, you're probably right."

~—◦—~

That spring, volunteers had to double up when feeding the red-tailed hawks. As they had in previous years, the females laid eggs and took turns at incubation. "It's feasible that one of them could foot us just for bringing them lunch." Jonathan pulled on his elbow-length handler's glove. "If you're taking food to them, I'll come with you to run interference."

We walked across the gravel path. He appeared serene, even happy. He'd been shocked and angry about getting kicked out of China's adoption program, but somehow he retained his springy stork-like stride, his ready smile.

I tried to focus on the birds, to distract myself. "So the eggs won't hatch?"

"Nah, they're not fertile. The hawks have a sort of Boston marriage thing going on—they've never mated with a male. But some of our birds lay, regardless. Hey, you'll like this story . . ."

He unlocked the door to the red-tails' mew and let himself inside. One bird sat on eggs in the corner. Jonathan stood ready for the other. She flew toward him, and he caught her by the jesses. Tethered, she settled on his glove and roused.

"You're a pro." I tiptoed in, eyes on the sitting hawk, and set a rat on each feeding platform. I knelt to pick up a pair of chicken feet and a ruddy flight feather, then backed out. "What's the story?"

Jonathan set the red-tail on her feeding platform. She sank her talons into the rat, and he backed out of the mew. "So you know Circe, the female harrier with one eye? She's a terrific foster mother."

"What d'you mean?"

We walked back to the clinic. Jonathan talked while he poured hot water into mugs of instant coffee crystals. He stirred hot chocolate mix into mine. "Few years before you got here, a guy on a haying machine disturbed a female harrier on the nest. He wasn't allowed to take a break from work, so he took the eggs and wrapped them in his shirt. Then he called us and we came to get them. Circe sat on them until they hatched, and taught the babies to be harriers."

"Did the male harrier . . . what's his name—Deva?—help?"

"Nah, too young. But in the wild, male harriers can provide for several nests at once. They're so busy hunting that they only have time to drop prey over the nest. The female jumps out and flips over to grab it in her talons, then brings it to the babies."

"Bet you're glad you only have one wife." I reached to kiss his rough cheek and put my hands on either side of his head, peering into his eyes. "Are you *really* okay with adopting from Vietnam?"

He shrugged. "I'm excited to visit the country, but . . . it does feel a bit like we're settling. I really wanted a daughter . . ."

Darcy walked in with a pie plate full of quail and planted herself at the counter to pluck shiny yellow eggs out of the carcasses. The eggs, loaded with cholesterol, got doled out one per day to the resident raven and crow, who regarded them with the same affection I had for chocolate truffles. "Don't let me interrupt you lovebirds," she said.

Jonathan downed his coffee. "I've gotta go help Louise with a perch in the spotteds' cage." He kissed me and pushed out the door.

Darcy looked up from her quail, thick braids hanging at either side of her head. "Hey, can you go catch up Deva and bring him in here? We need to give him his West Nile vaccination."

"Catch him? Me?"

Other, more seasoned volunteers like her were forever striding into mews and toting birds into the clinic for medical treatment, but I had no idea what such an operation entailed. "Um . . . you sure *I* should do it?"

She raised one brow, and the silver ring embedded in it caught the light. "Why on earth not?"

Because I'm a coward, I wanted to say.

Darcy worked a different shift. She didn't know that I'd picked up injured birds only in the treatment room, and then under Jonathan's careful direction. "The director's gonna be here in five minutes with the vaccine," she snapped. "Can you just do it?"

Pride goaded me forward, but embarrassment proved a more powerful motivator. Darcy struck me as just as skilled and confident and beautiful as the raptor handlers I'd admired at the High Desert Museum, at the zoo, at Bonney Butte. These women wouldn't let a little glitch in adoption plans or the threat of mouse blood stop them—they'd charge ahead and get the job done.

I picked up a pair of yellow leather gloves.

"Uh-uh. No gloves."

"No gloves?"

She handed me a cardboard pet carrier and a towel. "I'm training the harrier to be an education bird. I don't want him to associate gloves with the trauma of being picked up."

"Um . . . okay." I set the gloves on top of the computer and took up the carton and towel.

"Don't forget to weigh the carrier first." She handed me a small scale and a pencil. I reached to remove the towel. "Hel*lo* . . . you want to weigh that, too. The bird'll be on it when you bring it in, you know."

Cheeks flaming, I wrote the weight on the box beside other scribbled numbers and trudged out past the prey barn to the harriers' mew.

The female, Circe, sat on a high perch. She titled her squarish brown head and gazed at me out of her good eye. She looked oddly owl-like. Harriers' feathered facial discs help them to direct sound toward their ears; they rely on hearing as well as sight to catch a meal. Her long tail bobbed; up close, I could see how her sleek body structure would allow for low flight over fields and marshlands in search of rodents, were she not in this mew.

Deva sat on his feeding platform next to a feathered carcass. He shook his gray-and-white feathers and flew to a stump farther away from me. "Thank God it's a quail day," I muttered. "No mouse blood, no encephalitis."

I unlocked the door to the entryway and peeked in. Deva stood less than two feet, all of thirteen ounces, staring at me through bright yellow eyes. I breathed another prayer of thanks that Darcy hadn't sent me to carry the heftier female into the clinic. Both birds' talons looked to be half the length of Lorax's, and much thinner. Deva's skinny yellow toes gripped the stump as I unlatched the hook on the mew door. It swung open, and Circe let loose an alarm that sounded like my dogs mauling some poor, squeaky chew toy.

I stood in the closed entryway with my cardboard carrier and assessed the situation. I could creep slowly into the mew and spend half an hour chasing the bird—stressing him and myself to the point of exhaustion— or I could dart across the gravel, snatch him up, drop him in the box, and carry it in triumph to Darcy.

Before Deva could get feisty, I pushed open the inner door and rushed him.

Startled, he flew up and impaled my hand with one talon. Keratin tore through skin into muscle.

I dropped to the ground, dizzy with pain. "Help! Jonathan! Darcy! Help!"

Deva fell with me, shrieking and struggling to free himself from my hand.

I knew pain—I'd sprained my ankle, torn my trapezius, sailed over the handlebars of my mountain bike, and taken a rock to the head—but nothing prepared me for the agony of being footed by a harrier. It hurt more than anything I'd experienced in thirty-three years.

I whimpered on the gravel beside a pile of glistening quail guts as the bird screamed in my ear. His eyes blazed into mine. I'd hung out in the treatment room long enough to know that the only way to release a raptor's grip was to straighten the joints in its legs—difficult to do with one hand when the bird was busy trying to kill your other. I recalled how a rock climber, trapped by a rock slide, cut off his own hand to save himself. All I had in my pocket was a tube of ChapStick and my driver's license—hardly effective tools for self-mutilation.

Panic squeezed my chest.

"Jonathan! Someone! Help!"

At last Laurin came running. She opened the mew door and stepped over to me, deftly cradling the harrier in one gloved hand and straightening its leg joints with the other. The bird let go, and I bent over my hand, still prostrate on the ground. "I'm sorry for crying. It just *hurts* so badly."

"Of course it hurts." Laurin helped me to my feet and examined Deva, who'd returned to his perch. Satisfied that he seemed uninjured, she guided me out of the mew. "What on earth made you try to catch the bird with no gloves?"

I bit my lip, not wanting to implicate Darcy. "He needed a West Nile shot. I was supposed to carry him to the treatment room."

"Without gloves?"

I followed Laurin into the clinic, still clutching my hand to my chest. Puncture wounds don't bleed much, but when Darcy saw how the injured site had already begun to redden and swell, her lips tightened.

"Sorry. I thought you knew what you were doing."

I slunk into the bathroom and ran water over the wound, then disinfectant soap. I scrubbed it into the hole, sick with pain.

Jonathan walked in. "What happened?"

"Harrier." I held out my hand. "It wouldn't let go."

"Oh, love. I'm sorry." He held my hand to his cheek, then kissed it. I sank to the toilet seat next to the euthanasia chamber that staff had created from a Styrofoam cooler and a plastic tube connected to a tank of CO_2.

"What if the harrier had mouse blood on his talons?" I whispered so that Darcy couldn't hear. "I don't want to die."

"You'll be fine." Jonathan bandaged my hand and helped me up from the toilet seat. He lifted up his shirt, reminding me of the scar on his chest under his trio of tattooed ravens. "Initiation by peregrine. You're part of the club now."

I failed to appreciate the hazing. He handed me a clean towel from the treatment room. I scrubbed at my tear-stained cheeks and blew my nose. "I'm leaving," I muttered.

"I can't go yet. Gotta finish this broken perch first . . ."

"It's all right. I want to be alone."

I marched past Darcy and stalked out of the treatment room, across the lawn and down to the owls. At the crunch of my sneakers on gravel, Lorax raised her head and clacked her beak. I stood outside her mew and stared up at her, hand throbbing. "You wouldn't foot me, would you?"

She blinked and swiveled her head toward the sound of Jonathan hammering. Owls hear certain frequencies much better than we do; I wondered if the squeak of a nail being yanked from lumber offended her. Behind me in his mew, Archimedes honked. I walked over and sank onto the cement bench near his favorite stump. A yellow laminated sign hung on his door: STAFF ONLY. Jean had told me that Archimedes, because he wouldn't stop hanging off the glove, was no longer an education bird.

"Only staff and I can feed him and clean his mew," she reported. "And we're not allowed to try to get him on the glove."

I rested my chin in my good hand and watched him. Unlike Lorax, who regarded me only briefly before returning to whatever insect or songbird captivated her at the moment, Archimedes appeared to find me fascinating. He honked again and leaped off the stump and waddled to one corner. The education director had stuffed a plastic enrichment ball full of alpaca wool; he jumped on it now and began tearing out the wool with his beak.

"You look pissed," I observed. "I can relate. I'm a loser."

Sometimes we hold onto a self-image long after its accuracy has faded. Where once I couldn't tell a barn owl from a bat, a hawk from a falcon, raptors now populated my world. Screech owls called from the fir trees in my backyard, and Cooper's hawks swooped through the branches above the dog park. Ospreys and bald eagles sailed above the bike path along the Willamette River. Harriers and vultures flew alongside the I-5. I moved through the world now with Emily Dickinson's lines in my head:

> Several of nature's people
> I know, and they know me;
> I feel for them a transport
> Of cordiality.

I looked down at my hand, flaming red and swollen to twice its normal size. "I'm not giving up," I told Archimedes. "I'm going to Vietnam, and while I wait for this boy, whoever he is, I'm going to learn to train raptors."

The snowy owl looked over at me, surrounded by clumps of alpaca wool. He opened his beak and squawked. Full of the sudden hubris that comes from surviving one's more gruesome fears, I squawked back.

"Someday," I told him, "I might even train you."

Jonathan with a
Swainson's hawk
MELISSA HART

Messiah, the
golden eagle
JONATHAN B. SMITH

Chenoa, the Northern
spotted owl
JONATHAN B. SMITH

Lorax, the great
horned owl
JONATHAN B. SMITH

Archimedes, the snowy owl
JONATHAN B. SMITH

Bodhi, the barred owl
JONATHAN B. SMITH

Author and Bodhi
JONATHAN B. SMITH

Author and Archimedes
JONATHAN B. SMITH

Jonathan releasing a barn owl
MELISSA HART

14

Wish You Were My Daughter

"Darlin', can you help me?"

Jean hollered to me through the clinic window. Sodden and filthy, I bounced in from cleaning mews to find her standing with Lorax on her glove, a thick two-inch talon embedded in her right hand.

"I need you to pull it out."

Lorax's eyes glowed huge and yellow. The blond feathers on her outstretched leg trembled. No raptor *wants* to foot a human. "What the hell happened?"

"Shhh. I was medicating her feet and she got spooked by the UPS truck. Less talk, more assistance, what d'you think?"

"Sorry." I pulled on a pair of welder's gloves. "How d'you do this—do I need to straighten her leg?"

Lorax struggled to reclaim her foot, and Jean winced. "Grab the talon and pull straight up, so it doesn't sink in deeper."

"Grab her talon? She'll take off my face!"

Lorax clacked her black beak; the end of it resembled the type of can opener I'd historically utilized to puncture a can of Hershey's chocolate syrup. The gular patch at the owl's throat fluttered, and she croaked a low hoot.

"Holy moly—I don't think I can do this. Let me get Jonathan."

"Get a grip, Melissa," Jean said. "I'm dying here. Didn't you used to work in a group home?"

At nineteen I'd been a residential counselor in a group home for severely disabled adults. A young man prone to seizure-fed rages bit me in the arm. A woman named Sarah Nix, mute and deaf and legally blind, walked up behind me one day, dug her skinny fingers into my hair, and yanked, wrenching my neck so hard that I had to go on light duty a month.

Lorax had nothing on Sarah Nix.

I sucked in a breath. "Ready?"

"Ten minutes ago."

At arm's length I gripped the owl's talon between my gloved thumb and forefinger and tugged upward, extracting the tip from Jean's palm.

"God . . . thank you."

Lorax bated in a rush of flapping wings, then settled back on Jean's gloved arm. I ran to the bathroom for disinfectant cream.

"I'm fine, but her pads are cracked." Undaunted by the reddening puncture wound in her palm, Jean reached for a tub of Bag Balm, the menthol-scented emollient that farmers use for cow udders and bird handlers use for raptor feet. I winced as she picked up Lorax's foot and rubbed a fingerful of cream into its scaly pad.

"Their feet get dry from sitting on Astroturf perches." Jean pointed at the sink full of bobbing brown mice and held up a finger, indicating that I should retrieve one for her. "We don't want her to get bumblefoot."

"Bumblefoot?"

"Bacterial inflammation. Causes swelling. The balm's a preventative measure, like us rubbing lotion on our elbows and feet in the winter so they don't get chapped."

I appreciated Jean's willingness to explain the minutiae of bird handling like I might actually be worthy of the information. "Why don't you give her a mouse for good behavior?" she suggested.

"You mean put it on her feeding platform?"

"I mean hand it to her right here and now."

"Oh." I selected a limp brown mouse from the sink and held it between my thumb and forefinger. "What do I do?"

"Hold it up to her beak."

I stepped over to Lorax and looked at the acute edge of the upper bill overlapping the lower. That thing could crush small animals. "What if she takes my finger off?"

"Not a chance."

I held up the mouse, close enough that Lorax could reach out and take it in her beak. She clutched the mouse's head and swallowed the body. She paused when she got to the tail, though; the end stuck out of her beak like a piece of errant pasta.

"Um . . . that's hilarious."

"That wasn't so scary, was it?" Jean nudged my shoulder with her own.

"No." I flushed with sudden pride. "It wasn't."

Plenty of people who volunteered at the raptor center found themselves rehabilitated along with the birds. There was the soldier with PTSD, the fifty-something woman who'd just left an abusive relationship, the man who'd lost his job, the high school student who hated birds but had left his high school community service quota until the last minute and had no other choice. This last young volunteer found himself so enamored of the crow and raven, in particular, that he stayed months beyond the required school hours and returned after his first summer away at college to help out again.

There was Jonathan, left by his fiancée for another man on the day they were to sign papers on his dream house. There was me, in the midst of divorce and shell-shocked by my grandmother's death. There were countless other stories from countless other rehabbers at centers around the world—stories I could only guess at. Far more than they hurt us, raptors healed.

"You've built some good rapport with Lorax," Jean told me. "You and I should be the only ones feeding her for a while, so she associates us with her dinner. C'mon."

She wound Lorax's green nylon leash around her hand and clucked her tongue so that the owl stopped triangulating on the aquarium of crickets and focused on her. I followed them down to the owl mew and slipped inside, sat on the mute-streaked plastic chair and watched Jean back Lorax up to an Astroturf-covered perch. She stepped off and remained still as Jean unclipped the leash and handed her another mouse from her jacket pocket.

Across from us in a smaller mew, the sharp-shinned hawk flew back and forth, shrieking its displeasure at our presence. Lorax's cage mate retreated to a far corner and stared.

"Why's Lorax so calm when the rest of these birds are freaking out?"

"Human habituated." Jean unswiveled her jesses and stepped away. "Remember, she came to us as a baby after she fell from the nest. She's been handled by humans her whole life. We're all she knows, while these others . . ." She pointed at the other great horned and the crazed sharpie. "We rescued them from the wilderness when they were adults."

She knelt to pick up a brown-and-white feather and stroked the soft edge. "We have to make sure Lorax continues to like you. Different birds have different preferences for people. Some hate men, some hate eyeglasses, some despise baseball caps. Lorax hates Darcy."

I smothered a giggle. Lorax didn't appear to love me or hate me—she barely registered my presence. She stood on the perch and looked around the mew. Her feathers stayed unruffled, her head tufts at ease. Jean pulled off her glove and handed it to me. "Put this on. Let's try something."

"*What?*"

"I want her to step up on your glove. You've got to realize she's not gonna hurt you. Walk over to her perch and place your arm in front of her feet. She'll hop up."

"Yikes. Really?"

Jean had trained half a dozen birds and God knows how many women in the transitional program she directed for women just out of jail. I could think of no one more worthy of trust.

Slowly, I extended my arm until it lay parallel with Lorax's tawny feathered feet. She studied me an instant, then stepped one foot at a time on my glove and stood there. I sucked in my breath, shocked by the weight of her—impossibly light and alive, as if I'd caught up some woodland fairy.

"Give her a bit." Jean handed me a chunk of rat from the box at her waist. I took it in my bare hands, held it up to Lorax's beak.

She dropped it. Startled by its splash in her water trough, she gave a low hoot and sailed to her feeding platform. I jumped away, pressed my glove to my chest. "Wow. Wow, wow, wow. I could feel the air from her wings!"

"Cool, huh? Let's let her chill out now."

"She didn't scalp me!"

"Of course not."

Adrenaline can be marvelous stuff. Under the right conditions—catching a wave on a board, hurtling downhill on a bike, running a marathon—it empowers. I realized that day that bird handling must offer Jean and Jonathan and the others the same rush of hormones, the same mandate to live in the thrill of the moment.

"I've been researching enrichment online. What if I cut holes in a paper towel roll and stuff it with crumpled-up newspaper and lichen and mealworms? I think she'd have fun ripping it apart, and if I gave it to her, it might help to build rapport." In the reflection from Jean's glasses, I could see my eyes wide, almost manic.

"Darlin'..." Jean threw an arm around my shoulders and touched her forehead to mine. "This time last year, you couldn't even pick up a mealworm. You've come a long way."

⌒

Maybe so, but I still had a long way to go. Looking for a way to juggle adoption research with owl rapport-building, I read Vietnam travel guidebooks in the great horned owls' mew. "Vietnamese women cook this soup called *pho* right out on the sidewalk over burners," I reported to Lorax, "and people stand there and eat it for breakfast. There's a Vietnamese restaurant near here—do you think I should take Jonathan there for our anniversary?"

From her feeding platform, talons embedded in a quail, Lorax opened her beak wide. Her body undulated upward, the sign of an upcoming pellet.

I smothered laughter. "Thanks," I said. "I'll take that as a yes."

The next night, Jonathan and I drove to a small diner beside a lingerie boutique. A petite, wrinkled woman—white apron tied around a blue pantsuit—stepped over to the cash register. She handed us laminated menus, pointing to a red-cushioned booth under a shellacked wall clock in the shape of Vietnam.

Only three other patrons were dining there just then—a trio of college-age students drinking beer and laughing and talking in a language I guessed was Vietnamese.

"Wine?" I looked down at the menu, hoping for Cabernet.

"No wine." Our hostess poured water. "You like this coffee . . ." She tapped a finger against the beverage section of the menu; broken English text described coffee served Vietnamese style, thick with sweetened condensed milk.

"Yes, please." I grimaced an apology at Jonathan, barred from the drink because of lactose intolerance.

"Just a Coke, please." He glanced at the menu. "*Pho?*" He attempted the word for the Vietnamese soup.

"Fuh," she corrected him.

"As in 'What the fuh,'" I said, quoting a T-shirt pictured in my guidebook.

"You like the soup—very fine, very fresh." The woman trotted off to the kitchen.

Jonathan lifted his glass to clink mine. "Happy anniversary. Aren't we supposed to give each other gifts made out of paper or soap or something?"

He put down his glass and entwined his fingers with mine. Red-tailed hawks, during courtship displays, sometimes lock talons midair and spiral downward, shrieking. I squeezed his fingers and contemplated our postdinner rendezvous, grateful that he preferred my old boxer shorts and raptor center T-shirt to the silk teddies and garter belts on the mannequins next door.

"No gifts," I told him. "We've gotta save money for our trip."

Marissa had told us to plan for a three-week visit to Vietnam, during which we'd process paperwork and speak with all the right government officials. It looked good, too, we found out, to show up at our designated orphanage with presents for the kids and staff. After proving our worth there and at a barrage of meetings in Hanoi or Ho Chi Minh City, then finally at a formal adoption ceremony, we'd come home with a son.

I tried to get excited. "The Vietnamese like to say they're a country, not a war," I read from the book I'd tucked into my backpack. The hostess brought me the cup of coffee with condensed milk, and I gulped it, appreciating its sugary strength.

Jonathan sipped his Coke, looked away.

"You seem subdued," I told him.

"I just have a lot on my mind."

"You're craving nicotine, aren't you?"

After our wedding I'd asked him to give up smoking. He'd agreed, said he was happy to do it, but sometimes his eyes got a distant look, his attention focused on something that escaped me entirely. During those moments, he told me, the desire for cigarettes felt almost overpowering.

"I'm actually fine right now." He studied the cover of my guidebook. "Read me more."

Satisfied that I didn't need to run to the corner store for a pack of Nicorette, I opened the book. "They starting adopting out orphans right after the war, when the North Vietnamese invaded South Vietnam. The U.S. did an Operation Babylift thing there, same as in Korea in the fifties."

"Huh." He picked up a bottle of vermillion-colored condiment beside the soy sauce on our table. A rooster swelled proudly on the front of it. "Sriracha. Looks spicy."

"The Vietnamese eat a lot of fish sauce." I tapped the jar of brown liquid on the table; it gleamed like the dog park's mud. "Anchovies, fermented in barrels with salt and water for months." I lifted the lid and bent to inhale. "I'm skipping the fish sauce."

Our hostess returned and set down vast soup tureens in front of us. Beside them she placed saucers of bean sprouts, slivered basil, and crescents of lime. "For *pho*." She made a stirring motion with one index finger and pointed to the wooden chopsticks next to wide ceramic spoons.

Previously, I'd believed lime to be most palatable when shoved into the neck of a Corona bottle, but I squeezed a crescent into my soup and stirred in sprouts and basil. "Rice noodles at the bottom." I lifted up a gleaming tangle with my chopsticks and breathed in the unanticipated smell of cinnamon. "Fresh broccoli and carrots and tofu. Hey, we should have a Vietnamese dinner party for all our friends who filled out recommendations."

Part of the adoption application included recommendations from three couples who had to explain, in ten pages, why Jonathan and I would be good parents.

"I guess we could . . ." He lifted his bowl to his lips as the trio of students near us had done. "Seems pretty complicated, though."

"We'll get a cookbook from the library."

We finished our *pho* and stood up to pay our bill. Behind the cash register someone had taped up the photo of a bucktoothed Vietnamese boy.

His image didn't evoke the same excitement I'd felt upon seeing the Chinese girl after the flight show at the Oregon Zoo. But I felt a tiny green pinprick of hope, like the tips of early daffodils pushing up through the decomposed oak leaves in our backyard.

"We're adopting a little boy from *your* country," I said to our hostess.

The wrinkles in her forehead deepened. "Why?"

Before I could answer, another couple pushed through the door. She handed them menus and showed them to a booth.

"Why?" I repeated to Jonathan in the truck on the way to the library. "China was easy—mothers abandon their babies. But why *are* kids in Vietnam put up for adoption?"

Jonathan shook his head. "No idea."

We'd gone along without question when our agency switched countries on us, not bothering to investigate the potential political or social issues that broke up Vietnamese families. "Why boys?" I said now. "Are *they* being abandoned? I'm confused."

Jonathan parked outside our public library, distinctive with its stained glass windows. Rain pelted the windshield in the dark. "I've gotta tell you something."

My hands trembled from Vietnamese coffee and apprehension. Here it was—he'd reconsidered; he wanted to remain child-free and adopt a golden eagle instead. I told myself I could handle it. Plenty of organizations in Eugene were desperate for child mentors; I'd simply devote myself to some bereft eight-year-old with absentee parents. I didn't *need* to be a parent, did I?

I leaned my head against the window, the glass damp and cold against my ear. "All right . . . tell me."

He plucked at his brow. "So I'm in touch, on Facebook, with a cousin who adopted a boy from Vietnam last year. On his blog he said that before the signing ceremony, the kid's father biked three hours from his village to say good-bye to his son. Agency officials had to hold him back sobbing." Jonathan looked out the window at the bronze statue of Eugene Skinner sitting behatted on a log in front of the library.

"I don't understand. Why did the dad give up his son?"

"Economic reasons, maybe? Poor families adopt out their kids so they'll have a better life . . ."

"But that doesn't necessarily follow."

After my mother divorced my father, my siblings and I lived with her in a beachside duplex for a time, on her paychecks well below the poverty line. We shopped at thrift stores. We sat on the floor and ate rice and beans and played with plastic dolls that cost a dollar. We had a wonderful time until the judge's decree ripped us apart.

"Money doesn't guarantee a better life." At a loss for original explanation, I stated the obvious. "That dad obviously loves his kid."

"Exactly. That's what concerns me."

"Oh."

We walked into the library in silence. I found a cookbook and a documentary. Titled *Daughter from Danang*, it followed the journey of an Amerasian girl adopted out of Vietnam in the late 1960s and placed with a family in Tennessee. Twenty-two years later, Mai Thi Hiep—or Heidi, as her adoptive family called her—returned to her Vietnamese hometown to meet her biological family.

At home we curled up on the couch with the cats and watched Heidi's Vietnamese mother clutch her long-lost daughter, keening and sobbing into the young woman's shoulder. In a family meeting later, her biological brother suggested it was her turn to take care of their mom. Heidi could bring her to the States, or send a monthly stipend to Vietnam. During the gathering the mother sat and stared dully into the distance, suspecting the answer before the daughter she'd birthed nixed both choices.

The human brain can only hold so much contradiction, so much conflict, at one time. As the documentary's credits rolled, I fed the dogs and cats their evening snack, put on my pajamas, and climbed into bed. My amorous anniversary plans felt frivolous now, too exhausting to execute.

Usually, insomnia plagued me into the wee hours, but this night—overwhelmed by questions that had no satisfying answer—I plunged into sleep.

The next day, I covered Jean's shift at the raptor center. "I don't usually feed the diurnal guys," I told Darcy as I prepped quail plates. "Anything I should know?"

Much as I longed to give her the silent treatment for sending me gloveless to pick up a bird, I knew that an awkward silence as we moved through our shift duties around each other would be excruciating.

She fluffed up her hair with one hand, the one-eyed screech owl perched on her gloved wrist. "Don't go into the sharp-shinned hawk's mew. She's terrified of people. There's a little sliding door to the right of her door. Just drop her quail on the feeding platform and bail."

"Will do." I walked out the door with my pie plates.

"And Melissa . . ." She lifted her chin. I thought again of the pictures I'd seen depicting Athena, helmeted warrior goddess with an owl on her arm. "Watch out for the harriers."

I walked away muttering curses at her superiority, but glad of the insight into the sharp-shinned hawk. I'd paid little attention to the sharpie, smitten with owls as I was. They're typically smaller than Cooper's hawks, a blur of speed with short wings and a long tail that help them zip through dense forests on the hunt for songbirds. I had to admit that ours, missing the tip of one wing after failed surgery to fix a broken bone, struck me as mostly annoying. Whenever I walked around to feed the birds, she hurled herself back and forth in her mew, chattering a shrill alarm call over and over.

I'd steeled myself against feeling sorry for most of the raptors; after all, they got free medical care, stimulating enrichment toys, a good meal daily. But the sharpie struck me as different from most. As I approached her mew under a canopy of trees, she bounced from her perch and performed her usual back-and-forth dash, slamming her body into the wire sides of her enclosure. Sharpies like thick forest; this scattering of firs and maples wasn't working for her.

I turned my key in the padlock and slid back the door that led to her feeding platform, then dropped her quail on the plywood. I shut the door and felt the thump of her body hitting wood. Her shrieks hurt my ears. I escaped into Lorax's mew and ducked behind the plastic chair so the hawk would think I'd gone and stop screaming.

No one attempted to train the sharpie. I knew we were fortunate to display almost every type of raptor found in our region; still, I couldn't help questioning the presence of this hawk.

"We're thinking of euthanizing her." Darcy spoke from the screech owls' mew.

"Really?"

"Yeah. She seems miserable. Why cause emotional pain if we don't have to?"

Much as I didn't want to give Darcy credit, it seemed to me a good guiding question in the midst of confusion. I thought about applying it to Jonathan's and my conflicts about Vietnam. But the answer evaded me. Would our adoption cause emotional pain? Would we even know unless the boy's parents found their way to the orphanage to choke out a tearful good-bye to their son?

<hr />

"Why cause her more pain?"

My running partner, Kat, asked the question a few weeks later after pulling her eleven-year-old daughter, Andi, out of school. "Girls have been bullying her. I found her in the bathroom with my bottle of Ativan. She told me she wanted to commit suicide."

Kat sat on her living room carpet across from me, beside a stack of books on homeschooling. We balanced teacups on our knees, sugar cookies on a plate near our wool-socked feet. From upstairs the murmur of children's voices rose in a sibling spat, drowning out the patter of raindrops. Kat leaned close and spoke in a near whisper.

"The teacher knew what was going on. Andi's attitude just kept getting worse, but she thought the girls would work it out themselves. The instant my kid mentioned slitting her wrists, I yanked her out of that classroom."

Her eyes narrowed over her cup. "I'm going to homeschool her the rest of the year. She's so depressed she won't leave the house. We're waiting for junior high, hoping to lottery into the school across town."

"She could volunteer with me on Thursdays at the raptor center."

My friend brightened. "She loves biology . . . getting out in nature would distract her from the bullies."

"Right." I reached for another cookie. Kat and Andi had cut them in owl shapes, adding chocolate frosting with a candy-corn beak. "Jonathan and I moved our shift at the center to Thursday evenings so we can travel some weekends. If she's interested, I'll pick her up at three forty-five this week. Maybe come get her after a few hours, in case she doesn't like it. If she does, though, I'll pick her up and bring her home every week . . . ah . . . except for next Thursday. Our social worker's coming for our first home visit."

"Still thinking of Vietnam, eh?"

I shrugged, unwilling to plumb the depths of my ambivalence just then. "We'll see."

Kat dropped half a dozen cookies into a paper bag for me, an unusual humility softening her posture. "Thank you for the offer," she said. "I hope Andi likes the place. It could save her."

I nodded. "It saved me."

—◦—

Andi liked the raptor center—no doubt about that. From the moment we stepped into the clinic, she gravitated toward the tasks of prepping quail and rats for the birds and thawing bags of frozen mice in a sink full of warm water.

"Death is cool." In black yoga pants and a black T-shirt that read "Princess" in glittery letters, she plucked bright yellow eggs from splayed quail carcasses like a pro and fed one to the resident raven, holding it between thumb and forefinger toward the bird's thick black beak, like I showed her, without a trace of fear.

"I want to see the peregrine eat." Ponytail bouncing, she bounded over to the falcon's mew. The blue-gray bird flew to the far upper corner of her mew and clung to the wire. I began to admonish Andi, then registered her excitement and closed my mouth. "That's a cool bird! Last year at my friend's birthday party up here, a handler took her out. She ate a quail, and the feathers flew everywhere. Guts, too."

In the prey barn she grew quieter. "Aw . . . look at these cute little babies!"

I bent over the nest of pink wiggling creatures in one aquarium and showed her how to place each one carefully in a makeshift tea-box nest, and then to clean the glass and pile in fresh wood shavings along with food pellets and a water bottle.

"The mom won't stop feeding them because they smell like me?" Andi held one grub-like baby up to her eyes in wonder, then kissed it.

"That's a myth." I placed the trembling mother back in the aquarium and set down the metal exercise wheel. "She doesn't care how they smell. She just wants to protect them. Mothers . . . well, you know. They worry about their kids."

Andi stayed bent over the aquarium. I glanced at her pale, skinny forearms crisscrossed with hairline cuts. How could a person so young gravitate toward self-destruction? I wanted to engage her, to replace her chaotic self-image with a passion that would sustain her no matter what the mean girls of the world threw her way. The natural world could save her . . . if she let it in.

"Did you know male mice sing to attract a mate?" I took the lid off another aquarium and held up a black-and-white fellow with giant testicles. "Sometimes when I walk into the prey barn, I hear the mice squeaking and I think the tenors are having a competition—sort of an *America's Got Talent* for rodents."

Andi giggled and picked up the mouse in my hand. She lifted him to eye level and launched into the raunchy AC/DC song, "Big Balls," that had made me double over with laughter one summer at sixth-grade camp.

I cracked up now, so loudly that the education director stuck her head into the prey barn. "Don't scare the mice."

Andi went back to cleaning, her back hunched over another aquarium. A giggle escaped her. I shredded newspaper for mouse beds. Under the rustle I barely heard her next words. "I wish *you* were my mother."

Working alongside her, idly chatting about snowy owls and how peregrines could fly over 230 miles an hour before knocking out prey with balled-up talons, I felt a stab of longing. Although I knew Kat would be pissed, I couldn't stop the words from rushing to my lips.

"Thanks. I wish you were my daughter."

15

Parents in Progress

I'm a sucker for hard-luck cases. After I agreed to work alongside Kat's devastated daughter at the raptor center, a gray-and-white cat began stealing laundry off the wooden rack on our back lawn. He dragged my fifty-dollar Columbia sweater in his teeth to his owner's house two blocks away and dropped it in the muddy gutter, following this act by hauling a full-size bath towel across our backyard. I trailed him, discovered my sweater, and dialed the number on his tag.

A woman replied to my frustration with a hawk-like shriek. "Goddammit, Eeyore's gonna cost me a fortune in dry cleaning!"

She kicked him out of the house and ceased feeding him. When the thief—skinny and jonesing for love—began bringing us his previous owner's T-shirts and socks, and then a lime-green Victoria's Secret bra in my size, I surrendered.

"Cat, you have proven yourself." I poured him a bowl of kibble and invited him inside. He promptly developed flatulence.

"What's Marissa going to say when she walks in and our home smells like a giant cat fart?" I hollered across the house to where Jonathan knelt scrubbing the kitchen floor in preparation for a home visit from our adoption agency's social worker.

"Light some nag champa." He sat up. "Do you think she's gonna check behind the fridge?"

Adoptive parents reminisce about their social worker's home visits as the most stressful part of the child-procuring process. Someone in a position of power is mandated by law to spend hours in your personal space, a space that may or may not be occupied by three years' worth of unread

New Yorkers and ancient half-empty Merlot bottles, eight shedding pets, and your husband's collection of animal skulls.

"Think you could box those up before Marissa arrives?" I picked up a sheep skull on the hearth and swiped my dusting rag into the eyeholes.

"Okay." He took the skull and picked up a delicate rodent bone he'd left lying on the kitchen windowsill. "But I'm leaving the cow skull on the porch. She should get a sincere picture of who we are."

"Who we are . . ." I echoed. Would she find us too wrapped up in raptors? A statue of the Egyptian falcon god, Horus, stood on our mantel; owl photos hung on the walls beside Seattle Zoo's calendar; scrawled notes about shift obligations and training sessions and educational presentations filled almost every square. What if she found us too unconventional to parent a child?

Marissa had advised us over the phone not to clean before her arrival. "I just need to see where the smoke alarms are," she promised.

Still, we spent the weekend before her visit scrubbing every inch of our little house surrounded by firs and fur. Five cats and three dogs in 1,100 square feet during the rainy months meant mud and muck in every crevice, plus the occasional accident on our long-suffering couch and bath mat.

Jonathan wielded the broom above his head, brushing cobwebs and indignant daddy longlegs from the corners of the ceiling. "It's funny—we keep the raptor center cleaner than our house."

I failed to see the humor in this truth. Staff at the center required volunteers to keep the clinic, prey barn, treatment room, and visitors' center immaculate—we never knew when someone from Oregon Fish and Wildlife might pop in for a visit. Jonathan and I spent hours Thursday evenings scrubbing and bleaching and sweeping while our own home moldered.

I took out another Q-tip and attacked the grout around the kitchen faucet.

"Kat said friends of hers didn't get a child because the numbers outside their house weren't large enough for EMTs to see!" I hollered to Jonathan, busy in the next room. "And one of my colleagues at the J-School said she and her husband had to build another room for a potential child.

This process is so unfair." I scrubbed at the dog-nose prints smudging the kitchen window. "Birth parents don't have to clean their house before they get pregnant, but we've got to prove ourselves worthy before we even submit a dossier to Vietnam."

Jonathan walked over and put his arms around me. "Do we even want to submit our dossier?"

"*What?* You mean *not* adopt?"

I turned around to face him. He wanted a daughter even more than I did—I knew that. "Boy energy," as he called it, held little appeal. "I remember what *I* was like growing up," he'd told me. "No thanks." And yet here we stood, covered in cobwebs and dust bunnies, preparing our home for a little boy.

"Oh . . . wow. We better talk about all this. It's too late to cancel—she'll be here any minute."

Marissa appeared on the steps under our cedar. We waved out the window. "Don't tell her we're reconsidering," I whispered. "Let's at least hear what she has to say."

I hurried to open the door.

"Hi, guys." She marched up the porch steps past the cow skull. A fierce spring storm shook the oak branches that drooped dangerously over our front porch; she appeared oblivious to them and to the extra-large brass house numbers we'd nailed up under a blazing porch light.

I ushered her into the living room, offered to take her brocade coat, and pointed her in the direction of the feast we'd laid out on the table in her honor—smoked salmon, whole wheat crackers, sliced apples, brie. She ignored the food but handed me the coat.

"So give me the tour." She pursed her lips. "And relax. I'm not interested in the state of your linen closet. I just need to make sure your house is safe for a child."

I knew about safety checks. Volunteers at the raptor center had to begin each shift with a walk around each mew, looking for loose nails and broken perches—anything that might threaten the birds.

Social workers, too, look for potential dangers during a home visit—guns, knives, drugs, cockroaches, evidence of rodents, exposed wires, exposed pit bulls—those can be deal breakers.

I'd put all our kitchen knives into a drawer with a child-safe lock and stashed the Tylenol and my allergy medication on the top shelf of the medicine cabinet. We'd confiscated the cats; they sulked under bushes outside. The dogs hunkered down under the oaks, trying to stay out of the rain. I'd forgotten our yard sale G.I. Joe doll reclining on the mantel in a long pink nightgown, his muscle-bound arms raised in victory beside the picture of my moms.

I dropped Joe in a drawer as Jonathan led Marissa down the hall to the spare room. "I know we still need to get those little plastic covers for the outlets and locks on the cabinets, and we're getting a bed and some other furniture for the nursery . . ."

Marissa looked up at the smoke alarm mounted on the ceiling, wrote something on a notepad tucked into a leather portfolio, and walked into our bedroom. "Smoke alarm in here, too? Good." She turned and marched back through the nursery, pausing in the hallway to peer into the bathroom.

"What d'you think about the layout of our house? We have to walk through the nursery to get to our room. Is that a problem?"

"You have to remember where most of these kids are coming from. Orphanages, foster homes—a room of one's own on any terms is an incredible luxury." Marissa sat down at the table with her notebook. I saw our biographies—the multipage questionnaire we'd each had to fill out and that checklist of potential disabilities—tucked into the portfolio's pocket. She regarded us over the untouched platter of delicacies. "So what's up with the raptors?"

"The raptors?"

Under the table I squeezed Jonathan's hand. I'd assumed Marissa's questions would continue in the vein of Holt's intimate application; she'd demand to know what type of underwear we wore, and whether we preferred missionary or doggie style. Now I saw that she did indeed find our work with birds of prey suspect; cutting up rats and feeding dead quail to owls couldn't help but strike someone trained to spot red flags as the very antithesis of familial nurturing.

"Raptors are my passion." Jonathan recovered his composure before I did. "It's an incredible feeling to release them back into the wild after feeding and medicating them for weeks. Would you like to come see a raptor release? Once in a while, they're open to the public."

"Perhaps." Her eyes went briefly to a bookshelf, specifically to the forgotten lime-green bra I'd thrown there on top of my birder's handbook. "So . . . the way this works is I write up your adoption study, and then you compile your dossier. Birth certificates, marriage certificates, mortgage statements, certificates of good health, employment verification, passport photocopies, copies of your divorce decree, Melissa."

I busied myself stacking salmon on a cracker. "By when do we need all this?"

"You've got months. You'll get your referral in about a year and a half."

"A year and a half?" I calculated the timeline. "So how long do we have, postreferral, before we go to Vietnam?"

"Anywhere from four to six months."

"You're kidding. We applied over a year ago . . . now we have to wait two more years for a child?"

"Sorry, yes. Since China's restrictions, Vietnam's been inundated with applications. They should've told you that when you switched countries. In the meantime you can sign up for our two-month Parents in Progress class. It's never too early to start thinking about what you'll do when your kiddo hurls his Goldfish crackers at your owl."

Though we weren't entirely sure we wanted to stay with the adoption agency, we signed up for the parenting class a month in advance. While we waited we immersed ourselves in a formal workshop on how to train and handle birds.

In the old days at the raptor center, before I began volunteering, the process of training to become a bird handler was simple. Jonathan told me how staff needing an owl or hawk on the glove for an education program would simply approach a seasoned volunteer like himself and say, "Go get the red-tail," or "Take out the turkey vulture." But growth of the center meant refinement in procedure. Staff hired an education director to oversee training and the raptors' well-being. Now interested volunteers who'd put in a year or so of work could sign up for monthlong classes in bird handling.

One afternoon Darcy discovered me in Lorax's mew reading aloud from *Don't Shoot the Dog*. She snorted. "We never spent months building rapport with a raptor or cutting rats into bits for reward." She clapped her right hand against her left forearm. "We just grabbed the bird, stuck it on our glove, and called it trained."

Even I knew this wasn't the most skillful way to teach a wild animal to perform an unnatural behavior such as perching on someone's arm for an hour. The *Don't Shoot the Dog* author swore by the power of positive reinforcement. This made sense to me; I myself wouldn't think of running more than six miles at a time unless buoyed by the promise of a postworkout cream puff.

Staff at the center had just returned from a conference hosted by the International Association of Avian Trainers and Educators—a vast group of folks who work with raptors and parrots and other birds for nature centers and zoos around the world. They swooned over legendary trainer Steve Martin—not the actor, but a kindhearted evangelist for positive reinforcement. In a business where people sometimes let their raptors go hungry so they'll be more motivated to high-five a trainer with a talon or catch mealworms in midair to the delight of a paying crowd, Martin gave a presentation about working a bird at its natural weight using a reward-based system.

"But he also says to think beyond food." Jonathan and I read his paper, "What's In It for Me?" on the lumpy couch in the visitors' center one evening before handler classes. "Some birds like to have their head scratched—they'll actually work for massage instead of mice or quail." He rubbed the back of my neck.

I leaned into his fingers and closed my eyes. "I am *not* scratching Lorax's head."

"Yeah—if I tried that with the ferruginous hawk, she'd take off my hand."

Four volunteers pushed through the squeaking screen door and sprawled in folding chairs around the glass-topped table under which sat a display of bird eggs, from minuscule hummingbird to apple-size ostrich. The plucked African gray parrot peeked out from behind the curtained glass door and let out a belch. We giggled, earning a stern look from the education director.

She addressed our group over a clipboard, pencil stuck at a rakish angle in her ponytail. "I want to thank everyone for committing to these training sessions. All of us—new handlers and old—will follow these procedures whenever we work with a bird. First, we'll ask you to build rapport with your assigned raptor. As often as possible, hopefully every day, you'll sit in the mew and let the bird get to know you. Take in a chair and read, sing, whatever . . . but no gloves. And absolutely no picking up or touching a bird until we say you're ready."

She looked around the room, making eye contact with each of us. "We don't want the bird associating you with handling just yet. You'll see a variety of issues as you get to know your raptor. It may fly away from you, or clack its beaks or hiss. The turkey vultures might throw up. Your job is to stay calm and offer the birds a sense of security every step of the way."

My hand where the harrier had footed it pulsated with a phantom ache. But Jean assured me that I'd work only with gentle, human-habituated Lorax.

That first night of training, the education director covered the basics of behavior modification, then asked us each to walk from the visitors' center to the clinic while balancing a Dixie cup of water on our bare wrist. "The idea's to pretend you've got a bird on your glove. Remember, arm steady as a tree trunk."

Our free hand was eventually supposed to perform actions that ran the gamut from navigating door latches and fishing thawed mice from the sink to greasing leather ankle straps and medicating a raptor's feet . . . without spilling the water. I minced over to Jean, my Dixie cup empty and my shoes sodden. "So I'm supposed to oil Lorax's straps, feed her mice, put Bag Balm on her foot pads, and make sure she doesn't fly off the glove all at the same time?"

"And you also have to thread swivels through the jesses to clip them to your glove before you bring her out, and then when you're done with a program, unswivel them."

She took my cup and handed me strips of stiff tan leather—two jesses that would go around an education bird's ankles. "Grease these at home until they're butter-soft." She gave me a pair of silver swivels. "One ring gets threaded through the slit in the jess, and the other clips to your glove. Do the same with the other swivel and jess, and then clip the end of a leash to the swivels and wrap it around your hand so the bird doesn't get tangled. Practice without a bird until you can do it with your eyes closed. Literally."

"Why?"

She ran a hand through her hair, fluffing it. "Sometimes ed programs run late. You'll find yourself in a mew trying to navigate a flashlight and your bird. Believe me, it's easier to learn how to unswivel Lorax in the dark. You don't want her to bate."

I knew that *bate* meant to fly off the glove, and that shaking my wrist slightly would cause a bird to refocus on solid footing. In the workshop I began to learn a whole new skill set along with an expanded vocabulary. *Free flight* referred to a raptor's ability to fly from, say, a perch to a handler's glove without taking off for the tallest tree. A bird who bit into a handler's leg—as one of the turkey vultures had done to a volunteer, gashing a hole in her blue jeans—was a *Level Three bird*, available for training by only the most seasoned handlers who might or might not have a death wish. And a *fly-off?* That happened when a raptor, due to sloppy handling, took off into the sky and vanished forever.

The education director taught us what to do if we accidentally let a bird go. "Alert staff, put fresh mice on a stump, grab a net, and pray. That said," she added, and flashed us a ferocious look, "*don't* cause a fly-off."

⁓

The following month, in the frigid meeting room at the adoption agency, Jonathan and I memorized a different lexicon. The mother who gave birth to a baby was the *biological mom.* The baby went from being a *foster child* to an *adoptee*, while the adults who welcomed him or her into a forever home were *adoptive parents.* Jonathan and I, upon bringing home our child, would become a *transracial family.* Using a thick spiral-bound workbook as her guide, Marissa covered the behaviors we might observe after bringing our child home. "Anxiety, crying, anger, refusing to make eye contact, lying, stealing, pyromania, and caching food under the bed."

"That last one's a very corvid-like behavior." Jonathan looked up from his notebook at Marissa. "In the wild, crows and ravens stash nuts and seeds. Months later, they recall right where they put them."

The round couple sitting across from us, endlessly spirited in their green-and-yellow UO Ducks sweatshirts, widened their eyes at us and then at each other. We learned that they had two biological sons, then felt a calling to adopt a Chinese girl. They'd been married for two decades. "We passed China's new requirements with flying colors," the female half of the duo giggled.

I wanted to hate her. But at the break, she approached me. "Will this be your first child, honey?"

I nodded. "Probably our only."

Encouraged, she threw her arms around me and pressed my face into her shoulder. "Oh, honey, I'm so sorry you weren't able to conceive. This must be so hard on you."

Her hair smelled distinctly of the Avon perfume my great-aunt had fancied. I pulled out of the embrace and corrected her. "Actually, we haven't tried to conceive. We *want* to adopt."

The woman's face, full of sympathy, now clouded with confusion. "I don't get it. You guys didn't try to make a baby?"

"Nope."

"Why on earth not? You'd have beautiful children!"

I glanced down at a rack of the agency's magazines, each with a gorgeous overseas poster child on the cover. "Thanks . . ."

Jonathan and I had agreed not to launch into a political diatribe when people demanded to know why we were adopting someone else's kid instead of creating a little Helen or Adonis of our own. I found myself mumbling a vapid half-truth. "We volunteer to rehabilitate injured and orphaned raptors. We want to help a child in a similar situation."

"Dinosaurs?" The woman's pretty face scrunched up in further confusion.

"Birds of prey. Owls, hawks, falcons . . ."

"Oh, I get it."

But she didn't. Her brow furrowed under her Ducks cap, and she returned to her seat in the conference room and whispered in her husband's ear. He glanced at me and shook his head. Not to be outdone, I sat down and whispered in Jonathan's ear. "I think people think we can't have biological kids."

"It's okay. You don't have to correct them."

I bristled. I didn't care if a bunch of strangers assumed my eggs weren't hatching, but I wanted them to know that adoption was our personal preference. I'd just read a memoir by Seattle sex columnist Dan Savage, titled *The Kid: What Happened After My Boyfriend and I Decided to Go Get Pregnant*. He described the curriculum in their adoption classes as beginning with instruction on how to move past grief over one's infertility. For the couples surrounding him and his boyfriend, adoption seemed like a paltry consolation prize awarded in sympathy for failed conception. But it had been Dan's blue ribbon, too.

Surely there were other parents out there who didn't feel an overwhelming urge to procreate and, instead, wanted to help a child in need of a home.

"We couldn't have our own baby." A young red-headed couple that Jonathan and I would refer to ever after as Exhibit A walked into the meeting room toting an adorable little Korean boy in blue footie pajamas. Marissa had invited them in to relate their recent adoption experience, and they began—sitting rigid on folding chairs at the front of the room— by recounting their multiple attempts to procreate. "We tried every which way but upside down," the woman said. Before she could elaborate, the baby on the man's lap giggled, and the women around the table drew a collective gasp. "He's so beautiful!"

"It's almost time for his beddy-bye." The new mother reached for her son and rocked him in her arms. I pictured him swaying in time with the pendulums on all the biological clocks in the room. Did the woman see how hungrily we around the table stared at her little boy, how we coveted his smile, his tiny belch, his baby scowl as his father described their process of adopting him? I nudged Jonathan's foot with mine. "Maybe we should adopt from Korea."

"The reason we chose Korea is you don't have to go to that country." On the edge of his seat, the boy's father winked as if letting us all in on a magnificent secret. "They send the baby to you with an escort. All we had to do was drive up to the Portland airport to pick him up, easy as pie."

Most countries required adoptive parents to travel there, to attend governmental meetings and visit the orphanage or foster home and participate in a formal ceremony of transfer. Some, like Korea, were less demanding. Jonathan had told me how his sister and brother-in-law had a courier bring their Korean children over; the whole family had converged in Rochester's tiny airport lounge to welcome Nathan, and then Brynnli.

But we wanted to travel to our kid's country of origin, to see the foster home or orphanage, to take photographs, to meet the people and sample the food and explore the surrounding cities and countryside. I imagined what it would feel like to wander through Vietnamese rice paddies and navigate the frenetic streets of Hanoi with Jonathan and our new child. "*Chao.*" I practiced the greeting in my head. "Hello. *Cam on.* Thanks. Thanks for the kid."

Jonathan raised his hand. "I have a question."

The proud daddy at the front of the room took the yawning toddler from his wife and held him up for us to ogle. "Shoot, man."

"So . . . my sister has two children from Korea." Jonathan spoke in the eloquent, East Coast tenor that caused people and raptors around him to lift their heads and listen. "We've been talking in these classes about how to keep kids connected to their culture. My sister's worked hard to keep a sense of her children's heritage, but she says it's difficult, that there's more to cultural awareness than just introducing the kids to *kimchi* at the local Korean restaurant. How do *you* plan to do it?"

The man glanced at our social worker, then at his wife, and his face flushed redder than his hair.

"My son's an American."

He addressed a point over Jonathan's head—a point that happened to fall on a framed picture of the adoption agency's matriarch, resplendent in her snowy white updo and cascading kimono. "My son's gonna grow up to like apple pie, baseball, and hot dogs. Maybe when he's eighteen, if he asks us about Korea, we'll tell him, but for now, he's an American."

Beside him his wife repeated what I assumed was a household mantra. "He's an American."

Jonathan nodded gravely, and I resisted the urge to laugh. Along with the thick Parents in Progress book, we'd been given another spiral-bound tome about adopting from another country, the thesis of which appeared to be "Honor your child's culture, dammit."

This daddy obviously hadn't received the same book.

I thought of Archimedes, an Arctic bird sitting on a stump surrounded by Oregon rainforest. The weekend before, Jonathan and I had gone hiking up in the mountains and returned with a truck bed full of snow. We shoveled it into Archimedes' mew, thinking he would enjoy the reminder of his species' home turf. Instead, he remained on his stump and squawked.

"He's never lived in the Arctic," Darcy reminded us. "He was born in captivity back east."

The owl had sat on his stump all afternoon, watching the snow melt around him. Finally, he hopped down and stood in it, white on white, narrowed yellow eyes staring through the wire sides of his mew at something only he could see. Then I remembered another stanza from Rilke's poem about the panther at the zoo, in which the big cat can no longer see the world beyond its cage.

Wasn't keeping a child from his birth culture, from his world of origin, a form of imprisonment?

Marissa stood up and straightened her woven shawl. Beaded earrings twinkled in the fluorescent light. "Well, I'm sure you need to get your little one to bed." She shook hands with the couple, her face composed in a neutral half-smile. "Thanks so much for taking the time to talk with us tonight."

The couple bid us good-bye among a chorus of faint thank yous from the others around the table. When the glass door had closed behind them, she returned to the front of the room and regarded us all with arms folded against her brocade jacket. "I just want you to know . . ."

She chose her words carefully, and I saw how difficult it must be to navigate the different personalities in the room, all of us preoccupied with unanswered questions coupled with wild longing for a child.

"This couple's views on culture don't necessarily reflect those of our agency," she said. "For instance, our agency offers a yearly heritage camp . . ."

I barely heard her. My eyes sought the window and the sleepy little boy in the blue pajamas. Here was a prototype, a flesh-and-blood template of the child Jonathan and I might someday actually adopt. I longed to hold him in my arms. Boy or girl, I didn't care anymore. I just didn't want to let the kid go.

16

One False Move

A SAVVY RAPTOR HANDLER MASTERS THE NATURAL AND PERSONAL HIS-
tory of "her" bird, inside and out. "If you're working with an owl," the ed
director told volunteers in the handling workshop, "you'd better know
all about its particular eye, ear, and wing structure; its diet, mating, and
breeding habits. Everyone's an owl expert now, thanks to Harry Potter
and the *Guardians of Ga'hoole*. Don't let the third graders stump you."

Each afternoon, I sat on the plastic chair in Lorax's mew and read
about great horned owls. Biologists refer to the species, which dominates
the top of the food chain, as "tigers of the forest." They rule fields and
wetlands and people's backyards, as well, with bodies strong enough to
carry prey three times their own weight. Squirrels, rabbits, even osprey
and peregrine falcons never hear them coming—their soft, serrated feathers enable silent flight.

I learned about their mating and nesting habits, about the threats
posed by barbed-wire fencing and car collision, the power of their talons
to break the spines of large animals. Were Lorax to foot me, it would take
a force of almost thirty pounds to pry open her talons.

This fact, along with the threat of encephalitis, should have been
enough to deter me from handling her. But I'd come too far, felt the
thrill of air from her wings and the privilege of a growing bond that now
allowed me to hand her a rat and stand a foot away while she ate it.

Atop the carcass freezer with Jean after the final class in bird handling, I closed my eyes and threaded one circular swivel through the slit
in a jess, pulling the leather end through to tighten the bond. "I'd clip the
other ring in the swivel to the strap on my glove."

"Yup. Now you've gotta show me you can do it when the jesses are attached to an owl."

She motioned me down from the carcass freezer, opened the door, and extracted a box of Girl Scout Thin Mints from between bags of frozen rats. "I've been here too long." She handed me two cookies. "Why don't you come with Lorax and me to Gray's Garden Center on Saturday to meet shoppers? It'll be your coming-out party."

━━◆━━

Almost always, I'd volunteered with Jonathan—sat at educational booths with him and worked on building rapport with Lorax while he did the same with the spotted owl and ferruginous hawk. On Saturday morning, however, he didn't come to the garden center with me. "I'm going to work on photography." He reached to turn off the alarm and pulled me to him in bed. "I'll go up to the center later."

I showered and put on my new T-shirt screenprinted with the iconic blocky "female" symbol of public restroom fame, the figure's arm outstretched and holding a hawk. Jonathan kissed me and sent me out the door with a banana and my new leather glove, custom made from a tracing of my hand and arm sent in to the tailor. "You're gonna be great."

The manager of Gray's had invited Jean to bring Lorax, along with our center's literature, for a two-hour informal meet-and-greet with the owl. In the midst of shoppers contemplating begonias, employees barking over the intercom, and cash registers beeping, Jean sat with the great horned on her glove, calm as a Buddha.

I stood a few feet away. A small group gathered to stare. Jean wiggled the fingers of her right hand in a hello. Lorax remained unmoving.

"Remember, arm steady like a tree branch," she murmured. "It's busy here today, but shouldn't be a problem."

The owl maintained her tranquil demeanor—even when a customer dropped a plastic garden gnome near her, she merely lifted her ear tufts and stared at the offending creature, then settled back down on Jean's glove.

I sat down a little apart, near the folding table with a stack of brochures on how to attract raptors to a backyard with nest boxes and piles of brush. "I'm gonna be busy with the bird." Jean leaned over and spoke in my ear. "You'll need to field questions from the public."

"I hope I have answers."

But after the first half hour, I felt like a robot droning the same replies to predictable queries from people gone wide-eyed at the sight of a real live owl next to the display of plastic pink flamingos.

"Great horned," I replied. "Three pounds. Permanently injured wing. Sorry—can't pet her. She's a wild bird."

In a lull between visitors, Jean turned to me. "You bored? Yep. See it in your eyes. Get ready, darlin'—it's time for a glove transfer."

My glove had arrived via UPS that week—a sturdy, snug-fitting, chocolate-brown accessory that stretched up to my elbow. I wore it everywhere to soften it up. With the thick leather shielding my arm, I felt competent, powerful . . . until Jean asked me to hold Lorax.

I assessed the owl's strong toes, those talons. "What if she bates and hangs upside down like Archimedes?" I whispered so that two women carrying rhododendrons to the counter couldn't hear me. "What if she gets tangled in her jesses? What if she gets loose and takes off?"

Jean smiled, shook her head. "Relax. I'm right here with you."

She stood up, left arm low and steady, and positioned herself in front of me. "Got your glove ready?"

Transferring a bird from one handler to another can be a tricky business. You've got to be quick and decisive—not wishy-washy—or the bird will freak out. I'd watched others do it, but the process confounded me.

"I'll talk you through it." Leash in one hand, Jean unclipped Lorax's jesses from her glove. The owl appeared not to notice. "Now, lift your arm and move it until your glove touches the back of her feet."

I shifted my arm toward Lorax, and she clacked her beak with its tip sharp as an ice pick. I felt like a giant, vulnerable mouse. "I don't think I can do this."

"Course you can. You passed the handling classes with an A-plus."

Jean moved her own arm so that the back of Lorax's feet touched my wrist. The owl paused a moment, then stepped up to my glove.

"Breathe, Melissa."

"Now clip her jesses to you."

Hand sweating, I affixed the glove clip to Lorax's swivels. She hooted low in her throat, sounding surprised at her change of companion. Still, she didn't bate. Jean gave me the end of the nylon leash and showed me how to wrap it around my hand so that if Lorax did fly off, she wouldn't get tangled and I could reel her in.

"Well, look at that, darlin'." She stepped back and surveyed me. "You're holding an owl."

I gazed at her, my posture rigid as a soldier's. "I'm holding . . . an *owl*."

If Lorax minded the difference in handlers, she didn't let on—she perched on my gloved wrist and triangulated on a spider crawling across the floor.

"What's she looking . . . ew! A spider!" A little girl near us jumped backward. Lorax spread her wings and hooted. Alarmed, I lifted my wrist. She flew off, flapped in the air a moment, and then sailed back to my arm. Sweat broke out across my back and chest.

"Jean! What do I do?"

"Keep your arm steady," Jean murmured. "Resist the temptation to raise it when she flies off. Who wants to see the owl eat a mouse?" She held up a plastic container, distracting onlookers from the bate. "We brought Lorax's lunch box."

The group gasped collectively as she pulled out a limp brown mouse. "Gross." The little girl wrinkled her nose, but her eyes remained riveted on the bird. Lorax's talons tightened under my glove. I bit my lip. Could they puncture double-thick leather?

"Owls don't chew like we do. She'll swallow this down." Jean raised the mouse up to the bird's beak, and Lorax took it by the head. She held it for a long moment. But instead of eating it, she opened her beak wide and the mouse dropped onto my sneaker.

"Oh . . . yucky!" The girl backed away. The rest of the crowd tittered.

"It's early." Jean shrugged. "She usually eats in the evening. She's probably not hungry."

I looked down at the rodent draped across my shoe, and then up at the applauding onlookers.

I knew what my vaudevillian great-grandparents would have said if they could've seen me with an owl on my arm then—this was my public, and I had a duty to entertain them, even if they'd simply wandered into the garden center for a six-pack of broccoli seedlings.

Lorax had performed her role—it was time to fulfill mine.

Keeping my left arm immobile, I stretched my right arm down and plucked the mouse from my shoe. I held it out to Lorax, praying she wouldn't bite off my fingertips, and she took it delicately in her beak. Then she dropped it again, eliciting even louder laughter from the audience.

We performed our routine once more, and then I frowned, playing the weary mother. "Haven't I told you not to play with your food?"

That got a roar. Jean held up the donation jar. "All money goes directly toward the care and feeding of the raptors."

Several onlookers reached for their wallets. The little girl dropped a quarter into the donation jar. "I don't need a gumball," she confided to Lorax. "This'll buy you another mouse." She looked up at me, admiration in her eyes. "Will you buy her a white one?"

I grinned down at her. "Absolutely."

At the end of the hour, Jean held up our donation jar stuffed with bills and spare change. "They love you."

I clucked at the owl, looked into her yellow eyes. "They love *her*."

We transferred Lorax to Jean's glove. Jean walked to the car and backed her into a pet carrier, latched the door, and tied the leash end to the wire. "Nice work." She hugged me. "I'm gonna recommend you as Lorax's secondary handler."

⸺ ⁓ ⸺

"I took my daughter up to the raptor center yesterday." Marissa appeared at our house for a second home visit. This time, she didn't request a tour—she merely wanted to sit on the couch and talk. "We were a little confused by the 'Adopt a Raptor' signs on the cages. My kid said, 'Adoption means you take something home and love it.' But you can't do that with a raptor, right?"

I shook my head. "Those signs can be confusing. At the garden center the other day, a man told me he'd love to adopt Lorax, but first he'd have to build an addition on his house."

"People don't realize it's illegal to own a bird of prey without a permit," Jonathan added.

"Maybe you want to say 'Sponsor a Raptor' instead? More accurate." Marissa drummed her fingertips against her upper lip. "Tell me, you two, why do you want a girl?"

"A girl?"

I wondered if she'd mixed us up with another couple. The director of the Vietnam program had assured Jonathan and me that we would be assigned a boy. "Is there . . . is there a chance we could still adopt a girl?"

She shrugged. "Anything's possible. But what's wrong with adopting a boy?"

Excitement ricocheted through me. *Lydia. We might still get our Lydia.*

Jonathan countered Marissa's question with another. "Aren't girls easier to raise?"

Up until that moment, our social worker had come off as somewhat of a hard-ass, with a sort of clinical grimness I recognized from raptor center staff and volunteers who spent years ministering to injured birds who might or might not survive. But now she threw back her head and howled. "I've got a twelve-year-old soccer princess waiting for me in the van outside. Better go tell her she's supposed to be easier than her brother."

She recovered her gravitas. "Girls are no easier to raise than boys, and yet most adoptive parents request them with that misconception. Still, if that's what you want, why don't you check out our Waiting Child program? They offer special considerations in some countries for parents willing to adopt a disabled child. The disabilities range from mild to severe. Plenty of kids are just missing part of an arm or a foot."

Jonathan frowned. "I thought when we filled out the checklist of disabilities a while back that we'd automatically be considered for this program."

"Nope, you have to send a separate application, and then Waiting Child matches you with a kid. You can see the waiting children on our website and in a binder in our office."

I recalled the binder on the receptionist's desk during the orientation meeting—how the young woman with the brace on one leg had paused over the photo of a Haitian boy with cerebral palsy. I pictured her walking through the streets of Port-au-Prince now, hand in hand with her new son.

"Waiting children seldom get adopted as readily as their nondisabled counterparts." Marissa set down her notepad and leaned back in her chair. "Sometimes a country offers grant money to assist with surgeries and things like that. You'd likely be able to bring a waiting child home more quickly, and there's a chance of being matched with a girl . . . *if* you don't require a perfect kid."

A perfect kid. I laughed. "I have chronic insomnia, and Jonathan's got steel rods in his back. We work with disabled birds. We don't need perfection. We'll take a girl with a club foot. We can get special shoes so she can go hiking . . ."

Jonathan held up a hand, quieting my babble. "We understand our kid won't be perfect. But I admit we've been hoping for a daughter who'll love backpacking and hiking and camping and all the stuff we like to do."

Marissa snorted. "That guarantees she'll wear pink dresses and hate to get dirty. She'll want to stay inside all the time and play Fashion Show."

I thought of Andi—Kat's feisty, fashionable daughter who volunteered alongside me. That's the kind of child I wanted, and for the first time in months, I allowed myself to believe that I might get her.

Marissa stood up and pulled her velvet cloche over her head. "Keep an open mind, you two. You'll end up with the kid who's meant for you."

Andi had told me about an adopted girl from China who went to grammar school with her—a one-armed, formidable goalie whose mad soccer skills commanded the respect of every player on the field. "We could handle a child like her," I told Marissa.

"I worked on her case. She's a great kid."

Jonathan reached for my hand. "So how long are we talking now? Could we have a child in under a year?"

"It depends on so many factors." Eeyore, our gray-and-white laundry-stealing cat, strolled in and Marissa reached to scratch him under the chin. "I'll start sending you referrals, but you may find yourself rejecting them."

"Why on earth would we do that?"

"You'll see. Gotta go . . ."

After the silver minivan pulled away, I danced around the living room with Jonathan. He scooped up Eeyore and included him in the waltz. "Cat," he said, "you're gonna have a sister."

The next morning, I tied a bandana around my braids and pulled on my handler's T-shirt. "Jean wants me to take Lorax out onto the lawn today."

Jonathan walked in from the dog park and went to the bathroom to scrub his hands.

"Hold on—I'll go with you."

While he changed clothes I went to my laptop. I read an e-mail from Marissa. Then I screamed.

"Oh my God! We've got a referral!"

"Already?" Jonathan bounded into the office and read over my shoulder. "I have a healthy little girl from Vietnam whom I think will interest you. If you're willing, I'll bring over her biographical and health information."

"A healthy little girl!"

Jonathan dialed Marissa's number. "Yes, we're willing."

He listened for a moment, then hung up the phone. "She'll bring the paperwork over within the hour. Says we can have a day to think about it."

"Why would we need a day?" I threw my arms around him. "This is it. We're gonna be parents!"

His hazel eyes glowed down at me. "Looks like it's finally happening."

The child's name was Ahn, and she was five years old—slender and smiling in the blurry photo attached to a two-page biography that Marissa handed off before rushing her kid to a birthday party. "Happy. Healthy," the Vietnamese social worker had written in her report. "Gets along with her foster family and other children. Likes music and singing. She is always reading."

"She sounds perfect for us!"

But Jonathan frowned at the paper in my hands. "Keep reading . . ."

"Her mother is schizophrenic. Her sisters and aunts are also diagnosed with this mental illness." I looked up at him. "Wow . . . isn't it almost a given that she'll have schizophrenia, too?"

"Not necessarily," Marissa said when we called her. "And if she does, you'll be prepared. It's rare to have this much history about a child overseas. Likely, a lot of kids have families with a mental health diagnosis, but since they're abandoned or given up to orphanages without medical records, we simply don't know. You're actually lucky to have this information on Ahn, so you can take preventative measures early on."

Jonathan plucked at his unibrow. "So does the agency hold classes on how to work with schizophrenic kids?"

"Not specifically."

"Okay . . . thanks."

I sat down beside Jonathan and closed my eyes. In my two-year stint as a job coach for disabled adults in Santa Barbara, I'd worked with several schizophrenic people. One man—a pleasant, well-groomed individual in his late twenties—tried to hold down employment as a gate guard at the local lumberyard. But he'd forget to take his medication, and I'd find him wandering State Street ragged and filthy, muttering death threats to shoppers.

"Sam." I'd stand in front of him, one hand on the pager at my belt in case he attacked me the way he'd socked his last job coach in the jaw. "Go home and take your pills."

"The devil sent you," he'd reply and bare his teeth.

Schizophrenia scared me. A few years after I worked with Sam, my ex-husband's cousin suffered his first break in front of me. I'd been grading papers on the couch while Tony worked late one night, when I became aware of someone staring in through the living room window at me. The cousin, just twenty-one, demanded that I walk outside and sit in the dark with him. He talked on and on about how the government was out to get him because he had an implant in his head, put there by aliens—a cliché, to be sure, but terrifying for his conviction.

"I can't be sure," he said, searching my eyes so closely that our noses touched, "that you aren't one of them."

Shortly after that, I sat in Seattle's Elliot Bay Books and wept over an essay in *Brain, Child* magazine by the exhausted mother of a schizophrenic man.

"What preventative measures does Marissa mean?" I asked Jonathan now. "There's medication you can take if you have a schizophrenic break, but the illness itself isn't going to go away."

I stared down at the photo of the little girl. "I admit I have a horrible prejudice against this particular illness. What do *you* think, love?"

Jonathan studied the photo for a long time and reread the bio. "Right now, she looks like everything we want, but you know more about this than I do. Marissa's giving us twenty-four hours. Let's go up to the center and work with our birds, and we'll talk about this over dinner. Don't worry. It'll all become clear."

❦

It's impossible to think about anything else when you're working with raptors. One false move, and you'll find a talon through your hand or a beak impaled in your earlobe. You have to be constantly aware, attuned to your bird, ready to fade out unwanted behaviors and reinforce the more desirable ones.

"You gotta figure out what you want Lorax to do before you ever ask her to step on your glove." Outside the owl's mew Jean coached me. "Today, you want her to step from her perch onto your arm—so you break the action into increments, rewarding each one as she does it."

I practiced over and over. If Lorax didn't flinch when I lifted my arm to her feet at perch level, she got a piece of mouse from the plastic container strapped around my waist. If she touched a toe to my glove, she got another bit. If she placed her whole foot on my glove, she earned another bit, and so on, until—when she saw my arm raised— she stepped calmly onto my wrist and allowed me to swivel and clip her jesses.

"Now, very gently, open the door and guide her out, watching to make sure she doesn't bate in the doorway and bang up her wings."

I followed Jean's instructions and found myself standing in the open air with the owl on my wrist. My left elbow jabbed into my side. My hand squeezed into a fist. "Relax," Jean reminded me. "Stay calm. Now walk up the path, slowly. I've set up the T-perch on the lawn for you."

I crept up the gravel path toward the lawn. A handful of visitors stood looking at the kestrels. When they saw me approaching with the owl, they crowded around, voices rising with excitement.

"Step back a few feet," Jean commanded. She talked me through backing Lorax up to the three-foot-tall perch. Talons gripped the Astro-turf, found solid footing. "Good step-up. Now hold the leash in one hand

and unclip her jesses from your glove. Clip the leash to the carabineer on the perch, and you're good to go."

May sunshine warmed the lawn. Lorax lifted her head and blinked up at blue sky. Jean settled down beside the windmill where Jonathan and I had exchanged wedding vows before I ever knew I longed for a bird on my glove and a child in my arms. I stood beside Lorax and pushed thoughts of five-year-old Ahn from my mind, focused on the bird and her comfort level.

"This is Lorax, a great horned owl," I told the people around me. "See that lid that goes over her eyes sideways, like a windshield wiper? That's called a nictitating membrane—it protects a raptor's eyes from the prey's teeth and claws when it's hunting. These owls live from the Arctic all the way down to South America, year-round. If you hear crows going crazy in a tree, it's likely they're mobbing a great horned, trying to chase it away."

Suddenly, a man in a multipocketed vest jumped forward and stuck a telephoto lens inches from Lorax's head. "Mind if I take a picture?"

The owl hooted in alarm and leaped from the perch to land on the grass. Visitors jumped away, shrieking. I stood helpless while Lorax scuttled across the lawn and echoed the cry I'd sounded at the garden center.

"Jean! What do I do?"

"Stay quiet." She reached down for the leash and reeled Lorax in until the owl stepped backward onto her glove. "Everything's fine, folks. Just remember to keep five feet between you and the raptor."

She smiled pleasantly at the photographer who stood poised to shoot another picture. "Let's keep the lenses several feet away, too. These are wild birds, and their sharp parts . . ." She turned toward me, obscuring her face from the crowd, and jerked her head slightly toward the photographer, fury gleaming in her eyes. Then she swiveled around and plastered a generous smile across her face. "Well, folks, their sharp parts are really sharp."

Andi walked up in her boots and a cowboy hat, holding a box of Girl Scout cookies. Lorax lifted her ear tufts at the crunching but stayed put on the perch. "Hey," Andi said, "is it true owls can turn their heads all the way around like in *The Exorcist*?"

Jean nudged me. "You field this one."

A yellow jacket buzzed around the box strapped to my waist, enticed by the mouse within. I prayed it wouldn't sting me. "Owls can turn their heads about two hundred seventy degrees. Take a look at the owl skeletons in the visitors' center, and you'll see that they have way more vertebrae than we do. Now, who wants to see Lorax eat a mouse?"

Andi raised her hand. "Me!"

Lorax and I repeated our comedy routine from the garden center for visitors on the lawn, and then I returned her to the mew. She sat on my glove and allowed me to unclip her and lift her to a perch. I stood for a moment and looked at her. Gradually, the outside world began to creep into my consciousness, and I thought of Ahn.

I was no coward, but I knew my limits. I wouldn't dream of trying to handle a golden eagle or the four-pound ferruginous hawk. I didn't have the skill set; nor did I desire it.

Schizophrenia scared me. I didn't want to learn any more about it. I didn't want to get involved. The parents who adopted Ahn would be saints, and—I conceded with a sorrowful clarity—they wouldn't be Jonathan and me.

"In the end," he e-mailed Marissa that evening, "we've decided to pass on this referral. The mental illness isn't something we're prepared to handle. Please do send other referrals, though, as they come along."

I've never been a collector—even birthday cards go into the recycling bin after a month of display, and tax time leaves me in a perpetual quandary trying to locate discarded pay stubs. Still, I found myself tucking Ahn's biography and photo into a file folder in my closet. Shredding the two-page document felt too disrespectful, too dismissive of a life we'd opted to discard.

17

The Red Thread

AFTER MONTHS OF WORK LORAX AND I BECAME SO COMFORTABLE WITH
one another that staff had me take her to Eugene's gorgeous new library
for an educational presentation.

She immediately pooped on the floor.

"Oops." Red-faced, I fussed with the owl's jesses to cover my embarrassment. I'd remembered swivels and leash, raptor literature, thawed
mice. I'd forgotten a towel.

"I've got it." A tall, thin man a little older than me stooped down and
scrubbed at the mutes on the carpet with a tissue. Two African-American
preteens walked up to him. "We're gonna go check out the golden eagle,
okay, Dad? Mom's right there—she's got our books."

They rushed off. The man was obviously Anglo, as was his wife. I
studied their kids.

"Are they . . . are they adopted? I'm sorry—I don't mean to be rude.
It's just that . . ."

"No problem." He shot the tissue into a trash can. Lorax swiveled and
stared. "My wife and I adopted domestically, through DHS."

Seeing my blank look, he clarified. "Department of Human Services.
They've got lots of kids in the foster system, relinquished by their parents.
They need permanent homes. You adopting?"

"From Vietnam."

A woman with a stroller walked up then, so that her toddler could get
a better look at Lorax on my arm. The toddler reached tiny arms toward
Lorax, who hooted low in her throat at the creak of wheels. Her feather
tufts lifted. I tightened my grip on the leash.

"Well . . . thanks again for your help," I told the man.

"Thanks for being here." He stood a respectful distance from Lorax and studied her. "We just came in for books. We didn't know we'd find an owl. Fascinating, what you said about their ability to live almost anywhere. We live up near the Butte, and I'm pretty sure I've heard a great horned in the trees.

"Did it sound like this?" I launched into my owl call, perfected in the mew over months.

The woman picked up her toddler for a better look. I touched Lorax's toes with my arm, and she stepped up on my glove. I handed her a mouse. She dropped it on my shoe. The mother handed her child a juice box. The toddler threw it on the floor.

"Ha! Really, they're not so different," I quipped as purple liquid trickled from the straw.

"Hmm." The woman rubbed her red-rimmed eyes with one hand, then searched through a cavernous bag of diapers, sippy cups, wet wipes, and wooden zoo animals to extract a washcloth. "Really, they are."

—◆—

At home my sister called. "Sis, I'm pregnant again!"

She described how she'd taken three different home tests to make sure, and then tied up the sticks in pink and blue ribbons and brought them to her husband at his office. "I have a really good feeling this one's gonna stick."

And then babies began to appear out of nowhere in grocery carts and jogging strollers, flailing their skinny arms in car seats next to me at red lights. Toddlers walked hand in hand with their parents at the dog park in coats and tiny rubber boots decorated to look like ladybugs. Three months of summer stretched out, an unwelcome swath of unstructured time in which to contemplate how we'd been offered a child in need and turned our backs on her.

"You're not going to get kicked out of the program," Marissa assured me. "We'll work with you until we find a good match."

I wanted a child now, with a primal longing that startled and dismayed me. In my VW on the way to the grocery store, I pictured a car seat behind me, a little girl prattling and singing.

"You are my sunshine, my only sunshine . . ." I launched into the song my great-grandmother used to croon to her cockatiels on the back porch while performing bicep curls with cans of green beans. My time was my own, all summer to work on my book project. Most writers would kill for three months. But I thought of Milan Kundera's unbearable lightness of being and wished for a shopping cart burdened by a whimpering, pony-tailed toddler like the one next to me in the produce section.

"We're never gonna get another referral," I said to Jonathan at home. "We've ruined our chance for a child."

"Marissa says otherwise." He knelt outside, shaving his sheltie for the summer heat ahead. A wisp of orange-and-white fur caught the breeze and floated upward. "Bet we get one within a few weeks."

———

In fact, another referral arrived the next day. But it came from the raptor center, and it came for me alone.

"We're getting in a baby barred owl with a permanently injured wing."

The assistant director walked over as I stood on the lawn with Lorax, basking in the June sunshine. A chickadee called from a hanging feeder. The owl opened one yellow eye to regard it, but made no move to bate. "I know the university term's almost over," Laurin said, "and we're wondering if you might have time to glove-train the baby."

"*Me?*"

Startled, Lorax grew tall and wide-eyed on her perch, feather tufts on high alert.

"Sorry." I lowered my voice. "Are you sure I'm the right person for this?"

Bird handling was not bird training. Jean had taught Lorax everything she knew; she simply transferred the owl's behavior to me by teaching me her particular verbal and physical cues. As a trainer myself I'd be responsible for devising these cues, for shaping a young bird's behavior on glove and perch. Jean had excelled at teaching Lorax, a rock-solid education bird.

A car pulled up, and a handful of children spilled out. Lorax remained on the perch without bating. I reached into the plastic bits box at my waist and handed her a mouse. "Wait for it," I told the kids who gathered around, stunned into momentary silence. "It'll come back up."

Lauren continued her petition in a lower voice.

"I know training a bird's an enormous commitment. You'd have to be up here every day for a while to work with the baby. You'd be the only one feeding him and the only one training him until he's solid on the glove. You're patient and calm and smart . . ."

Lorax gave a hacking cough and spit the mouse onto my sneaker. The kids groaned. Lauren laughed. "Plus, you know your bird."

I lacked Laurin's conviction. A bad trainer, incognizant of a bird's needs and idiosyncrasies, can do some serious damage. I'd heard horror stories about raptors who were poorly trained; when asked to step onto a perch, a bird would fly back and forth in its mew until the handler snatched it up and bound it to a glove where it hunched, panting and terrified. Our education director constantly referred back to Steve Martin's philosophy; we had to train our birds to fly to a perch and step willingly onto the glove, tranquil and alert on our arm, in a relationship based on trust.

Was I even capable of such a commitment? Since I'd said no to little Ahn, my self-worth had sunk. Jonathan and I skulked around the house, avoiding each other's eyes. He went on hours-long walks with Cody, alone. I ran the Ridgeline Trail over and over, searching for some sign that I wasn't a total asshole. But now, redemption appeared before me with wings and a beak.

"Well . . ." I cocked my head at Laurin. "I did train our cat, Eeyore, to dance in a circle and jump to my shoulder."

"Perfect."

I moved my glove in front of Lorax's legs, and she stepped up to my wrist for the ride to her mew. "So . . . okay. Yes. I'll commit to training the baby owl."

—◆—

Barred owls resemble Northern spotted owls with their tuftless heads and dark eyes, but they've got brown horizontal stripes on cream-colored feathers, instead of white splotches. Deep in old-growth forests, spotteds utter a four-note series of barking hoots while barreds let loose a call that sounds like a question: "Who cooks for you? Who cooks for you all?"

"They used to be eastern birds," I told Jonathan at the dog park.

"Yep . . . in the Adirondacks, where we had my family reunion that time."

Kawliga dropped a slimy tennis ball at my foot. I scooped it up with the Chuckit! and hurled it toward an empty swath of field. "Then they expanded west and started crowding spotteds out of old growth. I read a story about a barred killing one. They've got a bad reputation in Oregon." I chuckled. "Like Californians."

"Barreds and spotteds have interbred, too." Jonathan kicked a ragged soccer ball for Cody. "Remember, I told you about sparred owls on our first date?"

I looked over his shoulder to Spencer Butte, and back at the Cooper's hawks skimming the tree line around us. How subdued I'd been when I moved to Eugene, how divorced from nature in my dark little office with no knowledge of the wilderness outside my door. I couldn't have fathomed—that day Jonathan invited me to pick up frozen rats in Portland—my new position as a baby barred owl trainer.

"He's flying in on United tomorrow," I said now. "Want to come meet him?"

"Of course. Who cooks for you?" Jonathan hooted. "You know, if you get good at their call, you might tempt the wild barreds around the center down on a limb to investigate."

"Like *Owl Moon*."

I told him of Jane Yolen's picture book about the father and child who trudge out to the woods on a winter night to call owls. "There's a gorgeous two-page spread of a great horned in flight."

A used copy of the book lay on a shelf in our empty nursery along with a beautifully illustrated children's guide to raptors and a ladybug magnifying glass for owl pellets. For a year they'd sat there growing dusty, waiting.

~~~

Staff assumed the baby barred was a male because of his size. He huddled on a skinny branch in the clinic's indoor mew, a diminutive bundle of brown and white with a dull yellow beak and round chocolate eyes. Without feather tufts his head looked tiny. The mew dwarfed him. A handwritten sign dangled from the wire door: MELISSA TO FEED.

I'd seen signs like this before; they let volunteers know that the bird was a special case, to be handled delicately and only by a few. Responsibility weighed on me. What if I messed up this bird?

The owl roused and pooped on the newspaper below his yellow toes. I stepped closer and murmured a greeting. "Good morning."

The baby clacked his beak and stretched his neck up, craning it to stare at a fly on the wall. Each down feather stuck out as if he'd received an electric shock. In a few months he'd lose all the down and grow sturdy, pinned flight feathers. For now he resembled the fluffy clumps of cottonwood seed that floated through the summer skies.

But he'd never fly. His left wing drooped below his feet.

The director walked by and peered through the screen. "Everything okay?"

"Absolutely." I reached into the refrigerator for a mouse.

A trainer's first interactions with her subject must be positive. To build rapport with the baby barred, I had to offer a gift of good faith.

"Here's a lovely brown mousie for you." I lifted the latch on his door and held out the freshly euthanized rodent.

Instantly, the baby puffed up his down in a defense posture and clacked his beak. I knew younger owls did this to look ferocious under threat of attack. This one seemed to double in size. The mouse trembled in my fingers.

The baby stared at it, then reached out and snapped it up in his beak. He held its head for a moment before choking down the body. His fluff lowered, and he relaxed on his perch, but only just.

I averted my eyes and began to sing softly as I arranged quail on pie plates for the afternoon shift. "You are my sunshine, my only sunshine . . ."

The little owl closed his eyes and settled his beak into the fluff at his chest.

"What'cha doing?" The director walked in and found me crooning beside the mew.

"Ah . . . building rapport." My cheeks went red. "I fed him a dark mouse, and he ate the whole thing."

Her eyes went to the scale in the closet beside the rack of volunteers' gloves. "Did you get a weight on him before you fed him?"

I shook my head.

"You're *always* supposed to weigh a baby bird before you feed it. It's the only way to get a true weight on him, and we need it in order to track his growth and health."

I bit my lip. On the perch beside me, the baby barred clacked his beak. "I'm sorry—I had no idea."

"It's *critical*."

"Okay, I'll do it now." I walked over to get the scale with its mute-festooned Astroturf pad.

"Too late now—he's already eaten. Make sure you remember from now on."

She walked out and I bowed my head, suddenly despondent. I had no idea what I was doing. I couldn't even train my dogs; the week before, Marley and Kawliga had hurtled across Morse Dog Park after a squirrel and dragged me by their leashes through the mud. Why would anyone believe I had what it took to train an owl?

Darcy walked in and saw me slumped at the desk. Her eyes went to the baby, dozing on his perch. "What's wrong?"

"I forgot to weigh him before I gave him food."

She snorted. "Birds in the wild don't weigh their babies before a meal. He'll be fine. Why do *you* get to train him?"

"I dunno. I had the time, I guess."

"Better you than me. I'm hiking the Pacific Crest Trail all summer." She tossed back her braids, and the baby clacked his beak again. "He's funny looking. What are they gonna call him? Someone suggested Achilles, but I think it was a joke."

The name struck me as too elegant for a bird whose feathers stuck out every which way. I'd been reading about bodhisattvas—those beings who vowed only to enter Nirvana after they'd helped everyone else to go first. Our education birds reminded me of bodhisattvas, in a way; whether they liked it or not, they were ambassadors for their species. Thanks to their sacrifice, visitors maybe stopped using rat poison, took down barbed-wire fences, and slowed down their cars.

"We could call him Bodhi . . ."

Darcy snorted. "Hilarious. That's the name the director suggested."

"Really?" I opened the door to hand the little owl another mouse, and his brown eyes flew open. He pounced on the snack with fierce talons and held it in his beak like a long, dark mustache. "Bodhi," I said, "or Genghis Kahn."

———

"You're training an *owl?*"

Kat regarded me over her glass of Pinot Noir at the cozy downtown restaurant where folksinger Lucy Kaplansky was about to begin her first set. "What do you train it to do?"

"Your kid could tell you—she watched me on shift the other day." I reached for a Parmesan stick from the basket on the table. "I'm teaching him to sit on my glove and a perch."

Lucy took the stage then. I'd discovered her sultry, smoky voice on a CD with Dar Williams. She explained that several of the songs on her latest CD, titled *The Red Thread*, were inspired by adopting her Chinese daughter.

"Did you know that?" Kat whispered.

Shaking my head, I sat up and listened.

In China, she explained, there's a proverb about an invisible red thread that connects those destined to meet. "The thread may stretch or tangle, the proverb says, but it will never break."

Lucy picked up her guitar and began to play. I pictured a crimson string connecting me with Kat as we polished off the cheese sticks and ordered another glass of Pinot. Could I close my eyes and see the same gossamer thread stretching from Jonathan and me in Eugene to a faceless child across the world in Vietnam?

I could not.

What if little Ahn had been Jonathan's and my destiny, and we'd severed our cord? Did infinite strands connect adoptive parents with dozens of potential sons and daughters, or did we get only one chance, one red thread?

I closed my eyes. All I could see were the thin leather jesses affixed around the bare ankles of a goofy-looking baby owl clipped to my glove.

Lucy paused between songs to tell a story about her child's games of make-believe. "Right now, she has two sons—a dog and a bear—and two dads."

The audience applauded. Lucy clapped, too, then launched into a song that settled into my soul and sold me on shelling out seventeen dollars for her latest CD. When she wrote "This Is Home," she told us, she and her husband didn't know anything about their daughter except that there was a little girl waiting for them in China, and that they would call her Molly.

After the song I stood up, fist pressed against my lips. "I've gotta go to the restroom," I choked out to Kat. I made my way to the back of the restaurant, sat on a toilet, and bawled.

Bodhi had successfully distracted me from the lack of Waiting Child referrals, from the difficult realization that those kids who appeared on the agency's website had profound disabilities that Jonathan and I weren't willing to take on. But away from the center, alcohol streaming through my veins and Lucy's lyrics echoing in my head, desire for a kid seized me so powerfully that I doubted my ability to return to the table without making a complete ass of myself.

I managed to collapse beside Kat during a more raucous song and sit stoic through the rest of the set. Afterward I stood in line to speak with Lucy. "Famous people freak me out," I whispered to Kat, "but I've got to meet her."

She took a long time chatting with the man in front of me, and I walked up to find that she looked tired, in need of a glass of Pinot herself. Still, she smiled and reached for the CD in my hand. "Want me to sign it?"

"Yes, please. I really liked your set." I blushed and stammered in my desire to forge some connection. "My husband and I . . . we're . . . we're trying to adopt a child from Vietnam."

Instantly, Lucy's demeanor changed. Exhaustion gave way to excitement, and she clasped my hands in hers. "You have no idea what wonderful thing is in store for you." She flashed me a wide, delighted smile. "You're gonna be so happy."

Glowing, I returned to Kat. "Feeling a little bipolar, are we? Andi says you're not sleeping." She put a hand on my arm. "I'm worried about you."

"I'm fine."

I shrugged off Kat's arm and told her good-bye. In my car I listened to "This Is Home" until I knew the words, until I could picture Jonathan and myself playing games of make-believe with a toddler on our bed, connected by a red thread like Lucy and her husband and Molly . . . like a family.

——

I threw myself into training Bodhi. After a week of building rapport with mice and folk songs, I coaxed him to step from his perch to my glove. I sat with him in the clinic for hours, rewarded him with bits when he allowed me to grease his new leather jesses and rub Bag Balm on his foot pads. On a Sunday in late June, I stepped from the clinic with the baby owl clipped to my glove and strolled to the lawn. He triangulated like crazy, bobbing his head on his skinny neck, trying to discern his location.

Jonathan stood a few feet away with one of the spotted owls on his glove. It was eight o'clock, and the deep gold of evening had just begun to gild the trees; summer nights in Eugene last until ten. We stood in the setting sun with our birds and talked quietly. Other couples that evening likely enjoyed dinner and a movie and a bottle of wine, but nothing could persuade me to trade these warm hours spent with the raptors.

Jean sat down on the bench with Lorax. "Have you tried scratching Bodhi's head? It's kind of like preening. I know some trainers use it as a bonding tool."

"I . . . I guess I could try . . ." Tentatively, I reached out a finger and touched the soft down on his head. For an instant he relaxed under my touch and closed his eyes. Then a wild owl hooted from the trees overhead. "Who cooks for you?"

He jerked his head up. I dropped my hand.

Jean laughed. "Still nervous around him, huh? That's probably good." She looked down at Lorax; the owl's eyes locked on a hummingbird near the clinic feeder. "Can't ever let your guard down."

Darcy walked out and stood by the raven's mew. "Bodhi's made himself so tall and skinny. Is he scared?"

"We just heard a wild owl."

"There's a pair of barreds been hanging around again."

From the mew below us, the center's resident elder barred, Loki, added his voice to the wild owls calling from the firs. Bodhi stared up into the trees, neck stretched high. "He looks like a Muppet."

My laughter died away as I spotted one of the owls on a low limb. It peered down at the bird on my glove and hooted. Bodhi saw it, too, and let loose a piteous screech.

Darcy's eyes glistened. "Oh . . . he's begging."

I turned toward her, confused. "He thinks that owl's his parent?"

"Something like that."

It had been too easy to see Bodhi as domesticated, a human-habituated pet who rode around on my arm and gazed into my eyes. His reaction to the owls in the trees reminded me that I was not his mother; I wasn't even preferable. The wildness within him lay dormant, but only just, ready to surface at any reminder of his first days of life as an unfettered bird.

Suddenly, the wild barred leaped off the branch and swooped down over my head, wings outstretched. Bodhi jumped off my glove. The pull of his jesses ricocheted through my whole body. I hunched over him, a protective shield. He flew back to my arm, panting.

"Whoa! Did you guys see that?"

The wild owl flew to another branch and sat there staring. Startled, the spotted owl bated off Jonathan's glove, and he walked off to calm her.

"Think I'll take Lorax back to her mew." Jean stood up and strolled down the gravel path, her eyes on the barred in the tree. "I sense a territorial dispute."

I began to grasp the enormity of what I'd taken on—once you commit to an abandoned creature, the red thread's nonnegotiable. If it hurts, you hurt. And if it's in danger, you do everything in your power to keep it safe. I checked Bodhi's jesses and the leash. "I'm gonna take him inside until the barreds move on."

"Good idea." Darcy's lips twisted into a wry smile. "I wouldn't turn your back on a wild raptor again, ever. Territory's a powerful motivator. Your bird could've been a goner."

"Could the wild barred really hurt him?"

"Absolutely. And you. Avoid the temptation to over-romanticize." She flashed me a look of warning. "You can't lose your focus for a second . . . otherwise, you'll get whacked in the head."

18

Ambiguity

"Uh . . . what exactly am I looking at, sis?"

My sister had called to tell me she'd e-mailed a couple of pictures; she wanted to be on the phone when I viewed them. I studied the abstract black-and-white images. They looked like the fine art photos I'd attempted to appreciate in galleries showcasing Jonathan's more post-modern colleagues.

"Have you taken up photography?"

"It's your nephew, dumbass. They're ultrasound photos."

"My nephew?" That amorphous, shadowy thing was a *child*?

She talked me through the bumps and crevices in each image. "See, there's his nose and chin, his hand, and that's either a foot or a penis—the doctor wasn't sure."

"Oh. He's so . . . cute?"

Katie laughed. "Yeah, I know. Totally weird. You're smart to adopt—you know going in what your kid's gonna look like. Hey . . ." Her bravado faded into a plaintive plea. "D'you think you could talk to me while I eat a peanut butter sandwich? I've been nauseous for weeks. The only time I can eat is when I talk to people."

"Of course." I didn't tell her about my own nausea. Jonathan and I had just gotten the bill for our dossier fee—twenty-five hundred dollars—and we were engaged in a rather large freak-out about how and where the money would be spent. Would it stay in this country, paying Marissa's pittance of a paycheck, or would it go to Vietnam, where it might enable questionable government activities?

Jonathan had clipped a newspaper article that worried us both. It told of how, in recent months, the Vietnamese government had arrested or sentenced a bunch of pro-democracy activists. We tried hard to vote with our few dollars. We bought local and organic, boycotting companies that violated human rights issues. In writing the dossier check, were we giving President Treit the green light on imprisoning those we'd likely champion?

I didn't mention any of this to my sister. Instead, I recounted the wild barred owl in the raptor center's tree, how Bodhi had begged, how the wild bird sailed down on three-foot wings toward my head.

"So you could've been scalped?"

"That's right."

"Why you do such crazy shit, sis? I mean, standing around with an owl on your arm?"

"I love it."

The Buddhists talk about something called the "wanting mind," that way of thinking that constantly craves security, affection, material possessions. In those hours with Bodhi and Lorax, my wanting mind took a breather. I tuned into the birds' needs, their fears, learned to appreciate the small excitement of a nuthatch in the cherry trees, two gray squirrels spiraling up a fir trunk. The world outside of me—outside the constant yearning for motherhood—presented the most marvelous intrigue when viewed through an owl's eyes.

My sister misconstrued my silence as sorrow. "Don't worry, Lissa. The right kid will come along . . . I know it."

⬥

A month later, the right kid did come along—perfect for me, and so very wrong for Jonathan.

The toddler, eighteen months old, beamed up at me from the Waiting Child website, in a yellow, blousy shirt. His wide, eager eyes shone with mirth. Fine black hair stuck up on his head like the down on a baby owl.

"No one's snapped him up yet." I dragged Jonathan away from his computer to look at the picture. "We have a good chance of getting this kid!"

Jonathan stood behind me and gripped my shoulder. "Did you read his bio? 'He's an outgoing, happy child reported to have ambiguous genitalia.' What does *that* mean?"

"It means he was born with genitals that aren't clearly male or female."

Gender issues interested me. I'd grown up watching *La Cage aux Folles* with my grandmother. My mother and I preferred front-row seats at drag shows in Portland and San Francisco. My first serious boyfriend in high school adored *The Rocky Horror Picture Show*; he revealed his desire for a sex change, and eventually had the operation. I'd read Jeffrey Eugenides's *Middlesex* three times, and so explained to Jonathan as much as I could understand about the child's diagnosis.

"It's a rare condition, genetic, I think, caused by two few male hormones in a boy fetus, or too many in a girl fetus. Ambiguous genitalia means the kid has either an enlarged clitoris or a very small penis. You know, he's like the protagonist in *Hedwig and the Angry Inch*."

I thought this last bit would win him over; my husband liked to listen to the musical's hard-rock soundtrack while he washed the dishes. But his unibrow gathered over dubious eyes. "So if the genitalia's ambiguous, why does the agency's website refer to this kid as a 'he'?"

"I don't know. Maybe the doctor had to pick a gender. *He* could grow up to be a *she*. Oh man, we'd be great parents for this kid!"

"I . . . don't know." Jonathan sat down beside me and picked up Cody, cradling the dog against his chest. "I want to hold out for a girl."

"What if he *is* a girl? I heard this story on *This American Life* about boys who know they're actually girls, and they meet at a camp for kids like them where they can wear dresses and play with dolls and, y'know, share a common frame of reference. Two of the parents were totally cool about it. We could be them . . ."

I found myself arguing desperately for the beautiful toddler. "We wouldn't care if the kid identified as male or female, homo- or heterosexual. And when the time came, if he wanted sex-reassignment surgery, we'd get it for him . . . right?"

I peered into Jonathan's face for affirmation, reached over and attempted to smooth the wrinkles in his forehead. He pulled away and went to the computer for another look at the child. "He *is* adorable—I'll give you that. Go ahead and ask for his longer bio." Then he walked toward the door. "Sorry—nicotine craving. It'll pass." He put on his jacket and grabbed his dog's leash. "I'm gonna go take Cody for a walk."

—◆—

After potential parents express interest in a child, the Waiting Child program sends a more detailed biography with as much medical and personal information as they possess. The next day, I called up Marissa to request the goods. "We want this child."

If the conviction in my voice surprised her, she didn't let on. "We're just curious—how come we didn't get his referral? He's perfect for us."

"He's from China. Hold on . . ." I heard the clack of computer keys. "I see what you mean—a real cutie. Lemme see what I can find out. In the meantime I'm e-mailing you a slightly longer bio."

I printed out the two pages. Jonathan and I discussed them that night over chili and corn bread. "Isn't he lovely?" I gazed at the little guy's picture again. "He looks like Bodhi, if Bodhi were a child."

Jonathan dropped his head into his hands and massaged his temples. "We've gotta do some research. I have no idea what we're getting into."

"Fine." I set my bowl down hard in the kitchen sink and retreated to our laptop. The Mayo Clinic's website offered a pretty thorough explanation of what we were in for. As veterinarians did with raptors, physicians could figure out the genetic sex of a kid through blood tests that measured hormone levels. They could also do a chromosome test and an ultrasound of the pelvis and abdomen to search for a vagina and uterus or testes that hadn't yet descended.

"So doctors, based on all these tests, suggest an appropriate sex for the baby." I read to Jonathan. "The website says, 'Parents should be aware that as the child grows up, he or she may make a different decision about gender identification. You may want to consider giving the baby a gender-neutral first name.'"

"That makes sense." He handed me a plate with half of a piece of chocolate cake from the local market—a dessert rumored among mothers in the community to have induced at least three births. For an instant I wished for a vast belly, for the comparable ease of Lamaze and a pair of stirrups.

"Look, I know this is weird, but do you think Marissa could get us photos? I need a clear idea of what's going on here."

"Photos of the *genitalia*?" Irritation sharpened my voice. We lived in a town with numerous transgender people; we'd marched alongside them in support of same-sex marriage with the local chapter of PFLAG.

"Are pictures *necessary*?"

"Yes," Jonathan said. "They are."

I e-mailed the request to Marissa. Then, sorry for my outburst, I sat down on the couch beside him and began to massage his shoulders. "Shall we retire to the bedroom?"

Jonathan closed his eyes. "I'm exhausted. If you don't mind, I'd rather just watch TV."

———

The ambiguous baby's Chinese foster mother sent photos the next day. Marissa printed them out and left them in a manila envelope under our doormat. We sat on the porch and looked through the stack. A long scar ran up the child's crotch; I could make out a short stub of flesh.

"I've seen more shocking stuff at the raptor center." I shrugged and slid the photos back into the envelope.

Jonathan took them out again and looked at them from several angles. "These photos are gonna keep people from adopting this kid, I guarantee it. He'll probably need penile construction surgery, and what if he can't get an erection? What if he can't have an orgasm? That's fine while he's still a kid, but what happens when he's a teenager?"

He took my hands in his and looked into my face. "I don't think I can handle a child like this."

"Of course you can."

Here was no terrifying mental illness; I had the tools to meet this particular challenge. Already, I saw our kid playing with stuffed Audubon raptors on a blanket on the lawn while Bodhi watched from my glove and Jonathan stood with the spotted owl. We wouldn't recoil in horror or disgust from this child—we'd approach him with openness and humor and respect.

But the Chinese government decided otherwise.

"Let me get this straight." On the phone with Marissa the next day, exhaustion pushed me to fury. "Jonathan and I haven't been married long enough to adopt a baby with ambiguous genitalia?"

"He's from China. Their same restrictions apply for kids in the Waiting Child program."

"There's no way to get him? No loophole? What if I apply as a single mother?"

"Not allowed. Sorry."

"What if he's not adopted in four years? Can we have him then?"

"Melissa, he's gonna get adopted."

I bit my lip to stop my vindictive retort. This was *my* child. I thrilled to the silken tug of thread that bound his little life to mine.

But China wouldn't budge.

I tucked the boy's bio into the folder with Ahn's and slumped on my office chair.

"Let me hold you." Jonathan held out his arms when at last I came to bed.

I despised his palpable relief, the buoyancy returned to his smile. Angry speculations circled in my head. If he'd fought a little harder for this child, maybe the combined force of our insistence would have swayed the Chinese government.

"I have a cold." I turned on my headlamp and opened *One Man's Owl*, staring at the words without comprehending until he began to snore beside me.

Sleep came without relief. I dreamed about hiking in the mountains with Bodhi. He sat on my glove, but I'd forgotten to bring his leash and swivels. I bent to hug the bird, but I couldn't hold onto him. He flew off my glove and fell into the ocean. Full of grief, I leaped in after him and drowned.

━ ⌒ ━

"What's it mean?" I stood on the raptor center's lawn with Bodhi the next day, after checking the firs for wild barreds. Jonathan paused on the way to the ferruginous hawks' mew.

"It's obviously a dream about loss . . ."

Bodhi stretched his neck up toward the sun, down feathers sticking out at ridiculous angles. He shifted on his T-perch as a UPS truck thundered up, but his talons remained attached to the Astroturf.

"Good bird." As the motor rumbled I found myself automatically touching the back of his head to comfort him, sinking my fingers into soft feathers and rubbing his skin. It felt scaly and warm and slightly slippery; at my touch he relaxed on the perch and closed his eyes, leaning into my fingertips.

"Wow . . . I'm scratching an owl's head."

The author of *One Man's Owl* writes about allopreening—that is, the way bonded birds preen each other's feathers with their beaks. I bent down and allowed Bodhi to comb through my hair; only once had I felt such a shocking tenderness, when my cat, Alger Hiss, put his paws on my face and looked into my eyes and purred. There's no connection like it, not even with a bonded mate of one's own species.

Jonathan's cell phone rang, and Bodhi shot into a downy arrow on my glove. "Number forty? I see. Okay, thanks for the update." He turned to me. "Director of the Vietnam program—regular, not Waiting Child. Just wanted to call and tell me we're number forty on the waiting list for referrals. Right now, they're placing about two kids a month."

My fingers found their way to Bodhi's head again. "It's never gonna happen, is it?"

He shrugged. "Sure, it'll happen. But do we still want it to?"

I saw despair in his hunched shoulders. He walked off toward the clinic, oblivious to the raven calling from her mew, "What'cha doing?"

The UPS driver dropped two boxes on the steps outside the visitors' center and waved at me. "Cool bird."

"Thanks."

Spooked by the truck starting up, Bodhi bated and tangled his legs in the leash. I unclipped it from the perch and put a hand on his back, guiding him to my glove, and then to the perch again. In the window of the visitors' center, I could see the education director giving a talk to third graders, holding up a bone. With her back to me, she hadn't witnessed Bodhi's bate.

Another car sped up as the UPS driver headed down the driveway, and two of my journalism students got out. They walked up the hill to the lawn, armed with a digital recorder and a video camera. "Whoa! What's that?" The twenty-one-year-old girl and guy, normally so blasé in my feature writing seminar, widened their eyes at Bodhi.

"Barred owl. Wild ones live around here, too."

"Okay if we make a short clip for photojournalism?"

"I'm cool with it, but go ask the education director to make sure. She's up in the visitors' center with some kids."

They disappeared up the stairs for a moment, then returned and gave me the thumbs-up. On the bench under the windmill, they checked their equipment looking vibrant and happy, not remotely preoccupied with orphaned toddlers.

I envied them.

Suddenly, one of the wild barreds called from overhead and Bodhi jumped off the perch again. He took off in a ragged flight away from me, trailing his leash behind him.

"Shit! I forgot to clip him in!"

His brief baby life flashed before me as he landed on top of the screech owl mew. Adrenaline shot me into the air, and I snatched up the end of his leash. Shaking, I reeled him in until he sat on my glove, panting and clacking his beak.

I looked toward the visitors' center. The education director's back was still turned. My students applauded from the bench. "That was a close one, Melissa."

"You didn't get that on film, did you?"

"Too bad. Our battery's dead."

"Thank God. I'm gonna take him to his mew."

I left my students and staggered back to the clinic, where I unclipped Bodhi and backed him up to his perch. For a long while I stood and scratched his head, trying not to think about the slow starvation he'd endure if he flew off again. Once more, he closed his eyes and leaned into my touch. I whispered a silent prayer of gratitude, gave him a freshly euthanized mouse, and headed for my car. Inside, I rested my forehead on the steering wheel and closed my eyes.

The image of Jonathan and me with a child grew blurred. I'd met bird trainers and wildlife rehabilitators who'd deliberately decided against having children so they could devote themselves to animals. An honorable existence, to be sure.

Jonathan could live a fine life, I thought. I'd channel my maternal desire into caring for Bodhi, pass on my avian knowledge to schoolkids. He'd keep working with the spotteds, the golden eagle, the ferruginous hawk. Maybe we didn't need a child to complete us; we just needed raptors.

I pulled Lucy Kaplansky's CD out of the player and put it back in its case. I didn't want to listen anymore, didn't want to know that somewhere across the country, Lucy and her husband sat laughing with their daughter. She had what I wanted . . . but perhaps I had something valuable, as well.

The wild barred owls began hooting in the trees above my car. I sat up and rubbed my eyes. When my vision cleared I saw it—a tiny, dark feather on my purple fleece like the fluff of fine hair on a Chinese toddler's head.

I plucked it off and blew it out the window.

19

Owl in the Living Room

I KEPT MY EYES ON BODHI. NO MORE TRIANGULATION—MY ENTIRE FOCUS became a baby owl with a naked head and long, awkward neck feathers. The bird's plumage so resembled the classic mullet hairstyle that staff and volunteers began to refer to him as "Jim-Bob."

Previously, I'd timed my visits to the raptor center so they meshed with Jonathan's work schedule. Now I had an owl to train. Every morning, I ran the dogs at the park for a few minutes, tossed food at them and the cats, then biked three miles up toward Spencer Butte and clocked in at the clinic. I pulled on my glove and took Bodhi out to the lawn. He learned to ride my wrist as I walked around the center, and I learned how to multitask—answering the phone, preparing cat food and tofu and grapes for the crow and raven, cleaning the clinic with a two-pound bird on my arm.

Sometimes we paused in front of Archimedes's mew. The snowy owl remained hunched over on his stump, peering out past the wire through his slitted yellow eyes. I wondered whether he registered Bodhi on my glove, whether he longed for the freedom of open air. I wanted to give him a chance. But a sign hung on his door: STAFF ONLY TO FEED. He wasn't allowed on a glove at all.

Owls take forever to train. A hawk can learn to jump to a mouse-baited perch and, from there, to a glove, in just a few practice sessions. Owls need a hundred times more instruction, and I read blog posts from snowy handlers who assured readers that this particular species was even more difficult.

It took Gary Gero, the trainer who worked with owls in the Harry Potter films, months to train the great gray to crash into bowls of potato chips and fall over. "Contrary to the stereotype," Gero told a journalist, "they're not necessarily intelligent."

Jean put it a different way as we stood on the lawn with Bodhi and Lorax. "Owls," she said, "are very good at being owls."

The center's other barred, Loki, wanted nothing to do with me. He freaked out every time I entered his mew with a rat or quail, sailing back and forth and staring at me through crazed, dark eyes.

"What's Loki gonna do when it's time for Bodhi to move in with him?"

Jean grimaced. "You'll have to watch them closely for a couple days to make sure they don't attack each other. Spend the first night in the mew with them."

"Spend the night?"

"Bring a sleeping bag and a book, darlin'. You camp, right? Anyhow, Bodhi's not gonna move for a while—his big-boy feathers aren't all grown in yet."

He'd begun to lose his down and grow mature plumage. His long flight feathers came in first—striped brown, and then smaller feathers that covered his breast and head. I stood with him in the sun and marveled at the three rows sprouting around his eyes like the petals of a marigold. A breeze whispered through the trees, displacing his fluffy head covering so I could see his naked scalp with the tiny pins that would grow into the last of his adult feathers.

The director walked out of her office and across the lawn. "Time to get him used to car rides, so you can start taking him to programs."

"Already?"

I'd seen the kestrel riding on a foot-tall perch in the front seat of her station wagon while the one-eyed screech owl hunkered down in a hollowed-out display log on the floor, but they were little birds. The larger raptors rode in pet carriers loaded in handlers' cars for festivals and retirement homes and Scout troop meetings. I assumed Bodhi needed a pet carrier, too. But I had no idea how to get him into one, or where on earth I was supposed to go with him.

Before I could ask, the phone rang, and the director walked off to the clinic. Jean caught my look of consternation. "Don't worry, darlin'. Back your wrist and your bird into a carrier with newspaper and a perch, then shut the door before he can come flying out. Cover the crate with a sheet to keep him calm, and don't forget to reward him with a little mouse." On her arm Lorax blinked at me placidly.

"Okay, fine. But where am I supposed to take him?"

"Well . . . your living room, to start."

"My living room?"

"Why not? Load a T-perch into your car and set it up in your house. Then you can take him out of the carrier and stick him up on the perch while you check your e-mail or wash the dishes. Have a cup of coffee with him. He won't mind."

I started down the path toward Bodhi's mew. Jean called out to me. "Hey, darlin'? Don't forget to put away your cats. Otherwise, he might try to eat them."

⌒

"There's an *owl* in your living room?"

My sister demanded a webcam so she could see Bodhi on his T-perch next to the woodstove.

"Sorry," I told her. "Don't have one. But really, sis, he's right here. I put all the cats and dogs outside, and I'm making coffee. He's totally cool."

"You let him in your *car*? Did he poop in it?"

"Nah, he rode in a carrier."

"Sweet Jesus. I thought he was free-flying all over your VW."

While she attempted to eat a bowl of mashed potatoes—the one food not nauseating her that week—I told her how one of the handlers liked to load the center's turkey vulture into the front seat of her car and drive it around Eugene to prepare it for off-site educational presentations. One day, a guy looked down from his big rig and spotted the bird in the car below him. Impressed, he put an ad in the local paper, hoping to entice the handler out to dinner and a movie.

"He titled it 'Vulture Girl,'" I said to Katie. "And she said yes."

"Well . . . that's one way to get a date."

I recounted Bodhi's and my inaugural car ride. Jittery with excitement, I'd prepped a pet carrier with newspaper and a perch and slid it into the trunk of the VW. I found an old sheet and dropped three mice into a plastic container. Then I went to get the bird.

"It'll be fun." I coaxed him onto my glove and jessed him up, double-checking the clasp on the leash. We walked out of the clinic and down to the car.

"I felt like a real owl trainer," I told my sister, "taking my bird out for his first car ride."

But then I'd stubbed my toe on a rock and almost went flying. Bodhi bated, and I panicked, raising my arm into the air instead of keeping it straight and steady. When we finally sorted ourselves out, he perched tall and tense, mute with fear.

"I knew staff were watching from their offices," I told my sister. "I thought they'd run out and take Bodhi away, call me an imposter, and kick me off the property."

But no one had come out to admonish me, and finally, I opened the hatchback and backed Bodhi from my glove into the pet crate.

I assumed he'd bate and struggle, and I'd have to return him to his mew. Instead, he stepped backward onto the unfamiliar perch as if he'd been loading into crates for years. I latched the door quietly and covered the crate with the sheet. "Then we took off down the hill."

"Ten miles an hour, right?"

"More like five."

And now here he sat. On his perch Bodhi whipped his head around to stare into a corner of my living room. I followed his eyes to the daddy longlegs creeping across the wall. Before I could stop him, he spread his wings and hurled his body upward off the perch toward the arachnid.

"Gotta go!"

I clapped the cell phone shut and grabbed his leash. My left hand reached for his jesses, so that when he came down from his ragged flight, he landed on my gloved wrist instead of on the hardwood floor.

"Good save." I congratulated us both, and reached for a cup to take the shivering daddy longlegs outside.

Bodhi triangulated, head bobbing from me to the front door in an attempt to figure out where the hell he was. Thank goodness his eyes remained fixed in their sockets—no rolling them in disgust at the clumps

of cat fur under the table or the thick line of dirt from muddy dogs rubbing themselves along the wall post–park visit. "I need to clean," I said.
He clacked his beak, neutral.

I sat on a barstool and picked up my mug, smiled at the absurdity
of our kaffeeklatsch. Bodhi stared out the window at the oak and maple
leaves swaying in the summer breeze and curled up one foot. Jean had
told me to talk to him as much as possible, so he'd get used to the sound
of my voice.

"Next month, Jonathan and I are taking the ferry from Washington
to Alaska," I began. "There're bald eagles everywhere, and you can see
whales and dolphins from the top deck."

The vacation represented an attempt to bring romance back into
our marriage. For weeks we'd sidestepped each other in our small house,
avoiding eye contact, irritable over our first big disagreement—whether
or not we had the capacity to raise a child with androgynous genitalia.

I resented the way Jonathan clinked the spoon against his upper teeth
when he ate yogurt at night, snarled at him for leaving the lid off the bin
of cat kibble, turned up my nose when he arrived home from work smell-
ing like cigarettes from a coffee break with a still-smoking coworker. "It
stinks," I snapped, and Jonathan closed his eyes and told me in a tight
voice that he had to go and walk his dog.

We sold our king-size bed and bought two twins. "I'm sorry I have
insomnia," I said, "but I just can't try to sleep anymore with your restless
leg syndrome and your snoring." Grief made me phenomenally undiplo-
matic. "And I can't make love right now. Things are just too intense."

He nodded, eyes veiled. I remembered how stoic he'd seemed those
first days at the dog park; now, once again, he withdrew into silence,
stayed up late listening to hard rock through his iPod and processing
photos of skulls.

"He gave up smoking for you," Kat told me. "He's a keeper—figure
it out."

I tried. "Let's go on vacation." I told him about an article I'd clipped
from *Sunset* explaining how to catch a ferry from Bellingham, Washington. "We can pitch a tent on deck and travel up the Alaska Marine Highway, to Sitka. There's a huge raptor center there. Let's go see it."

"Fine."Tight-lipped, he returned to his *New Yorker*.

———

"We used to be so in love," I told Bodhi on my stool. "The adoption angst is killing us."

The owl blinked at me. I glimpsed the nictitating membrane that swept across his eyes. When I offered him a mouse, he took it, then dropped it on the floor. "Great. The cats'll love that."

I picked up the mouse and the phone rang. Bodhi shot into defensive posture and glared at my cell. "It's okay, Bod-ster." I clucked my tongue. "Hello?"

"Melissa? I'm from the Vietnam program . . . not the Waiting Child program, but the regular one. Just calling to give you an update."

I willed the snarkiness out of my voice. "Okay . . . shoot."

"You're number twenty-four on the waiting list. You should have a referral within the next six months, if all goes well."

The month before, we'd been number forty.

"Referrals are coming more quickly than we expected."

"Six months, huh? And then it's another six before we go to Vietnam to pick up the child?" I touched Bodhi's head, rubbing the sweet spot behind his ear holes. I'd peered into them, attempting to see his long eye sockets, without success.

The woman cleared her throat. "That's right."

"Okay . . . well, thanks." I closed my phone and sat down.

It's impossible to be depressed about a lethargic adoption process when a baby barred owl with a bad mullet sits on a perch in your living room. The agency's phone call neither excited nor discouraged me—starting a family now seemed as implausible as training a raptor had six months ago. I recalled something Jack Kornfield said in one of his audio lectures, quoting his Buddhist monk teacher, Ajahn Chah: "Why don't you want what you have, and don't want what you don't have?"

I handed Bodhi the mouse again. This time, he swallowed it down, and then gazed unblinking into my eyes.

At that moment I had exactly what I wanted.

The next day, Kat's daughter called to tell me she wouldn't be volunteering anymore. "I'm gonna play softball," she said, "and we have practice."

"Anytime you want to visit, give me a call."

"Will do," she said. "I gotta go. My friend's calling."

"I'll miss you," I said, but she'd hung up.

At the center a dreadlocked couple with a child walked up and paused a respectful three feet from Bodhi. The woman, in a long skirt and a hemp bandana worn like a halter above a silver navel ring, clasped her hands. "Oh, look!" She picked up her child. With its shoulder-length hair and brown T-shirt and shorts, it looked—like so many kids in Eugene—gender neutral. "What type of owl is that, honey?"

The kid's face wrinkled up. "A horned owl?"

"He's actually a baby barred." I launched into my spiel about how Bodhi had come to live at the center. "He's from Texas. His drooping wing means he can't fly well enough to hunt, so he lives here as an ambassador for other barred owls."

The parents in hemp and dreadlocks saw enough of Bodhi to be inspired to become members at the center. While they signed up and paid the fee, I bent to give their child a better look at the owl. "If you know you're coming up for a visit, call us and I'll bring him out on the glove for you."

The kid peered at me through a tangle of brown hair. "He's really pretty."

Bodhi, spooked by a yellow jacket buzzing around the bits box at my waist, spread his wings. I stood up and twisted my wrist, distracting him from the bate and myself from the sight of the mother who returned to put her arms around her child. "We're so glad we discovered this place. I have a feeling we'll be up here all the time."

These were the goals of the center, of course: to inspire curiosity and commitment from visitors entranced by the beauty of the birds. But I hoped, watching the couple walk hand in hand down the driveway with their beautiful little son or daughter, that I wouldn't be around the next time they visited.

The education director walked out to me. "I was listening to you just now, and I've gotta say that Bodhi's not a baby anymore. He's juvenile, ready to move into an outdoor mew. Let's shoot for next week."

"Next week?" My hand went to his jesses. "But he's so young."

"Mature plumage means a bird's waterproof. You've been doing good work with him—he'll be fine."

"I know you're right." I looked down at Bodhi's small, silly head with its patches of fluff and flight feathers. "But I hate to see him grow up."

She shrugged. "That's what they do."

I bent and buried my nose into his head feathers. They smelled like grain, like the feed stores my mother had taken me to as a child when we needed chicken and rabbit food. Bodhi lifted his beak and tugged at my hair, reminding me of the child who'd reached up to the dreadlocked woman's hand on the way down the hill.

"Don't anthropomorphize." Darcy, cleaning the great gray owl's mew, called out a caution. "He's gotta grow up, you know. He's not your kid."

"I know."

I retreated to the clinic before I could retort that, earlier that week, I'd spotted her kissing the saw-whet owl's head.

———

We moved Bodhi into the outdoor mew with Loki the following week. I didn't spend the night, but I sat on a stump long into the evening, watching for any sign of discord between the younger and older bird. Loki hooted as I walked into his living space with Bodhi, then flew to a far corner to observe. The younger owl stalked up and down each perch on his skinny legs, checking out the new pad. I brought quail and an extra mouse each as a housewarming present; the owls crouched on feeding platforms across from each other and tore into the quail.

"They look calm."

Jonathan walked up behind me. "They're not trying to attack each other, and the mew looks big enough for both of them."

"Unlike our house," I muttered.

He stepped back, hurt in his eyes. "I can spend more time in the back-yard studio if you need to be alone . . ."

I shook my head. "Sorry. I'm just sad. I'm gonna hate walking into the clinic and not seeing him there."

"He'll be happier away from all the noise and people, down here under the trees."

I shrugged, just wanting to be alone with my owl. But only a faint glow of sun remained in the sky, so I followed Jonathan up the hill.

"Did you hear John Hendrickson's coming to town?" He paused under the windmill. "He's that nature photographer who did the raptor book your mom gave me. We've got his poster of the barn owl in the tree, one wing stretched out . . ."

I looked up at the windmill, remembered how we'd stood under it years ago, vowing to love and care for each other, to treat each other as best friends, always. What had gone wrong?

I tried to smile, to look interested. "He's coming here?"

"He's doing a benefit slide show and lecture for the center, over at the university. We're bringing birds. Maybe it's a good time for Bodhi to make his debut."

I twisted the owl charm on the beaded necklace I'd made. "D'you think he's ready?" It was one thing to chauffeur an owl to our house, and another to stroll across campus with him on my glove and sit quietly for a slide show surrounded by birders and photography buffs.

"We have to try." He bent to kiss me.

I tilted my face up toward his. At the touch of his lips on mine, tears seeped from the corners of my eyes. I echoed his words. "We have to try."

～

John Hendrickson's presentation took place at the law school—an elegant brick building with a long, wide lobby ordinarily inhabited by modish students and now replete with raptors. I carried Bodhi's crate into the bathroom, away from the crowd around our center's tables of literature and other handlers with their birds. He stepped onto my glove, eyes half-lidded and muscles relaxed.

"Ready to meet your fans?" I lay my cheek against his new head feathers. He leaned in, pressing against my face.

Should he bate and tangle himself in the leash or stick out his wings at a grotesque angle and commence defensive beak clacking, we'd have to excuse ourselves from the program and revisit his role as an education bird. Part of me wanted him to stay safe at the center, unstressed by public appearances, but the other part flushed with pride as we stepped into the crowded hall and he remained calm on my arm.

"Oh, how cute! Can I pet him?" A woman in a velvet caftan glided over, ropy black hair swinging. Bodhi stiffened and narrowed on my arm.

"He does that when he's scared, to look more like a tree," I explained. "You can't pet him, but I'll tell you all about him. He's Bodhi, a four-month-old barred owl."

The woman drew back her hand. Her pleasant face soured. "A *barred* owl? I thought it was a spotted." She sneered at the two-pound bird on my glove. "Why on earth would your center keep one of those? The government's right—they *should* be shot."

I stepped back, baffled by her ferocity. Most raptor centers across the country display barred owls. Our staff asked us to avoid political discussion about their migration and the displacement of spotteds; we had to remain neutral, exhibit the birds and let the public come to its own conclusions. But I never dreamed someone might look at Bodhi and threaten murder.

"I need to take him to the auditorium now."

During Hendrickson's slide show, Bodhi sat quietly. I looked at the photographer's pictures of baby screech owls, at the barn owl with a mouse in its beak, at the more sobering silhouette of a gunshot golden eagle hanging dead from barbed wire, and fumed. "It's not your fault," I whispered to Bodhi. Humans likely caused the species' migration west of the Mississippi, by planting trees across the Great Plains. This change in the landscape may have allowed barreds to hopscotch from one side of the country to the other.

Still, Northwest environmentalists, watching their forests fall to clear-cutting and their spotted owls die off for lack of territory and food, were pissed. At my laptop that night, I found an article from *High Country News* describing how a bird-watcher in Redwood National Park discovered the mangled body of an owl lying on the ground. Overhead in a branch, a barred perched with spotted feathers still stuck to its talons.

I recalled the velvet woman's bizarre governmental praise. "What's up with that?" I asked Jonathan as we packed for our trip to Alaska.

He pushed his sleeping bag into his backpack, tossed in wool socks and a stocking cap. "U.S. Fish and Wildlife's proposing to shoot hundreds of barreds, to see if they can recover the spotted population."

"Shoot them as in *kill* them?"

"Like nutria."

We'd just watched Ted Gesing's short documentary showing similar hunting of orange-tusked water rats in the Deep South. One scene in which hunters whooped and fired from the back of a pickup struck us both as eerily similar to a video game.

"Give some yahoo a gun and permission to blow barred owls out of the sky," I told Jonathan, "and all hell's gonna break loose."

He paused in his packing. "I wouldn't mention that at your handler talk tomorrow, especially since it's your first one with Bodhi. You never know how the public's gonna respond."

I thought of the barred owl, small and helpless, wing drooping below my glove and dark eyes guileless. The government's plan seemed to me asinine. No matter how many owls they shot, wouldn't more take their place, based on the species' sheer resiliency?

"I can be neutral." I shoved sleeping bag and pillow and running shoes into my backpack. "But no one better mess with my bird."

20

Everything's Political

FOUR YEARS BEFORE HER DEATH, MOLLY IVINS, *TEXAS OBSERVER* columnist, gave a talk at the McDonald Theatre about her particular position as Washington, DC, hell-raiser, and Jonathan and I went to hear her. "Everything is political," she told the audience.

Her words resonated in my head as I stood in the raptor center's education pavilion surrounded by maples and snowberry bushes to deliver a talk with Bodhi on my glove.

Most raptor centers, at zoos or otherwise, offer educational presentations. Sometimes they're formal, polished half hours with music over speakers and bird trainers speaking into headsets. At our center handler talks became intimate exchanges between trainers and visitors, inspired by the raptors they got to see up close.

The UO Ducks played a game that day, so only a handful of people— some of them in green and yellow sports gear—sat on the benches while I related Bodhi's personal and species information. Beside me Jonathan introduced Amazon on a T-perch and told the visitors about the center. "We rehabilitate up to two hundred birds a year," he said, "and we're able to release about half back into the wild. Your admission fee goes toward food and medical treatment for the birds."

We fielded people's questions about what and how we fed them, whether or not owl pellets were poop, and what people might do to attract raptors to their property. "Nest boxes, brush piles, no pesticides. Leave snags—that is, dead trees—alone unless they're threatening your house." Jonathan rattled off the list. "We'll stick around a while, in case you'd like to see the birds up close."

Most visitors stood up, murmured their thanks, and wandered over toward the mews, but a tall man with shoulder-length gray hair stalked over to me, his face long and grim. He scowled at the owl on my arm. "So that's the culprit, huh?"

Bodhi raised his neck feathers. I drew him closer to me. "This is a permanently injured barred owl. He fell out of his nest as a baby." I pursed my lips. "He hasn't done anything . . ."

"Look, hon." The guy towered over me, one index finger raised. I made myself look away from his Timberlines, up into his unshaven face. "I don't agree with Fish and Wildlife wanting to blow owls out of the trees, but something's gotta be done. We've worked too long and hard to save Spotty. Now these guys are coming in, taking over what we've tried to protect?"

"What about preserving old-growth forests?" I countered. "Then there'd be territory enough for both species."

"Melissa," Jonathan said at my elbow.

I ignored him and told the man how, in North Carolina, suburban home owners celebrate barred owls. The birds nest in trees above their sidewalks, and the city mounts webcams so residents can see parents tending to fledglings on their TVs. "People are hosting owl-watching parties in their living rooms."

The man shrugged, unmoved. "Ain't gonna happen here." He straightened up and turned his back on Bodhi. "I'm all for saving forests, but people 'round here lost their jobs and homes 'cause of Spotty. We can't turn our backs on him now. No one in Oregon's gonna celebrate your owl."

"Melissa? Bodhi needs to get back to his mew." Jonathan stepped closer to me. "It's his first handler talk," he told the man. "We don't want to overdo it."

Outside Bodhi's mew with the bird safely inside, I smacked my forehead with the palm of one hand. "Would Molly Ivins stay neutral? I don't think so."

Jonathan refrained from pointing out that I was no political columnist and Ivins was no owl trainer. Instead, he lowered his unibrow and slunk up the hill, the golden eagle perched like a familiar on his arm.

I doubted the wisdom of our setting off for Alaska just then, alone with each other for a week. Caught in a tide of backpackers rushing up from Bellingham's dock to claim a spot on the USS *Malaspina*'s top deck, Jonathan glowered. I gnashed my teeth as I struggled to put up our tent. But once the ferry took off, we stood and gazed over the railing at the endless evergreen forests. His hand found mine. We relaxed.

By the second morning of our trip, we'd seen a breaching humpbacked whale, pods of dolphins, and bald eagles hanging out on the beaches of Ketchikan like truant teens. "Dumpster ducks." The old man beside me on deck hocked a gob of spit overboard. "Come in and take over, eating garbage and crapping on everything. I hate 'em."

"Our national bird," I marveled to Jonathan, who roamed the decks for hours taking photographs. "I thought they looked incredible out there flocking on the beach, but that guy just saw them as pests."

He slung his camera over one shoulder and drew me close, kissed the top of my head. I'd braided my hair and pulled on a stocking cap against the almost constant wind. "You look perfectly at home out here," he said.

On deck for hours, wind in our faces and cetaceans leaping from the water, we became our best selves. I thought of John Muir's words from *Our National Parks*—they referred to mountain climbing but worked just as well on the ferry:

Nature's peace will flow into you as sunshine flows into trees. The winds will blow their own freshness into you, and the storms their energy, while cares will drop off like autumn leaves.

While other campers on the top deck played guitars and did yoga, or read on chaise lounges, we reveled in nature's peace and peered through our binoculars, checking off species in our bird book.

"Comin' up on your left," the jovial young Forest Service ranger called over the intercom, "you'll glimpse the rarely seen species *lawnus ornamentus*."

We dashed to the other side of the ferry in time to see a flock of pink plastic flamingos that someone had placed high in a fir. "Lawnus ornamentus," I giggled. "That's hilarious."

Jonathan put his arms around me. I leaned back into his chest and pointed at the baseball-like head of a bald eagle high up in a tree. We avoided talk about our stalled adoption plan, about our raptors. Three days on the boat reminded me that here was the man I'd fallen in love with at the dog park, the husband I cherished.

We walked down to the cafeteria for bread and soup, then sat in the windowed observation room to watch the ranger demonstrate, in a vigorous physical performance that involved a lot of rolling around on the floor, how to defend oneself in case of bear attack.

A copy of *Alaska* magazine lay on the seat next to me; on the cover, a female snowy owl half-obscured by mist. The photos inside showed the big white birds sitting on boulders and flying across an endless expanse of tundra.

I swiped the publication to read in the tent. That night, as the ferry's thundering motor lulled us to sleep, I told Jonathan about my plan for a covert owl operation. "Remember how staff said at the last ed team meeting that we still aren't allowed to work with Archimedes?"

"Of course."

We'd sat in the meeting the week before and listened while Darcy begged to be allowed to handle the snowy. "He needs to come out on a T-perch." She'd flipped her braids aside; they bounced like aggrieved reptiles. "I was working with him. I almost had him on the glove."

"Snatch and grab isn't a viable training method." The volunteer coordinator frowned. "When I went in to feed him the other day, he bolted away from me and hung upside down from one corner of his mew. He never used to be afraid of people. *Someone's* spooked him."

The ed director narrowed her eyes. "*No one* is cleared to train or handle Archimedes right now." She let her gaze fall on Darcy for an instant. "The last thing that owl needs is more trauma."

I agreed with the complex politics regarding the snowy—Darcy had a reputation for heavy hands and little patience. But I felt sorry for him. He seemed, hunched low on his stump, to be mired in depression. Though he'd been raised in a mew, I couldn't help believing—especially now that I found myself in Alaska—some part of him longed instinctively for the Arctic plains.

Still, my proposed plan was selfish. I'd been in love with Archimedes since the first day he'd leaped onto my sneakers. Most birds either ignored me when I brought the day's quail or rat, or flew as far away from me as possible. When I approached him he met my eyes and honked as if in greeting.

"Bodhi's my baby," I whispered to Jonathan in the tent, lest the young man in the enormous nylon pavilion next to us hear our pillow talk. "But Lorax feels like my peer. I feel that way about Archimedes, too. I want to get to know him. Does that make sense?"

"It does," he admitted. "You're talking about bonding. But love, he's not an ed bird. You're not allowed to work with him."

"It's better to ask forgiveness than to ask permission." I quoted our neighbor—another Molly who liked to deliver such witticisms on our porch on a wine-soaked Friday night—but I didn't tell him about the day I'd lingered in Archimedes' mew after placing a quail on the stump. I'd looked around for staff and volunteers, then sat on the steps leading down to his gravel floor while he ate his dinner. One eye on the path, I read to him from *Don't Shoot the Dog*—a whole chapter on positive reinforcement. When I stood up to leave, he honked at me. I could've sworn I glimpsed a gossamer red thread that led from his big feathered feet to my wrist.

⌁

The ferry left Jonathan and me in Sitka, where we'd reserved a basement in a local artist's house within walking distance of downtown. "Not much to see," she told us in the parlor space she'd created on the bottom floor of her house, complete with DVD player and a pile of movies, books, and magazines. "Couple restaurants, a bookstore, some art galleries. Whole town's quiet except when the cruise ships come to town."

By cruise ships, she meant the mammoth Princess and Carnival vessels that docked off the coast and boated people over in smaller crafts to walk the town, eat fish chowder, and buy fudge and silver whale-tail pendants. Numerous passengers ventured through a forested park full of chattering ravens to the Alaska Raptor Center—our own end-point destination.

The first morning of our visit, Jonathan and I wandered past ultra-modern mews and flight cages and meeting spaces, and peered through a public observation window into the large, gleaming clinic. "How on earth can they afford all this?" I whispered. "They're a nonprofit like ours."

"Cruise ship money." The PR director led us past eagles and falcons tethered outside on display. "People come in off the boats for two hours, pay their admission, maybe sign up to sponsor a bird, then leave. In the winter, though, we get nothing."

I thought of the artist we were staying with—she'd confessed that locals tolerated fair-weather invaders in their sleepy town because without them, the economy would crumble. "If only," I told Jonathan on our flight back to Seattle, "spotted owls and barreds could get along in the same way."

"But tourists aren't threatening the locals." He explained that the analogy made no sense. "Spotteds are no longer breeding or raising young birds. They're vanishing. Their whole population's been compromised."

"Ugh." In the car heading south on the I-5, I peered out the window at the Willamette River sparkling under the bridge between Washington and Oregon. "Molly Ivins was right. *Everything* is political. I just want to go to Powell's and bury my head in the stacks."

～◆～

Powell's City of Books takes up several blocks, so large that when shoppers walk in the front door, staff offer them a color-coded map. People lose each other among the various floors and rooms. Jonathan headed up to the photography section with a promise that if he left it, he'd come and find me on the ground floor among the magazines.

I walked past the racks, picking up *Sierra, Audubon, High Country News, Orion*. A title in *Mother Jones* caught my eye: "Did I Steal My Daughter? The Tribulations of Global Adoption."

I scanned the tagline. "The answers are never easy when you enter the labyrinth of global adoption."

I sank down on a bench near the front door. Outside, men hawked newspapers to benefit the homeless, and car horns blared. I barely heard them. The other magazines slipped to my side as I opened to the article and read without stopping.

The author, Elizabeth Larsen, had adopted a toddler from Guatemala. Later, she discovered how some "orphans" in that country are stolen from their parents, while other birth mothers and fathers are coerced into giving up their children. She began questioning the ethics of having adopted little Flora. Her article examined the theories behind closed and open adoption and gave a history of international adoption in the United States, with a timeline that highlighted celebrities and their foreign-born babies. I thought of Kat's implication that I wanted an Asian child as an accessory, like a lapdog.

Closed adoption, in which birth parents and children don't have any contact with each other, was apparently unique to international adoption. A quote from one advocate shook me. "When you read the adoption boards online," the source said, "it seems like parents go overseas because they don't want some pesky birth mother or relative showing up."

Jonathan and I cringed at the idea of meeting our child's birth parents. So did the author of the *Mother Jones* article, until she thought about what it would mean to take Flora away from her culture and her birth mother forever. She ended up finding and meeting the birth mom in a McDonald's, with her husband and the little girl, and the two women wept and exchanged information and agreed to keep in touch.

Their particular situation had worked out best for everyone; still, the story and my own ignorance blew my mind. In the twenty-one months Jonathan and I had worked toward adopting a child, I'd thought very little about what it would feel like to be spirited away from your homeland, your culture, your relatives, with no records and no way of contacting them. I'd thought even less about what it would feel like to be unable to keep your child because of politics or poverty, to watch her disappear forever in a stranger's arms.

In a daze I bought the magazine and headed upstairs, pushing past crowds of people to find Jonathan. He sat immersed in a book of Andy Goldsworthy's photos. I collapsed beside him. "We need to talk about something, when you're ready to go."

He looked up from the book. "You okay? No . . . you're not." He stood up and took my hand, led me down the stairs and out of the bookstore to the car. On the way back to Eugene, I read him the article.

"I feel like we can't be a hundred percent sure that any child we adopt from Vietnam wasn't taken from his or her birth parents. Our agency's ethical, but even they can't know what Vietnam's government is really up to, whether we're taking a baby away from a parent who could otherwise keep it if we sent the thousand dollars we just spent on our Alaskan vacation."

"That might be an oversimplification." He pointed out a red-tail hawk on a fence post, and another in a tree. "Then again, we're pretty ignorant about the politics over there."

I stared out the window at a flock of starlings mobbing a third hawk in a field beside the highway. We'd spent thousands already attempting to adopt overseas. If we pulled out now, we'd lose the money and our child.

The complexity of the situation overwhelmed me, and I struck my forehead with my hand for the second time in two weeks. I needed to run, as hard and fast as some wildcat, up the trail to Spencer Butte. Above the city perhaps the winds would blow their own freshness into me and I could figure out what the hell to do.

21

Love People, and Feed Them

During one lecture in *The Roots of Buddhist Psychology*, Jack Kornfield speaks of a man who longed desperately for enlightenment. "Love people, and feed them," the man's teacher suggested. But that wasn't good enough for the guy. He wanted peace and serenity and balance in the midst of chaos.

"Love people, and feed them," his teacher said over and over, until at last the message stuck.

I thought of the story as I carried a thawed quail down to Archimedes and placed it on the rectangle of Astroturf zip-tied to his log perch—ostensibly on the exact spot he'd stand before stepping up to a handler's glove. From his stump he honked, insistent as a noisemaker from a kids' birthday party.

"If you get on my glove, we can go all sorts of places," I told him. "We can stand in the trees, go down to the ed pavilion, get out to programs downtown."

I clucked and tapped the perch; he glanced at it, then looked down at my white sneakers and honked again. I braced myself for a round of foot sex, but he remained on his stump until I let myself out of the mew and turned the key in the padlock. Instantly, he flew to the perch and seized the quail in one enormous foot. A raptor seldom eats in front of someone unless he trusts her absolutely.

Once again, I thought of our neighbor's belief that it's better to ask forgiveness than to ask permission. Though I was tempted to commence snowy owl training on the sly, I mustered up my courage and approached Laurin as she stood outside with the turkey vulture on her glove.

"D'you think it would be okay if I . . . well . . . if I hung out in Archimedes' mew for a few minutes a day? I'd like to build some rapport with him—not glove-train him or anything—but just give him some company. I thought, maybe since he's a human imprint, he might like it."

She looked down the hill toward Archimedes' mew; he sat on the perch, a bright white spot just visible through the trees. "Hmm. You've done a great job with Bodhi. Let me ask the staff. Guess there's no harm in sitting with him, as long as you don't try to get him on the glove. He's a difficult bird, but you're sensitive to that. And you're right—he'd probably enjoy the company."

She reached into the back pocket of her jeans and handed me a rolled-up newsletter. "Here, you can read to him about the IAATE conference near Amsterdam. It's tons of fun—maybe you and Jonathan could go in February?"

"IAATE?" I looked down at the image of a green feather on the newsletter.

"Remember, it's the International Association of Avian Trainers and Educators? I know Louise is hoping to go."

"The Netherlands?" I flipped the page to a photo of a laughing young woman with a macaw, wings outspread, astride her shoulder. "Too bad we're broke."

"Sorry . . . I forgot about the adoption. Hey, how's that going?"

The couple who'd brought their new Korean son to our agency's Parents in Progress meeting had told us the worst part of the process was the wait and how their friends and family eventually stopped asking for updates. I felt grateful to Laurin for asking about our adoption, but baffled about how to answer. No polite sound bite could capture my new concerns about adopting a child from Vietnam, and Jonathan and I had no idea what we'd do if we decided to bail on our agency altogether.

"It's . . . slow," I said finally.

"Good thing you're both so patient."

I snorted mirthlessly. Jonathan was the patient one, living in the present, wanting what he had at any given moment. I was a nut job, my heart breaking in my chest every time we saw a little kid in a coffeehouse or store. But I didn't correct Laurin.

The vulture on her glove spread its wings, basking, and she stepped out of the shade into sunlight with an indulgent smile. "If you're here every day training Bodhi, you might as well take Archimedes his dinner, too. Wouldn't hurt for him to start associating you with food."

———

Now I worked with Bodhi an hour each day, then walked down to Archimedes' mew with a book and a rat or quail. He honked when he saw me but made no move to fly to the perch. Sometimes I sat on the wooden steps and sang to him. Visitors heard me crooning "You Are My Sunshine" and laughed on their promenade around the center

After two weeks he deigned to rip up a quail in my presence. A few days later, I offered him a rat from my bare hand. He chirruped as he took it in his beak—a begging call that struck me as more friendly, less piteous than Bodhi's.

"I know I could train him to jump on my glove," I told Jonathan on the way to the grocery store one afternoon. "If I were allowed."

He found a parking space and gathered our cloth bags from the back of the car. "Write a behavior plan for him—break the glove-training into steps. Then submit it to the staff."

"Like a task analysis."

As a counselor in a group home, I'd written task analyses for disabled residents, deconstructing their various chores—brief documents along the lines of: "Step one: Put soap on the sponge in the kitchen sink. Step two: Apply sponge to a plate. Step three: Rub sponge in a circular motion."

For Archimedes I'd need to do something similar: "Step one: Fly to your perch. Step two: Stay put. Step three: Put your feet on my glove."

"You've gotta reward him for every step," Jonathan said. "The trick's finding just the right reinforcement. Lots of birds like freshly euthanized mice . . ."

I winced. "Yeah, but who's going to kill them?"

Somehow, I'd managed to volunteer at the raptor center for years without euthanizing prey. I sensed my good fortune was about to run out, but Jonathan flashed me a chivalrous smile. "I'll do it."

One of Eugene's omnipresent Subarus pulled up beside us. An Anglo woman who looked to be my age got out and walked around to the other side of the car. She opened the door, and a little Asian girl leaped from the passenger's seat onto the woman's back and flung her arms around her neck. They walked toward the store, laughing.

Jonathan took my hand, chattered maniacally on our way past the outdoor displays of pumpkins and cornstalks. "It's still relatively warm. I'm gonna grill us some salmon tonight. What do you think about dining alfresco on the patio?" Then, glancing at my face, he dropped his voice into Barry White anesthetic. "Don't worry, love, that'll be you soon with a child."

I looked away toward Spencer Butte swelling high above the South Hills. Dense fir growth hid the raptor center from view, but I could feel Lorax and Bodhi and Archimedes there, sitting on their perches, simply being.

━━━

We spent the last weeks of summer at the raptor center, lounging in the waning sunlight with our birds and successfully avoiding any conversation about whether to pull out of the Vietnam program.

Then our social worker called. "I've got a referral for you. He's a baby from Vietnam, and he's healthy. I'll drop off the paperwork on your front porch."

I hesitated. "Is he . . ." We'd shied away from telling her about the *Mother Jones* article about baby theft, not wanting to insult her work, but I had to know more about the baby's background. "Is he a *real* orphan?"

"Left alone under a bridge," she said. "No question—he needs a home."

She dropped off a manila envelope and rushed away to her kid's soccer practice. On the porch I pulled out a two-page document and held it out to Jonathan. "Our future son."

"Oh . . . *my gosh.*"

The baby looked like a just-hatched barn owl, naked and purple and horribly emaciated. His cheeks were sunken, his face contorted. Jonathan put on his glasses. "Wow. He looks sick."

I clutched my stomach. "Oh, love—what's *wrong* with him?"

As our social work had reported, the child was a bona fide orphan, abandoned under a bridge at birth with no note, no blanket, nothing. His destiny, should an adoptive family not take him, lay in a Vietnamese orphanage. Even the journalist from *Mother Jones* couldn't argue that this child needed a home . . . but something didn't feel right.

Marissa wasn't answering her cell. Jonathan found the number to the Vietnam program, and I called the staff there. "We've got a referral. The little boy doesn't look healthy. Is he part of the Waiting Child program?"

"He is." The woman on the other line explained the baby's situation in a patient, upbeat tone. "He was found under a bridge, turning blue from lack of oxygen. But the latest medical reports say he's doing fine."

"He looks so ill . . ."

"Are you still holding out for a girl?" Irritation displaced the woman's cheeriness. "Because I have to tell you that if you reject this child based on his gender, you'll get kicked out of the Vietnam program."

I stared down at the photograph. "How long do we have to make a decision?"

"A couple of days. After that, we'll assign him to the next family in line."

I hung up the phone and related the conversation to Jonathan. "We can take the paperwork to a pediatrician and see what she says. If the baby didn't get oxygen at birth, there's a good chance of brain damage." I looked again at the baby's photo. "I'm not sure I can handle that."

"But they said he's healthy." Jonathan dumped kibble into bowls for the cats. "Maybe he's just, well, unfortunate looking. When I was a few months old, my mother worried because I couldn't sit up. She took me to the doctor for a diagnosis."

I paused in rereading the baby's bio. "You've never told me this. What did the doc say?"

"Said my mom had nothing to worry about. I was just fat."

"I'm calling my mother."

I reached for my cell. She answered, and I launched into my question without explanation.

"Mom, tell me the truth. Was I an unattractive baby?"

She chuckled. "Since you ask, honey, you did look a little like a plucked chicken."

"Thanks."

"Glad I could be of help." Her voice held its usual bemusement; as always, she asked for no backstory, trusting I'd divulge it when ready. "For the record, honey," she added, "you don't look like a plucked chicken now."

"Good to know. Social worker's calling—gotta go."

Marissa told me she'd e-mailed an update from the baby's Vietnamese foster mother, along with new photos. "At present he weighs three kilograms," I read to Jonathan. "He doesn't roll over yet, but he can grasp objects. He eats well, finishing a hundred milliliters of formula each time. He has eight meals every day, but . . ." I raised my palms, mystified. "She says he's malnourished at the third level."

The photos showed the same sickly baby, his mouth wrenched and squalling. But baby barn owls, those naked scrawny little apparitions, grow into superb creatures with heart-shaped faces and lovely tawny feathers. Who were we to deny this little boy the potential to fly?

"What does 'malnourished at the third level' mean?" Jonathan went to the computer. "I'm e-mailing the program's director." He copied me on the note:

Thanks so much for the referral of this little boy—we've been looking through his paperwork, and we have a few questions. From what we know of malnutrition, it sounds as though there may be a good chance of developmental delays. We'd like to know more about his condition before we move on. Some specific questions are: What does 'malnourished to the third degree' mean? What are the long-term effects of malnourishment at such an early age, and is he improving?

A staff member's reply came the next morning.

I'll confirm what malnourished at the third level means. I'll also find out if they believe there are developmental delays. We suggest checking with a pediatrician or international doctor to find out the effects of malnourishment over the long term.

We waited. Marissa had told us not to cut out any potential child's photo and put it up on our refrigerator. "You'll set yourself up for disappointment," she'd said. I had no desire to put the Vietnamese baby's picture out where we could see it; the image unnerved me, challenged the boundaries of my compassion.

Love people, and feed them. Would adoption fill out this child's sunken cheeks and replace his pained grimace with a smile?

———

With two weeks to go until the fall term, I blew off class prep and immersed myself in the study of snowy owls. I learned that the parents, if babies are threatened, fly at humans.

"In Europe you can buy one as a pet," I told Jonathan. "People want them because of Harry Potter's bird, and then they abandon them because they're so big and powerful." I told him how staff at other raptor centers had difficulty training snowy owls. "This one handler blogged about how hers jumps off the glove and hangs there, just like Archimedes does."

We stood in the fifty-foot flight mew, catching a quartet of rehabbed screech owls for their final weighing and release. Jonathan reached up with a long-handled net and expertly caught one little bird on its flight from one perch to another. He brought the net down to the gravel and gently scooped up the owl in gloved hands, transferring it to a towel in a pet carrier. "Are you gonna ask staff for permission to start glove-training?"

"They'd say no. For now I'm just feeding him." I leaped up with my net, but I missed, and the remaining three screech owls took off for a high corner of the mew. "Sorry, love. By the way, know how snowy owls mate?"

"Nope. But I bet I'm about to find out."

"The male flies around with a lemming, then drops to the ground. When the female flies up, he lowers his head like he's bowing and fans out his tail feathers."

"Would you settle for a chocolate truffle? I'm fresh out of lemmings." Jonathan ducked his head and kissed me. "I've gotta get these owls to Louise. Probably easier to do by myself . . ."

I left him to his work. In the clinic I folded my glove into my jacket pocket and prepped a thawed rat with vitamin powder, then carried it down to Archimedes' mew. Next door on his perch, Bodhi clacked his beak. "Your dinner's next," I promised.

The snowy squawked from his stump and lifted his head as I unlocked his door. I turned away from him and pulled on my glove, then hid it behind my back as I stepped into the mew. We sat together for a few minutes, until he relaxed his posture and closed his beak. I glanced around to make sure no one stood nearby, and stretched out my arm with the dead rat in my gloved hand. The owl screeched and flew from his stump on wide white wings, clung to the side of the mew and panted.

Dismayed, I dropped the food onto his perch and left.

The next day, I left my glove in the clinic. He refused to take the mice Jonathan euthanized. I draped them artistically across the Astroturf, but he waited until I'd walked to the top of the path near the lawn before flying over to eat them.

"Well, yeah. He's not going to eat in front of you if he doesn't trust you. Sounds like he was pretty spooked the day before," Jonathan said.

"Crap. Can I earn back his trust?"

"Sure. But it might take a while."

The next day, I walked down to find Archimedes standing on the perch. He allowed me to approach him, but when I touched his jesses with a cautious finger, he launched himself up into the air and whirled around his mew, shrieking so loudly that the education director stalked down the path.

"What's going on in here?" She peered through the wire at me. I'd had just enough time to return to the steps and open up *Don't Shoot the Dog*. Archimedes stood with his feet splayed on the gravel next to his water trough, feathers fluffed to twice his normal size and black beak gaping.

I looked up, feigning innocence. Her eyes went to the glove at my feet. I bowed my head, expecting excommunication. Instead, she regarded me, hands on hips, for a long moment. "Laurin told me you've been building rapport with him. Don't force him," she said at last. "He either makes the choice to step on the glove or you stop working with him."

Granted permission, I flashed a grateful smile. "I'm working on a behavior plan," I told her. "I've just got to deal with some adoption stuff, and then I'll give you a finished draft."

She turned as Darcy appeared at the great gray owl's door with a bucket and hose. "Be smart," she said and walked back to the clinic.

⌁

That afternoon, a new report came in from the Vietnam program. Our baby appeared to be healthy, eating well, with no developmental delays. "If we take him," I told Jonathan in bed that night, "and give him a good home and five nutritious meals a day, he'll gain weight and color. Maybe he'll even smile."

"A boy," he said. "I thought we'd decided to adopt a girl."

"If we reject this child, we're through with Vietnam."

"Weren't we through, anyway? I don't want to feel forced into this."

Alarmed by his tone, I changed the subject. "How am I gonna get that snowy on my glove?"

He took the bait. "What if you cut his mice into small bits? Animal behaviorists say it creates psychological hunger, like if we eat M&M's one by one over an hour instead of chowing down a whole bag in five minutes."

"Yeah, I get it. But who's going to cut up the mice?"

I waited. He shook his head. "If you're gonna be a bird handler, you've gotta get used to this stuff, my love. Think of it like cooking—people cut up chicken and pig every day. Archimedes is an obligate carnivore—if he doesn't eat meat, he'll die."

The next morning, I squeezed my eyes shut and cut a dead mouse into bits, whispering the lovingkindness prayer for the poor, soft creature. I slid the carnage into a plastic box and strapped it on my waist, left my glove in the clinic, and walked down to the mew.

Archimedes lifted his head as I unlocked the door but stayed put on his stump. I sat on the steps and sang, accompanied by the buzz of yellow jackets swooning over the bits box. At last I stood up and offered him a bite-size piece of mouse from my bare fingers. He chirped and took it from my hand, gashing my thumb with his beak.

A year before, pain and fear would have unraveled me. Now I wiped the blood off on my jeans, pulled on my glove, and offered another bit. At the sight of brown leather, he screamed and flew into the air, hanging upside down from his wire ceiling.

"He's not afraid of you—he's afraid of your glove." Laurin stood outside and watched. "What if you leave it on his perch overnight with the mice draped on it?"

"Worth a try."

The next morning, I walked down to the mew to retrieve my glove. Would Archimedes regard it as less of a threat, now that he'd spent the night with it?

He greeted me from his stump with a honk, and I looked over at the perch. The mice had vanished and my hundred-dollar glove, still draped across the Astroturf, sported a long white streak of bird poop.

I took it up to the clinic. Jonathan sat at the desk. "Look at this!"

He glanced up from the photos he'd taken of some of the resident raptors, shot against a black velvet curtain I'd held at a safe distance behind them. The dark background brought out the beauty of individual feathers, the yellow of the bald eagle's eyes, the red of the turkey vulture's beak. He'd taken no photos of Archimedes; the snowy had flown at the black cloth and attempted to kill it with all of his talons outstretched.

Jonathan examined my glove. "Maybe your reinforcement's wrong. I wonder if he'd work for lemmings."

But the Gourmet Rodent didn't offer lemmings; nor did any of the local pet stores we called. Nauseous, I cut up chunks of rabbit usually reserved for the eagles and dropped them into the bits box, murmuring apologies to my childhood pet, Frisky. With the box at my waist, I wore my glove into Archimedes' mew, hiding it behind my back as I stepped through the door. I sat down and talked to him a while, then popped open the lid. He stared at the box as if he knew what bloody new treasures lurked within.

I moved closer, holding out a piece of meat in my right hand. He took it, chortling. With slow, cautious movements, I brought out my gloved left hand. He spread his wings but remained on the stump. I picked up a bit in my leather-clad fingers and reached toward him. He shrieked and flew up into the air, wheeled around his mew, and banged into one side. A white feather floated down to the gravel at my feet.

"Dude, you've got no love for the glove." I sighed and vacated the mew. On my way up the path, I thought about a trainer who'd presented at the IAATE conference the year before. Staff told me she couldn't get her snowy on the glove, but she'd taught him to walk in and out of a pet carrier and jump to a perch for programs.

"Sounds good in theory, but Archimedes won't even leave his stump when I'm in there except to fly up to the roof."

In the treatment room, feeding skinned chicken bits to an injured hawk, Jonathan flashed me a sympathetic look. "He's an owl, love. It takes time."

"I don't have time."

In ten days I had to return to the university. Even though I taught only two classes, I knew I wouldn't be able to get up to the center every evening. The days would grow shorter—by December the Northwest sun set at four thirty—and Archimedes would huddle in his mew through the winter, untrained, while depression crept in and slaughtered me come January, when my little sister was due to give birth. My family would gather around her new baby in warm, sunny Orange County while I flailed alone in cold, dark failure.

"Let's take this Vietnamese boy," I told Jonathan. "We'll love him and feed him and he'll be fine. We'll be good for him, you know?"

He finished feeding the hawk and replaced the rolled-up towel in the pet carrier before latching the door. "I'll consider it if we can take his paperwork to a pediatrician tomorrow. I have questions . . ."

"Fair enough." I put my box of rabbit in the refrigerator and called our pediatrician, then our social worker. "Jonathan and I decided we'll take the little boy from Vietnam, contingent on a doctor reviewing his paperwork tomorrow."

"Not necessary."

Marissa's voice, usually clinical, grew quiet, even awkward. "I don't know how to tell you this, so I'm just going to have to come out with it."

I held the phone against my ear, waiting. "Did we get kicked out of the Vietnam program?"

"No."

Across the clinic Jonathan looked a question at me. I shook my head and held up a finger.

"I'm sorry to have to say this." She paused to clear her throat. "The little boy you were going to adopt has died."

22

Prostitutes and Bird Trainers

I DON'T KNOW WHY JONATHAN AND I WERE SHOCKED TO LEARN THAT the boy assigned to be our son had died. Between us we had fifteen years of experience in raptor rehabilitation; we were smart. We knew that every bird's a gamble. You find an emaciated owl or hawk at the side of the road and tube-feed it four times a day, and then—if it's still breathing—you offer it bits of skinned chicken from forceps every two hours, but there's always a chance it'll expire. It's the same for abandoned infants. Marissa told me over the phone that one in three hundred of an agency's babies die.

"But they said he was healthy!" I lay in bed that night staring out the window at the dark, drooping fir branches illuminated by a dim streetlight. "Why would they tell us that? Why would they assign us a horribly malnourished child and say he was okay?"

Jonathan hit the mute button on the remote and refocused from the television to me with a mixture of sadness and relief in his eyes. "It doesn't matter, love. He wasn't the right child for us. And now we won't get kicked out of the Vietnam program."

But distrust gripped me. I regarded our agency, the Vietnamese social workers, their entire country with a fierce new suspicion.

"Can we even believe what they tell us?"

Newspaper reports rumbled about human trafficking violations. In April Vietnamese government officials were scheduled to renew something called a Memorandum of Agreement, mandating a national oversight of adoptions so that everyone played by the rules. They'd been accused of shady transactions in the past, and US officials had refused to work with the country until they signed the MOA. If they didn't renew it this spring, our agency and others would refuse to adopt out kids from Vietnam.

"Where does that leave us?" I fumed. "If they don't sign, we'll be foisted off on another country, last on the waiting list again. There's gotta be a better option."

"How about private adoption from this country? We haven't really talked about that . . ."

"Too expensive. We've already spent thousands of dollars. Honestly . . ." I sucked in a ragged breath and burrowed down under my pillow. "I think I might be ready to call it quits."

~~~

In the middle of the night, I sat up and gasped, so loudly that Jonathan woke from a sound sleep. "What's wrong?"

"I forgot to feed Archimedes! His rabbit . . . it's still in the clinic refrigerator!"

Jonathan pulled me to him and lay my head against his chest. "It's fine. He's not gonna starve. Anyhow, I'm sure someone figured it out and gave him the food."

But they didn't. In the clinic the next morning, we found a note from staff asking who'd left the rabbit in the fridge; they'd finally given up on the mystery and fed the bits to the golden eagle. Jonathan euthanized four mice for me, and I dropped them into my bits box. We avoided each other's eyes, still too upset about the Vietnamese boy to concentrate on anything besides feeding raptors. But he put a warm hand on my neck for an instant. "Good luck."

At the sound of my footsteps, Archimedes raised his head and honked. "Morning, owl." I spoke to him absently, latching the door behind me. I fished out a mouse and held it toward the stump in my glove, expecting his traditional fly-off. Instead, Archimedes chirped and snatched the mouse from my leather-clad fingers.

"What the . . ." I stared at him. His eyes blazed round and yellow, riveted on the box at my waist. "You're hungry?"

I stepped over to his perch and set another mouse on the Astroturf. He stared at the still brown body a moment, then let loose a shriek and sailed over, gulping it down.

"Good work!"

I murmured the words over and over as he stood on the perch and ate the other two mice from my gloved hand. "So this is what happens when you skip dinner?"

He swallowed down the final mouse tail, wiped his beak on the Astroturf, and flew back to his stump. He turned to look at me, feathery white mustache trembling. He chittered, then opened his beak wide and honked.

"Thank *you*!" I backed out of the mew and ran up the path to the clinic, calling for Jonathan.

He wasn't there. I raced around the center, peering into mews, until I found him walking out of the ferruginous hawk's enclosure.

His unibrow shot up. "Another referral?"

"No, no. Archimedes . . ." I panted. "Flew to his perch . . . ate from my glove. He was hungry!"

"Hungry?"

"I didn't feed him last night, remember?"

"Ah." Jonathan nodded, comprehending immediately. "Will work for food."

What's in it for me? Steve Martin had written about how the answer to that question is critical. Now I understood. When Archimedes felt sated, he had no motivation to dine from my leather accessory, much less from a patch of plastic grass. But hungry after thirty-six hours without a meal, he'd eat wherever I told him to.

And now I found myself facing a dilemma—whether to withhold food to get him to stand on my glove. Bodhi had taught me that, eventually, I could move from food as reward to head-scratching. But Archimedes was nowhere near that stage. Food was all I had.

In every flight show, every Sea World program, every trained cat performance I'd ever watched, handlers got their animals to fly and dance and jump on command by offering mice and fish and freeze-dried liver. I could offer my services as head masseuse later; for now I had to use fresh mice.

"Be careful." Jonathan cautioned me in a low voice as we walked past the prey barn where two volunteers stood cleaning mice aquariums. "I once heard of a trainer who withheld too much food and his bird got anemic. It almost died."

My hand flew to my chest. "I'd never do that."

"It's a delicate balance—you've got to weigh him every day to make sure he's not getting too thin. Check this with the ed director, okay? I'm glad he ate from your glove, but this is serious stuff."

The education director sat in her office, organizing school programs on the October calendar. I sat down in a folding chair beside her.

"Archimedes flew to his perch and ate from my glove."

Her head shot up, and she stuck her pencil in her ponytail. "You're kidding."

I shook my head. "No joke. He was hungry—that was his rabbit in the fridge from last night. I know I can have him standing on the glove in a week. But I think I need to withhold his food for another night. Would that be okay?"

She grimaced. "Let me talk with staff. We don't like to do that . . ."

"Yeah, I know."

I walked to the wooden bin of stuffed toy birds and rearranged them so the three snowy owls stood side by side, flanked by a couple of velvety turkey vultures. "If I could get Archimedes out on the glove, these things would sell like crazy."

"Melissa, are you okay? You seem dazed."

What do you say to a casual acquaintance about a child who was supposed to be yours, but died?

"I'm fine." I drummed my fingers on the empty bits box at my waist. "So you'll talk with staff, and I'll work on finding a secondary reinforcement for Archimedes. Somehow, I don't think it'll be my singing."

After discussion, staff agreed that for training purposes, Archimedes could skip another meal. "But you've got to weigh him daily to make sure he's not in danger of emaciation," the ed director told me. "We don't want him getting anemic."

"Of course." I thought again of the baby boy from Vietnam. Had his caregivers weighed him regularly? Had they really offered eight meals daily, or was that a fiction designed to comfort ignorant adoptive parents overseas? Had *he* died of anemia, emaciated beyond help?

I loved and fed the snowy owl. For a few evenings he received regular meals: I cut his prey into bits, and he ate from my fingers. But the glove sent him flying, and he showed no interest in jumping to his perch, even for a whole mouse. "He's stuffed," I told Jonathan. "Completely unmotivated."

On Friday night I withheld his rat and commenced a twenty-four-hour juice fast in solidarity. The next afternoon, I bicycled up to the center, swerving to avoid piles of wet leaves. Hunger clawed at my stomach. I clocked in and cut up four mice, grabbed my bits box and glove, and walked down to Archimedes. From his mew Bodhi clacked his beak at me. "I'll take you out later today," I promised.

The snowy squawked and spread his wings on his stump, eyes fixed on the Astroturf tied to his perch.

"Is your stomach growling, too?"

I sat on his steps and composed myself for the training session. Too easy to rush in and mess the bird up—I had to approach these few minutes deliberately. Couldn't think about my own hunger, the dead baby, my childless state. The maple trees above us dangled only a few remaining leaves after the previous night's rainstorm, and a cool wind rustled them with the promise of a downpour this afternoon. I breathed in through my nose, sound of the ocean in the back of my throat as a yoga teacher had once taught me, gently blew air out through parted lips and stood up to begin a mindfulness practice that would've shocked the socks off the Dalai Lama.

I walked to the perch and set a bit of mouse on the Astroturf. Archimedes chortled, flew over, and gobbled it up. I drummed my fingertips against the bits box. He stared at my hand. His feet splayed on the green plastic, curved talons gleaming. For an instant I recalled the anguish of a hawk's talon impaled in my hand. *Breathe.* I held my gloved arm flat, parallel to the perch, and offered a bit in my other hand. Archimedes touched his right foot to my glove and chirped his begging call as I gave him the food.

My heart pounded under my ed team jacket. "You touched the glove."

But how to get him to put both feet on it so I could jess him up and walk him around? Again, my fingers drummed the bits box and his head swiveled, ears focused on the sound.

Professional trainers called this an auditory cue. I understood vaguely that the tapping represented a starting bell, of sorts, an indication that work had begun. I lifted my glove to his perch once more, holding up a bit. He set his entire right foot on my wrist. I handed him food. "Good bird."

We practiced over and over—me drumming fingers on the bits box, him stepping his right foot on the glove for food—until, when he'd performed the task correctly ten times, I reached into the bits box to find it empty.

He looked up at me. I tapped his left foot. He paused and spread his wings as if to fly, then chirruped and stepped both feet onto my arm.

"Good work!"

Archimedes weighed twice as much as Bodhi, that is to say, a good three pounds. His powerful toes squeezed my wrist. This close, I could see his beak needed trimming—the hooked end curved dangerously close to my face. Still, he stood solid on my glove.

There's a technique in behavior modification called "jackpotting"—you offer an animal a giant reward for highly desirable behavior, a holiday bonus of sorts. Archimedes had jackpotted me. In return, as he stepped backward off my glove and onto his perch, I reached into my pocket and pulled out the chick I'd been saving for Bodhi.

He swallowed it whole, then rose and soared around his mew in what looked less like consternation, and more like an exuberant white victory lap.

———

In the clinic I told Jonathan what Archimedes had accomplished. He walked to the sink to wash his hands. "That's wonderful, love. Good day for the ferruginous, too—she ate a whole quail on the glove. Course, she tried to eat my finger, too."

"Training birds is prepping you two for parenthood." Laurin looked up from cutting a swath of leather into jess strips and smiled.

"Not gonna happen." I examined Jonathan's gashed finger. "Vietnam's a bust."

He didn't argue otherwise. "It's a mess over there. We've got to pull out."

We hadn't told anyone about the referral of the Vietnamese baby, and we didn't reveal his death now. But Laurin looked at us with sad eyes. "I'm so sorry, you guys."

"It's okay."

Jonathan and I spoke the words synonymously. At that moment we honestly believed them.

Between working with two owls and visiting Lorax in her mew to maintain rapport, I found myself up at the center two and three hours a day. Archimedes learned to stand on my glove as I threaded swivels into his jesses. I walked meditative circles around his mew and trained him to step onto a scale. At three pounds, he stood on the small side for a snowy. Jonathan taught me to bury my fingers in his fluffy white chest to feel the muscles around his keel, testing for tone. "If you can feel that bone prominently, you've gotta feed him up."

Inside the mew I prodded Archimedes' chest with tentative fingers. Jean was right—it felt like putting my hand inside a down comforter. He roused under my fingers, and I stepped back.

"From the looks of him, he's doing great." From outside the mew Jonathan regarded the owl sitting calmly on my glove. His voice grew teasing. "To think that six years ago, you were the girl who didn't even know what a raptor was. Let's go grab a burrito."

I didn't dare look away from the owl. "Not right now. I want to work with him some more."

"I'll bring you back something."

"Junior veggie, no cilantro or sour cream, yes guacamole."

When he'd walked off I tapped the bits box at my side, distracting the owl from our move through the doorway and out into the open air. I handed him a bit and he chirped as he swallowed it, looking about at the trees and bushes, at Lorax pouncing on a stuffed Audubon hawk in her mew.

Unlike Bodhi and Lorax, Archimedes didn't triangulate. His body remained still, calm, as if he knew exactly where he was. At the sound of Jonathan's truck rumbling down the driveway, he swiveled his head, squeezing my arm with his toes. I looked up, too—thought I glimpsed something white between my husband's fingers. The owl shifted on my wrist and gave a low woof.

I wiped my hands on my jeans and, without thinking, reached up to scratch his head. He went rigid under my fingers, then relaxed into them.

Scratching an owl is like petting a cat—it's intuitive. The animal under your hand lets you know through subtle movements where the preening feels best. Archimedes leaned into my fingertips, telling me to scratch behind his ears, and then under the feathered discs surrounding his eyes. He closed his eyes and I rubbed the naked lids, stifling laughter.

Darcy appeared at the top of the path, the red-shouldered hawk on her glove. "Didn't think you had it in you," she told me. "You're too sensitive about everything. Still, you must be doing something right. IAATE's looking for papers for the Amsterdam conference. You should totally write one about training Archimedes. Jonathan could take photos for a slide show."

I looked up at her, surprised. "But I'm not a real trainer." Below us the UPS truck began its thunderous ascent up the driveway. The bird on my glove spread his wings. "I'd better get him back to the mew."

The owl bated as we walked through his door, spooked by the mosquito netting, and I had to kneel beside him on the ground as Jean had done, to untangle his feet from the leash and unclip his jesses. He returned to my glove panting and clacking his beak. I breathed deeply, waiting for him to calm down, then gave him a mouse and returned him to his perch. He flew to his stump and puffed up his feathers, chittering madly as the truck rumbled back down the road.

He wasn't perfectly trained, but now I had two reinforcements—food and massage. I had bargaining power and an undeniable bond with the bird. I tossed him his plastic ball stuffed with new alpaca wool, and he leaped on it, ripping the fluffy stuff out with his beak. In the next mew Bodhi stood meticulously extracting mealworms and shredded newspaper from the paper towel tube I'd made him.

Outside the mew, headed for the clinic, I became aware of an ache in my hand. Archimedes had footed it; a small puncture wound reddened on my palm. I wiped the blood off on my jeans and walked up to the bathroom to wash out the hole. Jonathan walked in with a bag of burritos. "Thanks." I unwrapped mine and kissed him, wrinkled my nose. "What smells like cigarettes?"

"There was a guy smoking outside the burrito place. Inside was so crowded, I had to stand there for a while waiting for our order."

"Doesn't the smell make you want to smoke again?"

He unwrapped his burrito and let himself out the clinic door. "I get cravings. It's no big deal. Are you gonna go to work with Bodhi?"

I shook my head, followed him outside. "He's busy with his meal-worm tube."

We sat on the carcass freezer to eat. The first drops of the new storm pattered on corrugated plastic above our heads. "What about adopting from Korea?" Jonathan said. "My sister says the foster parents hug the kids constantly; they're not left alone to languish in cribs like babies from some countries. They're played with and talked to, and they're healthy."

"I can't even think about this right now." I told him what Darcy had said about proposing a paper for the IAATE conference. "It's held in February at the largest bird park in the Netherlands. Three days of work-shops and lectures, nights spent boating down the river and touring the red-light district. Doesn't it sound like fun?"

"Prostitutes and bird trainers? Sounds like a blast."

"We'd have to pay our own way."

The organization didn't compensate presenters, and we'd have to cover airfare, hotel, and food. We had just enough money in our savings account to handle the expense . . . if we gave up our plans of international adoption.

"What if you write the paper and I take photos of you and Archi-medes, and we'll figure out the rest later?" Jonathan reached for my hand, looked into my eyes. "I want you to do this, Melissa. It'll help you heal."

With his encouragement I penned a humorous essay about my experi-ences as a naive but well-intentioned volunteer who, with help from fel-low volunteers and staff, managed to get an irascible snowy owl up on the glove. Jonathan read it a few days later, sitting on the couch with Cody on his lap.

"A Love for the Glove." He repeated my title. "It's smart and witty. You've got a good chance of this getting accepted." He set the pages down and picked up the dog brush. "Most of the papers are written by zoo professionals, and you're a volunteer. I'll bet the conference directors find your perspective unique."

"Or stupid," I laughed.

I e-mailed the paper. For weeks I didn't hear back. Ridiculous to think such an association would even consider my experience as worthy. I threw myself into teaching, took my feature writing class up to the center for a field trip and brought Bodhi and Archimedes out on the glove for them.

"I want to volunteer." One of the twenty-somethings—a fearless rock climber and an already impressive essayist—appeared at my elbow with an application in hand.

"You'll love it," I told her. "It's endlessly surprising. I learn something every single day."

What I'd learned that morning, meditating in Bodhi's mew before my class arrived, was that I had no desire to pursue international adoption any further. I knew enough now about behavior modification to understand that punishment is a powerful motivator. You scare an owl by yelling and rushing and strapping it to your glove, and the bird's going to fly up into the highest reaches of the mew where you can't get at it. Likewise, you frighten a couple of potential parents by offering them an ultimatum and a baby who dies, and that hopeful mommy and daddy will run for the hills . . . or in our case, the Netherlands.

Six weeks after Archimedes made his debut outdoors on the glove in front of his mew, I got an e-mail from IAATE's secretary. "We'd like to invite you to present your paper at our annual conference in February."

I thought about the decision for about five minutes. Jonathan and I could spend the next months preparing for an exotic overseas conference, or we could sit at home wondering when and if we'd ever adopt a kid. One felt exciting, the other just sad.

I closed my laptop and called him at work.

"My love, grab your camera. We're going to Amsterdam."

23

A Baby Who Hasn't Been Harmed

ON THE SHUTTLE TO THE AVIFAUNA HOTEL IN ALPHEN AAN DEN RIJN outside of Amsterdam, a young Texan with a huge belt buckle and an attitude to match flashed us a wide, lazy smile. "Bird trainers know how to par-tay!"

He scanned the shuttle, letting his eyes rest on a young blond woman in a tight red dress and knee-high boots. "Elephant trainers go to bed way too early, and the big cat trainers are sensitive and prissy. But us bird people . . ." He let out a whistle that sounded remarkably like our director's African gray parrot. "Let's just say the dance tonight is gonna be *wild*."

The dance, hosted by IAATE, functioned as an icebreaker before the weekend-long conference. But Jonathan and I, enamored of our hotel room overlooking the bird park with its free-ranging ostriches and cranes, disdained the dance and climbed instead into the king-size bed with the sliding glass door open, the better to hear the park's owls. While other trainers competed in the ballroom to see who could imitate the best bird-mating dance, Jonathan and I engaged in our own. "Bird trainers," I whispered a Texas drawl into his ear, "know how to par-tay!"

Later, jet-lagged and logy from a late-night order of French fries with mayonnaise, I fell asleep with my head against the trio of ravens tattooed on his chest and the screech of resident barn owls in my ears.

The next day, I woke early and walked the grounds of the park, past flocks of ducks and cages of hornbills and Egyptian vultures—their skinny necks encased in white-feathered ruffs. Five snowy owls stood around a crumbling miniature stone castle. I missed Archimedes. Jean had promised to feed him in my absence, building rapport so she could eventually work with him, as well. A crane sailed overhead, and I glanced at my watch, then jogged back to the hotel.

I liked to give my journalism students an essay from the *Utne Reader* titled "How I Got My DIY Degree at the University of Planet Earth." In it the writer talks about how he learned about the world through attending global conferences on a variety of subjects. I wondered what he'd think of the IAATE lectures with their topics that ranged from how to teach your buzzard to run an obstacle course to how to use telemetry to find your hawk when it takes off during a show and disappears into the sky.

"Oh god, I'm nervous." At a break I clutched Jonathan's arm. Most of the people around us got paid to do what we did as volunteers. Would they even consider me legitimate, with my temperamental snowy owl who neither ran obstacle courses nor free-flew on command to a rat-bated perch?

"I mean, all he does is sit on the glove. Big deal."

"You'll be great." Jonathan led me over to the raffle table. The big prize, the one I and everyone else coveted, was a week at Natural Encounters, studying with Steve Martin and his bird-training colleagues.

"Where is Steve?" I wondered.

The woman next to me nodded toward the podium, where three people stood with their heads together over the sound system. "He's right there."

The man appeared unassuming, in jeans and a white button-up shirt; still, when it was my turn to walk up to the podium to give my presentation, I locked eyes with him and nearly passed out.

And yet something comes over me when I hit a stage. The vaudevillian spirit of my great-grandparents goads me to deliver the goods, and fear seems an undeserved luxury. I looked away from Steve and scanned the audience, their faces upturned and waiting. Louise met my eyes. I thought of how, years ago, I'd begun volunteering at her center simply to get close to Jonathan. I never dreamed I'd be standing at a podium in front of her and hundreds of professional bird handlers, presenting a paper on a volunteer position I adored.

"My improbable work as a snowy owl trainer," I said into the microphone, "began with a chicken."

The crowd burst into laughter. I continued with my speech and Jonathan's images on the screen behind me, ending with film footage of Archimedes eating mice on my glove. Applause echoed in the cavernous ballroom, and I walked down the steps shaking, grateful to sink into my seat.

"Love, that was terrific." Jonathan put his arm around me, then removed it and stood up as Steve Martin walked over. I stood up, too, and the man clasped my hand.

"Wonderful." He smiled into my eyes. "Simply delightful. Thank you."

IAATE's director called a break then. Jonathan went to refresh his coffee, and I walked around the auditorium, looking at bird books and training paraphernalia for sale.

"Would you like to buy one?" A young Dutch man, observing my interest in a photo of a fuzzy fledgling snowy owl, stepped up to me with a binder full of raptor pictures.

"Oh no." I shook my head. "My husband's a photographer, and our house is full of photos already. But thank you."

The man raised an eyebrow. "We're not selling the pictures. We're selling the owls."

"The *actual* owls?"

He nodded. "Yes, miss. Trainers like to get them just hatched. They're easier to work with that way."

He cocked his head and twisted his lips into a wry smile. "Look, I did like your talk—it was funny—but the truth is, most trainers would never attempt to work with your raptors. They're orphaned and injured—*traumatized*, is that the right word? It's much easier to start with a baby who hasn't been harmed."

I nodded. "I know what you mean."

After the presentations that day, Jonathan and I wandered through the bird park to a giant playground that boasted the longest slide in the Netherlands. He wielded his camera, and I climbed the stairs up into the tower painted to look like a bird. "I'm exhausted!" I panted from the top.

Down below, children skittered around the swings and lesser slides. They hollered from the merry-go-round and pulled themselves across a small stream on a wooden raft. Two of them clambered up after me—a red-cheeked little girl and boy. "You gonna go down?" they asked.

"You bet."

I hurled myself down the slide and into darkness. It lasted much longer than I expected, and when the slide finally propelled me out into the late-afternoon sunlight, I blinked at the kids and parents around me, befuddled.

"Got a good shot of you," Jonathan called, but I couldn't answer. A sharp sadness propelled me through the park as if sprinting for some finish line, and I huddled behind the falling-down castle with its comforting quintet of snowy owls.

Jonathan found me at last. I looked up at him, stricken. "Oh, love. We've spent all our money . . . but I still want a child."

⚬

That winter, my sister gave birth to her little boy. The first order of business was a bris. She and her husband planned to host the celebration of their baby's circumcision in their pretty Orange County condo.

"That's the weekend of a major opening at the museum." Jonathan shook his head over the invitation. "No way I can go."

I booked a flight and a hotel room, hoping the time away from each other would bring clarity. We hadn't officially pulled out of the Vietnam program, but we'd received no referrals for months. I had no idea what we'd say if the agency sent us another profile and photo.

Distracted and distraught at the idea of meeting my new nephew without even the promise of a child of my own, I left my wallet on a chair in San Francisco's airport. Without cab fare I had to call my mother and her partner to pick me up from John Wayne Airport. "Honey, I'll put the hotel room on my credit card," my mother said, "and we can loan you money for food."

"Thanks," I muttered. Inadequacy overwhelmed me. I longed to get on the next plane back to Eugene. Instead, I walked into my sister's sunny living room to find a cloth-covered table on which sat a pillow and two silver candlesticks. A tray of gleaming silver instruments lay nearby.

All I knew of the bris ceremony came from a *South Park* episode titled "Ike's Wee Wee." My sister set me straight. "The circumcision's a physical sign of the covenant between God and Jewish people, followed by a damned good meal."

She led me into the dining room and pointed out the sumptuous deli platters and introduced a crowd of modish friends and in-laws. Confused about the dress code and delighted with a Southern California reprieve from the Northwest winter, I'd put on sports sandals and shorts and my "Seize the prey" T-shirt.

"You can borrow a dress," my sister whispered.

"I'm okay. Hey, where's my nephew?"

"Sleeping."

She led me up the stairs to the nursery. I registered the room's perfection—the matching crib and nursing chair, the baby's name painted in wooden letters and hung on the cream-colored wall, the little bureau with one drawer half open to reveal dozens of symmetrically folded cloth diapers. I tiptoed across the white carpet and peeked down at the infant in his white onesie.

"Isn't he beautiful?" Without warning my sister's serenity crumpled. "Oh, Lissa, what if something goes wrong with the procedure? He's still so little . . ."

"I . . . don't know." We had no comparable ceremony in the world of raptors. There were coping parties—weekends devoted to trimming our resident birds' beaks and talons—but I sensed it would be imprudent to make such a comparison now. All I could do was hug Katie, and then leave her alone with her new son for a few minutes before the ceremony.

I paused at the door and watched her bend to pick him up. For an instant I saw her again at eight, blond and pigtailed and clasping her doll dressed in pink gingham. But then she stood up, mid-thirties and beautiful, with a baby at her breast.

I closed the door and walked downstairs to greet the mohel.

He was the guy, trained in both religion and medicine, who'd perform the circumcision. He barreled into my sister's living room like Topol, straight out of *Fiddler on the Roof,* with his yarmulke and prayer shawl and prominent Brooklyn accent. He shook my hand and beamed. "Mazel tov, big sister. This your first bris? Mine, too."

Three minutes later, he used the same line on my mother.

The ego can be a ridiculous thing, robbing a day of wonder and fun. That morning, I stood in a corner of the living room half-hidden behind a bassinet and tried to focus on the celebration, but desperate thoughts circled in my head. As the big sister I was used to hitting all the milestones first—lost baby teeth, graduation, a career. Now Katie raced ahead of me in motherhood. She knew how to feed and diaper a baby, how to throw a great party a week after his birth, immersing herself in a world I might never get to share.

I stood on the hall steps with my mother, and we parted respectfully as my sister and her husband descended with their swaddled infant. I'd done enough research to know that in some Jewish families, a childless couple carries the infant to the mother as a sort of charm to ensure that they'll soon have a baby of their own. I'd hoped for the honor as a sort of last-ditch appeal to whatever god might have influence over Jonathan's and my adoption, but Katie simply handed the baby to the mohel, who offered the kid a cloth soaked in Manischewitz to suck on.

My mother elbowed me. "I'd like a piece of that cloth."

"He's also had a topical painkiller and some Tylenol," the mohel assured us. My sister clutched her husband's arm, her eyes full of tears. The mohel made a speech, a sort of call-and-response answered in turn by the grandparents and parents. "I invite those of you who would like to step into the kitchen for a glass of celebratory wine to do so now." The big man let his gaze sweep the room, and my mother whispered in my ear.

"He's about to do the operation. This is his way of giving squeamish people an out."

"You leaving?"

"Hell, no. You?"

I shook my head. In-laws in the front row crowded close, murmuring Yiddish words. Katie handed over her baby and buried her head in her husband's chest. The father-in-law placed the child on the pillow and held onto one leg. My brother-in-law held onto the other, and my sister held her son's tiny hands. The circumcision took all of a minute. Afterward the mohel bandaged up the boy. He dispelled the room's tension by holding up an infant-size prayer shawl that bore a sticker with his website.

The crowd laughed, excepting my sister. I longed to embrace her post-ceremony, but she clutched her wailing baby to her chest and headed for the stairs, pushing past my mother and me. "Be back . . . just need a few minutes."

Katie's mother-in-law walked over and hugged me. "Mazel tov! If you and Jonathan have a baby, it'll look like your nephew's twin."

"We're not having a baby. We're . . . we're trying to adopt."

I knew then that I couldn't give up on my hope of having a family. Jonathan and I would figure it out, somehow. But I didn't tell this to the elegant woman in front of me.

"*Adopt?*" she repeated, lip curled. She rolled her eyes at my mother. "Well . . . at least it's something."

Angry words flew to my lips. I bit them back and laid one trembling hand on my mother's arm. "Ah . . . pardon me for a minute. I'm gonna go call Jonathan, let him know I made it."

I walked outside to dial and told him what had happened. Behind a line of arborvitae, I gave in to self-pity and wept. "No one understands how hard the wait's been. Katie's son is beautiful, and—oh, Jonathan, I still want a child."

"It's okay." He dropped into his most mellifluous voice, reassuring me as if I were some freaked-out hawk. "We're still adopting. Nothing has changed."

My mother appeared at the door, heard my voice, and peered behind the row of scrubby trees. "Everything all right?"

I nodded. "I have to go."

"Stay strong," Jonathan said, and again, "Nothing has changed."

But he was wrong. In my mind everything felt altered.

In the dining room Katie's friends from high school gathered around the platters of lox and cheese and salads in their miniskirts and stilettos. Two years older, I'd known them only slightly, reporting on their cheer-leading and drill team troupes for the yearbook and closing my bedroom door against their incessant giggling as I labored over math homework.

Now they held babies and toddlers in their arms and fed their kids pieces of bagel. "How are you up there in Oregon?" they asked with urgent kindness. "Do you like it? What do you do for fun?"

I stopped their kind, incessant questioning with a sentence for which I knew they had no frame of reference, a sentence that buoyed my self-worth just enough that I didn't have to follow my sister up the stairs and collapse sobbing on her guest bed.

"I train owls."

I flew from Orange County back to Eugene without telling my family about the little dead Vietnamese boy. As I waited near baggage claim for my suitcase, three large-format photos of children caught my eye. I'd seen the pictures at the airport before, each framed on an easel; vaguely, I recalled them as images of Oregon foster kids. One eye on the carousel, I wandered over to the display and read a brochure at the bottom of one easel.

The photos represented part of the Heart Gallery, a national project alerting people to foster children available for adoption. Apparently, over one hundred twenty thousand kids waited for families—not temporary, but permanent. Fourteen thousand of the children lived in Oregon.

One picture showed a five-year-old boy laughing in a pile of autumn leaves. In another, three little boys embraced. The last picture showed a beautiful twelve-year-old girl nuzzling a white rat. I stared at her image, dismayed. What must it feel like to reach the seventh grade with only a rodent for comfort?

I pocketed a brochure and ran over to the carousel for my suitcase. On the way home from the airport, I called Jonathan at work. "Look up the Heart Gallery when you have time. I think it might be the answer to our problems."

"Do you know about the Heart Gallery kids?"

I called Marissa that evening, after dutifully reporting the details of my nephew's bris to Jonathan. If our social worker felt dismay at being summoned during her dinner hour, she hid it behind her laconic tone.

"Of course. They're children from DHS—Department of Human Services—relinquished by biological parents and up for adoption."

"So Jonathan and I could adopt one of these kids?"

"Well . . . yes."

"How much does it cost? Are we talking another twenty thousand?"

"It's free."

"*Free?*"

Jonathan's brow shot up. "Free?"

"So how come this is the first time we've heard about it?"

"You applied to adopt internationally, my dear."

"How exactly do we get one of these kids?"

"Fill out an application at the local DHS office and go to their orientation meeting. It's all day on a Saturday, in a couple weeks, I think. Your home study's done; I can rewrite it so it's applicable to their program. Hold on a sec . . ."

She paused and I heard her speak in a muffled voice, telling someone to finish a casserole if that person wanted chocolate cake for dessert. "Sorry. If you're really interested," she said, "come by my office and look at the binder. Every week, DHS sends bulletins—bios and photos of foster kids up for adoption. About thirty a month. You can look at them and get a better idea of what you'd be getting into."

"Do you know much about the program?"

In the background I heard children laughing and a dog barking. "Well, sure." She chuckled. "I adopted my child through DHS."

"Wow. Okay, then. How does it work? Caseworkers match us with a kid?"

"Nope, you choose. It's like our agency's Waiting Child program—you have control over what disabilities you're willing to take on. Only this way, you've got more information because the kids are from this country with tons of documentation."

"Disabilities? These kids are disabled?"

At the stove, grilling salmon, Jonathan frowned.

"DHS kids are mostly taken from parents because of abuse and neglect. Sometimes the kids have mental and/or physical issues. You choose the ones you're comfortable with. Or none. That's fine, too."

"Okay. Thanks." I hung up and updated Jonathan. "Can we handle this?"

He looked up from the brochure and the photo of the girl with the rat. "Is it any crazier than going to the Netherlands to give a lecture on training snowy owls?" He pulled me to him and kissed me. "This feels like the right thing to do."

<hr />

We hadn't been to our agency in almost a year, since our final Parents in Progress meeting. The place remained unchanged. Same play area with its shelf of kids' toys, same rack of magazines, same photos of the matriarch in her kimono and elegant updo.

Jonathan walked up to the receptionist's desk. "Is Marissa here? We're interested in taking a look at the kids from DHS."

She disappeared behind a partition, then emerged with a thick red binder. "She's gone, but she left a note saying you two are welcome to look through this. Careful—it's heavy."

We sat on the couch in the play area and opened the binder to the picture of a little African-American boy with a wide, happy smile. "His legal name is Peanut?" Jonathan shook his head. "Who does that to a kid?"

"Four years old," I read. "Slight global developmental delays, born exposed to methamphetamines. Loves cars and airplanes and plastic dinosaurs."

I read through the biography of a little blond girl named Chrissy. "Mother did cocaine while pregnant, father busted for armed robbery. Both parents homeless; she's been in foster care since birth. These kids sound like characters in a Charles Dickens novel."

Jonathan kept reading. "She loves cats and books and playing princess."

"*Princess?*"

"Doesn't her love of cats and books cancel out that transgression?"

We bantered that afternoon, excitement quickening our words. But most of the biographies unsettled us. We couldn't fathom adopting three siblings who'd been sexually abused, or any child older than, say, five. We wanted a girl, and preferably one without severe developmental delays, which left us with three choices in a binder of hundreds.

Jonathan dog-eared the pages. "Can you make photocopies of these for us?" he appealed to the young woman behind the counter. "We're supposed to give the case numbers to Marissa so she can submit our home study."

The woman glanced at Chrissy's photo. "What a cutie."

Jonathan and I beamed at each other. "That's what we thought."

We regrouped at Papa's Soul Food Kitchen over fried catfish and yams and black-eyed peas. While we waited for our food, I called Marissa. She explained that our home study could be rolled over from international to domestic, as could our fingerprints and our recommendation forms. But we'd have to sit through another eight weeks of parenting classes.

"Even though we already took your agency's workshop?"

"Look, most of the classes will be repeats, I know, but we don't want anything to go wrong. If someone at DHS decides when you're about to go to committee for a child that you haven't jumped through the right hoops, you're gonna be really sorry."

"Go to committee?"

"The kid's caseworker chooses three families from the submitted home studies. A committee decides on a match."

Our food arrived. I thanked Marissa and hung up. Over the meal Jonathan and I quietly discussed the photocopied bulletins folded up in my backpack. She'd cautioned us to keep them to ourselves; some of the children and their foster and birth parents might live in Eugene.

As we stood up to pay our bill, an Anglo couple walked in with their young Chinese daughter. She was gorgeous, with silky black ponytails and a lively high-pitched voice.

So often, we think we can guess our destiny. We're so certain we know what it looks like that we forget to open ourselves up to the pleasure of surprise.

Sometimes surprise can be a bitch. The next afternoon, Marissa called as I cleaned Archimedes' mew. He barked at the buzzing in my back pocket. I carried my cell to the entryway and rolled his wool-stuffed ball toward his stump.

Marissa kept her voice neutral. "I have an ethical dilemma you probably don't want to deal with today, but you have to. There's a referral for you, from Vietnam."

"Another kid from the Waiting Child program?"

"No. A healthy baby boy with a sparkling biography. Not a single red flag. And Melissa . . . he's gorgeous."

24

A Rescue Attempt

MARISSA SAT DOWN BESIDE ME ON THE PORCH STEPS. DAFFODILS lifted their bright heads from the English ivy around us, and new leaves trembled on the Japanese maples outside the front door. "Yep," I agreed. "He's adorable."

The Vietnamese boy was six months old, chubby-cheeked, with big black eyes and a head full of hair. "Found at birth blue and shivering," I read, "but developmentally on track and able to form attachments. Are they *sure*?"

"They are." She flipped to a page of handwritten notes. "I spoke to the foster mother myself, and we've got several doctors' reports. This kid looks great."

"But travel to Vietnam will cost thousands."

"Correct."

"And DHS is free."

"Correct."

"And his bio mom might have done drugs and drank while she was pregnant?"

"You'll never know the whole story about any child you adopt."

I looked into her eyes. "You can't tell me what you'd recommend, can you?"

"Sorry."

"All right, then." We stood up, and she headed down the steps. "Jonathan and I will talk about it when he gets home from work and e-mail you our decision."

"Sleep on it if you need to. We want to make sure this little guy gets a great home."

That afternoon, Jonathan and I stood in the prey barn together and cleaned mouse aquariums and talked about the new child. He admitted the little guy's biography ranked among the least frightening we'd seen.

"We'd need to go to Hanoi to get him in six months." I transferred a litter of pink baby mice to an empty tea box while I scrubbed out their cage. "But now, after our trip to Amsterdam, we've got no money and no time off."

Jonathan held a black-and-white spotted mouse in his palm, stroking its long, silky fur with a finger. He thought a long time before he spoke. "I think of the family who will get this boy if we don't take him. They're gonna be so excited." He placed the mouse on its exercise wheel. "Doesn't he deserve their excitement instead of our ambivalence?"

I peeled off my gloves and wrapped my arms around Jonathan's neck. "I want a little girl who really needs *us*."

He nodded, kissed me full on the mouth while baby chicks peeped in our ears. "That's my feeling, too."

That night, he e-mailed Marissa:

After much discussion and thought, Melissa and I have decided that we're finding ourselves more excited about adopting from DHS. I think it's the right choice for us, as we've noticed a marked difference in our reactions to the children. I hope this is acceptable, and I hope that no one will be hurt by this decision.

She sent a reply the next morning:

I commend your decision—I know it wasn't easy. No one but you knew what was right for your family, and this was the right choice for you.

That weekend, Jonathan and I stood in our nursery and hung the owl-print curtains I'd sewn. We still had no crib, no changing table, no rocking chair or dresser. But now, after a year and a half, we finally had conviction.

In DHS classes led by two wry social workers who spent their own money providing parents-to-be with a table full of refreshments each week, we discovered that—like raptors—some children fared no better at the hands of unskilled adults. We learned of babies born addicted to every substance imaginable, toddlers who'd been burned and molested and abandoned wailing twelve hours a day in their own excrement, preteens who—having survived to twelve years old—couldn't tolerate physical touch or eye contact or the thought that they might not be completely and utterly worthless.

At the raptor center we cared for a screech owl whose feathers had been singed off. A couple had heard the bird calling from their chimney and built a fire, hoping to smoke it out.

"All you had to do was call us for help." The director examined the bird with her mouth set and her eyes fierce. "One of our volunteers would have rushed over with a net and a box and caught the bird for you."

The owl's tiny talons had melted, along with its feather shafts, and for weeks those of us working in the clinic held our breath against the nauseating scent of burnt keratin.

Injuries to raptors sometimes took the form of accidental actions involving beaver traps, tree removal, and rodenticides. For months we'd been ministering to a screech owl perched in a treatment room carrier with its head tilted at a ninety-degree angle—quizzical and cute for an instant, but ultimately tragic because the bird had ingested a hell of a lot of rat poison.

"The center's like a big foster family," I told Jonathan as I held skinned chicken up to the screech owl's beak. "We care for the birds while they heal, and then hopefully they go on to a permanent home."

But not all birds moved on, and some children languished in foster homes until high school graduation, when they found themselves out on the street.

"Foster farms." That's how the more jaded young adults in DHS described houses run by some foster parents who appeared interested only in cashing the state's slim paycheck for each child and providing a Spartan bed-and-breakfast before shooing their charges out the door to school, after which the kids would catch a bus to the Boys and Girls Club or to the station downtown until dinner and bedtime.

Other foster parents seemed to Jonathan and me just short of candidates for sainthood. People in our weekly class spoke in reverent tones about a woman named Molly who'd been taking on the most difficult boys in foster care for decades—severely disabled little guys with intense medical needs and something called reactive attachment disorder, which manifested itself in all sorts of unsavory ways.

Our social workers mentioned Molly on the night they discussed RAD, and explained that kids afflicted with the disorder could be withdrawn, angry, even murderous. I'd listened to a story on *This American Life* by a mother who'd adopted a six-year-old Romanian orphan—a victim of Nicolae Ceaușescu's rule—with reactive attachment disorder, a child who'd tried to kill her before the mother hit upon the novel idea of tying him to her body night and day for months, and holding him close even while he trembled with rage. Here was the neediest child imaginable. I knew, with a guilty heart, that I could never mother a boy like that. Thank goodness some parents could rise to the challenge.

"I guess you could call me the mini-Molly." The frizzy-haired woman sitting beside me in a skull-and-crossbones T-shirt and an ankle-length gypsy skirt stood up numerous times that night to share tales from her own foster parenting frontlines. She stuck her hands on her hips and flashed an accusatory look around the room. "I have a thirteen-year-old boy in my house right now whose parents sexually abused him, and he still poops in his pants. Then he tosses them into the dryer with my clean laundry."

Collectively, the crowd around her gasped. She smiled grimly, satisfied with the reaction, and bobbed her head like an owl. "No one puts shit in with my good bath towels, y'hear?"

One of the social workers held up a big bowl of candy—rewards for our answering questions and sharing anecdotes such as those delivered by Mini-Molly. The social worker's eyes sparkled behind her glasses. "Give this woman some candy . . . but for God's sake, don't give her a Tootsie Roll."

⌒⌒

"Most parents adopting from DHS look for healthy white babies."

Marissa delivered an envelope of new bulletins one afternoon and lingered on the doorstep to chat. A dozen gray bushtits congregated on the suet feeder dangling from the porch eaves. Above us I heard the playful squeaks of Cooper's hawks flirting in the firs. "Only one or two of them come up each month for adoption, so you can imagine the hundreds of home studies their social workers get. I know you're tired of waiting. As you're going through this batch of bulletins, think outside the box. I'm not saying adopt a teen, but you might look beyond a perfectly healthy white one-year-old child."

"Of course." The three girls we'd chosen from the agency's binder had already gone to committee and found homes, and so we were looking at those kids who'd just become legally free of parents who'd relinquished them. "We're totally open to kids of other ethnicities. I mean, we were going to adopt from Asia."

Marissa nodded. "Sure, but I don't just mean race. You're gonna see disabilities that scare you—babies born exposed and addicted, with developmental delays. Don't automatically write them off—most kids in foster care have some delays that go away with good parenting and therapeutic support."

The obvious hierarchy of state adoption bothered me more than I cared to admit. Most people wanted the easy kids, the ones who wouldn't present bizarre challenges like RAD or feces in the clothes dryer. I understood this desire from my work at the raptor center. Handlers loved to work with the Level One birds—the imprinted kestrel and the one-eyed screech owl and Lorax—who'd step up on almost anyone's glove if offered a mouse. Level One birds seldom offered surprises, and new handlers gained confidence and skill working with a raptor that essentially trained them.

Level Two birds were trickier—the equivalent of, say, a three-year-old who's seen some hard times already. They demanded more attention, more finesse in their training plans, but—like the spotted owl Jonathan worked with—once they appeared out on the glove, the handler could relish a certain satisfaction in having conquered footing and biting and bating behaviors to shape those more pleasing for public display.

The Level Three birds, Archimedes among them, reminded me of the battle-scarred foster teens I met outside the DHS office. Committing to one of these raptors or kids required an incredible amount of patience.

In spite of a trainer's best efforts, he or she might not have success in extinguishing undesirable actions. Even now, if a baby stroller or wheelchair got too close to Archimedes, he'd leap off my glove and hang until I guided him back to my arm with one hand on his back. Still, I could handle a Level Three owl; at any time, if the pressure overwhelmed us, I could walk away from him and his mew.

I couldn't walk away from my child.

Jonathan returned from work, and we sat down on the window seat to look at the bulletins. We bypassed several teen boys and girls, feeling like assholes as we discarded their bios without reading them. "I think there's no one here for . . . wait, what about this one?"

The toddler's name was Minerva, not a lyrical moniker, to be sure, but I appreciated the mythological reference. She was fifteen months old, of indeterminate race, with straight black hair and dark eyebrows, eager brown eyes, and a pretty smile. She wore a pink sleeveless dress dotted with blue flowers.

"Look at the way her little ears stick out!" I swooned against Jonathan's shoulder. "How cute."

Jonathan studied the bulletin. "Should we tell Marissa we're interested?"

At DHS we'd learned that the bulletins were designed to lure us in with an adorable photo, whereas the bio was supposed to scare the crap out of us. Minerva's bio struck us as suitably frightening. Her mother did drugs during the pregnancy and relinquished her daughter at birth to medical foster parents who specialized in babies born addicted. Her father was homeless, and no one could find him. According to the bio the baby had developmental delays, but she could crawl and make sounds.

"She likes to rub her face on objects with fur." I reached to pick up Alger Hiss and turned him over like a baby to scratch under his chin. "Wouldn't our house be perfect for her?"

Jonathan read the end of the biography out loud. "Minerva is a very sweet, beautiful child. She'll be easy to fall in love with and deserves the best opportunity to reach her potential."

Sometimes we took in a hard-luck case at the raptor center simply because the bird charmed us. We worked our butts off feeding it around the clock, finding just the right medications, serving its every need in an outside rehab mew for months and months.

Sometimes the bird was worth the gamble, and we released it into the wilderness with effervescent hearts. Other times we had to concede to euthanization.

Aware of my folly, but powerless to stop, I cut Minerva's photo out of the bulletin and stuck it on the refrigerator. "I think we should call Marissa and apply to adopt this child."

Jonathan smiled and picked up his phone.

———— ⌐ ————

A few days after Marissa sent in our home study, I jogged down the hill to the post office and pulled a thick manila envelope from our box. I recognized the name on the return address as Minerva's DHS caseworker. Inside, a stack of reports by Minerva's doctors and early intervention specialists and the caseworker herself.

"Why are we getting this much information already? We just applied three days ago."

Jonathan reached for his cell and put Marissa on speaker phone. "You've been chosen to go to committee for Minerva, so the caseworker sent you her Adoption Child Summary." She paused, and I heard children squabbling in the background. "*Don't* get excited."

I ignored her and hopped up and down in the kitchen, to the delight of all three dogs. "Oh, love! We're going to committee for Minerva." I tapped the photo taped to the refrigerator. "She's gonna be our daughter!"

"Didn't Marissa say you never get the first child you apply for?" Jonathan poured a cup of coffee and doctored it with teaspoons of sugar and nondairy creamer. "Let's read her whole bio before we go too crazy."

The thirty-page packet expanded on the background we'd gotten in Minerva's initial bulletin. Her life story, by page two, hurt to read. Her mother had suffered sexual abuse as a teen, and DHS removed her from her own mom and sent her to foster care, then transferred her to mental health services for threatening to commit suicide. Later, she got arrested for prostitution. Minerva's father had been raised in foster care, too. Homeless, he had a record based on theft, trespassing, and drug abuse.

Both parents were meth addicts, and the bio mom admitted to taking drugs up to the time of Minerva's birth.

"The mother's got two half sisters," I read. "They're drug addicts, too." I closed my eyes, pressed my fingers against my eyelids. "Minerva's parents want an open adoption. How much contact would we have to have? Marissa said most bio families are fine with letters and cards, but what if they want to see her?"

Jonathan stared into his coffee cup. "I'm not sure we want to have contact with them. I mean . . . they're addicts."

"Her doctor says Minerva has trouble eating—she's easily distracted and can't suck on a bottle." I skimmed the grim numbers on her growth charts. "Let's at least take her report to our pediatrician. The doctor'll tell us whether we should be concerned about the meth. Maybe it's not a big deal."

Online, I researched the effects of meth addiction on babies. Oregon's governor had declared the drug of epidemic proportions in our state. Adoptive parents on listservs seemed evenly divided on the subject. Some wrote to say their children were flourishing, top of their class. Others replied in despair with stories of unmanageable ADD and fits of rage. Over and over, I read through Minerva's adoption study, highlighting sentences of concern until most of the paragraphs glowed yellow.

The next day, we hauled the paperwork to the pediatrician near our house and dumped it on her desk. "We need you to give us your assessment of this little girl."

She'd seen such studies before and didn't mind offering her insight to couples hoping to adopt from the state. "Based on this little one's medical history . . ." She pulled her long, dark hair into a hasty ponytail and looked from Jonathan to me in an office filled with children's picture books and pastel drawings of serenely smiling pandas. "You're probably going to see some mental illness and some developmental delays. Her physical development shows her to be very small, and she's not talking. These are problems at her age."

"But in her photo she looks so healthy."

The pediatrician flipped to the front of the packet and Minerva's initial bulletin. "She *is* a beautiful child." She turned the paperwork. "I encourage you to keep tabs on kids born addicted to meth. We used to think crack babies would suffer all sorts of illness as children and teens, but it turns out they're pretty resilient. We may find something similar with this batch of new meth-addicted babies . . . but they haven't grown up enough yet to provide us with a clear longitudinal study."

— ❦ —

I left the doctor's office and headed up to the raptor center. Jean had planned a trip down to see her daughter and wanted me to feed the peregrine falcon she'd been training. Out on the lawn Jean transferred the stunning buff and blue-gray bird to my arm. "Feed her daily on the glove so she gets used to you.

Peregrines had once faced a drug epidemic of sorts. During World War II farmers began to spray DDT on their crops. Smaller birds fed on poisoned seeds and insects; the peregrines ate the birds, and pesticide buildup in their bodies prevented calcium production. The falcon's eggshells got so flimsy that brooding mothers crushed them. Twenty years later, there were no peregrines in the eastern United States. Then, in 1970, government officials listed the birds as endangered.

"Scientists at Cornell began to hatch them in captivity and put them in artificial nests," Jean told me. "They fed them—invisibly, of course— until they were old enough to fly and hunt on their own. Eventually, the population recovered. Now they're no longer endangered."

"And the DDT?"

"Banned from use on crops." She handed me a quail.

The falcon, seeing the prey, snatched it out of my hand and ripped off its head.

"They're pretty messy eaters."

"Ah . . . I see that."

Unlike owls, peregrines don't swallow their prey whole, but instead dismember feathers and feet and wings and pull out the guts in a carnal B-movie horror scene. By the time the bird had finished her meal, tiny brown and white feathers flecked my fleece jacket, and loops of blue-gray and pinkish guts festooned my sneakers. I missed the tidiness of Lorax and Bodhi and Archimedes, the neat pellets they produced.

"How's the adoption going?" Jean stood behind me and tapped the falcon's bare, skinny legs with her glove so it stepped back on her wrist.

I looked around for other volunteers and dropped my voice. "We're looking at a toddler born addicted to meth."

For an instant Jean's face clouded, and then she flashed her broad smile. "Well, that's just great, darlin'. You know, I did crack when I was pregnant, and my daughter went to college at age sixteen. She's twenty-one now, just got a job at Microsoft."

"You did *crack*?"

She nodded. "Addict. Then I got sober and went to work at the women's transitional home and this place. A life of service changes a person."

"No kidding."

I returned her bird and walked away to the clinic with new hope. Jonathan and I didn't have to reject Minerva. Working in her service, we could save her.

⌒‿⌒

At all our previous DHS meetings, potential adoptive parents and those training to be foster parents congregated together in the same cavernous room at the DHS office, united by Styrofoam cups of strong coffee and Oreos and the vast bowl of candy. On the last evening the bespectacled social worker met us in the hall and pointed down a corridor. "Foster parents in this room. You guys looking to adopt a kiddo permanently, here's your place."

She ushered Jonathan and me into a small meeting room and stood in front of a handful of adults—some single, some coupled—most of them around our age, including two men who clasped each other's hands as tightly as Jonathan and I did. Unlike us in our jeans and worn fleece jackets, they gave the distinct impression of having just stepped out of a J. Crew catalog.

"So, just to reiterate . . ." The social worker sat down on the edge of a long table and flashed her bemused grin. "If a committee selects you to be the parent or parents, you have ten days to say no. If you say yes and take the kiddo into your home, we'll visit you once a month for six months to make sure things are working out."

I raised my hand. "Can we spend time with the child before we go to committee?"

If Jonathan and I could just hold Minerva and look into her eyes, I knew we'd be okay.

"Nope. There's no situation room, so to speak. We can't do that to our kiddos—get their hopes up like that. The committee gives you a child, and you get to think about it for ten days. Then you commit, or you don't."

She hopped off the desk and walked to the door. "And now for the fun part of this series—I've invited a panel to share their adoption experiences with you."

A man and woman walked in toting a giant pink scrapbook. They were followed by a bearded man a little older than us with a sandy-haired girl who looked to be about eleven. They took seats at the table in front of us and looked over at the social worker. She pointed at the couple with the scrapbook. "Why don't you go first."

The woman flushed, but she opened the book and held it up with obvious pride, displaying page after page of her child's photos surrounded by press-on letters, colorful geometric cutouts, and little wooden doodads in the shapes of balloons and horses. "This is our daughter's life book," she told us. "We had two biological kids already, and we had so much fun with them that we wanted to open up our home to another child, you know, to be of service. They all get along beautifully. Here's our family at the coast, and camping at Crater Lake, and skiing at Hoodoo . . ." She chuckled self-consciously. "Why don't I pass it around so the people in the back can see it, too."

When the book came to me, I looked down at the happy family portraits with dismay. I'm no scrapbooker; half the time, I forget to transfer my photos off the camera and onto the computer, much less have them printed. Jonathan and I had to make a book for DHS caseworkers depicting us and our house and our immediate family members, but ours was a Spartan affair with a line of handwritten text below each photo and not a single horsey sticker.

"Kiddos need a solid sense of their history," the social worker told us. "We try to send our kids to their forever home with their own life book, and pictures of their birth and foster families. Adoption's not a secret anymore."

"So where are the photos of your daughter's bio parents?" I flipped through the pages of the beautiful scrapbook once more but found none.

The woman pursed her lips. "Well . . . birth mama's in and out of treatment centers, and her daddy's gone. We don't have any photos of them. But . . ." She took back the book and turned to the first page to point at the photo of a gaunt, hairless infant, the picture mounted at a jaunty angle on top of a piece of pink paper festooned with green-and-yellow mallards. "This is a snapshot our baby's foster mama took. We're so glad to have it."

I studied the photo. Had this couple's baby been born addicted to drugs? Her cheeks looked sunken, her eyes dull. The question burned on my lips. The social worker had encouraged us to ask the parents anything, but even I, as a journalism teacher, couldn't put this nice couple on the spot in a room full of strangers.

"Thanks so much for sharing your experience." The social worker turned to the bearded man and the preteen. "How 'bout you two?"

During the woman's presentation the man had looked interested, but I'd detected several suppressed yawns from the girl. He spoke now, in an easy, friendly manner. "My wife's at home with our younger child, also adopted from DHS." He paused and looked at the girl beside him; she snorted but flashed a tiny, shy smile.

"Just tell them, Dad."

He turned his attention back to us. "Adoption's gonna blow your mind. One minute, you're going out to dinner spur of the moment or stopping after work for a drink. The next, you've got this child. The rewards are marvelous, though."

"Thanks a lot."

Father and daughter exchanged a look so full of bantering adoration that goose bumps ran down my back. A decade from now, would Jonathan and Minerva sit at a panel with the same joyful camaraderie?

"Our older daughter came from a difficult situation," the man said. "We had a pretty rough first year, but things are better now." He put an arm around his child's shoulders. "We're a big fan of the nurture side of that old argument."

I pressed my knee against Jonathan's. A safe home, organic vegetables, ballet lessons—these would surely negate any lasting effects from pesky prenatal methamphetamines.

One of the modish men beside us raised his hand and asked the question I couldn't: "We've heard that most kids from DHS are born exposed or addicted to drugs. Was that the case with your two children?"

I sucked in my breath, desperate to know the answer but horrified on behalf of the girl. She couldn't possibly have signed up for this level of disclosure when she agreed to sit on the panel.

Her father looked at her, and she shrugged again. "Both of my girls were exposed to drugs in utero. This one's an honors student at the junior high down the road."

Relief filled the room. The social worker stood up. "If you're going to committee for a kiddo and you've got concerns, we can usually put you in contact with the foster parents and therapists. They'll be able to give you a better picture of the situation than you get on paper."

I had a pretty clear picture already. I could see Minerva pattering around the living room in her little pink dress, scooping out cookie dough onto trays with her tiny fingers, rubbing her face against Eeyore's fur and smiling that sweet smile.

Jonathan looked after the man and his daughter as they walked down the hall ahead of us. Could he see Minerva, a preteen, reaching out to take his hand as this girl did with her father? From his distant expression, I couldn't tell.

"We should speak with Minerva's foster mother," I said. "I'll call her tomorrow."

———

Foster farms exist, to be sure, but for every money-motivated shyster, there are skilled parents devoted to helping kids in need. Minerva's foster mother was one such mom. She'd been acting as a temporary parent for seventeen years, she told me, caring for over 150 children.

"Minerva needs a bottle every two hours." Her voice, over the phone, sounded kind and matter-of-fact. "Feeding's difficult because she has a weak suck, which is a common effect of meth exposure. She doesn't like to smile, and she cries when she's around too many people. She'll need parents who can accept her as she is. I think she presents as autistic."

"Autistic? That's not in her adoption summary."

"Her behavior could be drug related, but it could be autism. Hard to say."

I'd worked with a few autistic folks as a job coach and special ed teacher. I'd read Temple Grandin's memoir and seen *Rain Man* a couple of times. While the diagnosis didn't chill me as much as schizophrenia might, I found myself reluctant to meet it with the can-do attitude I might give to, say, a kid with a missing arm.

"And what about her bio parents?" I looked at Minerva's photo and traced her pretty face with my finger. How had the photographer managed to capture such a happy, open expression if the baby seldom smiled? "Our Adoption Study says they've asked to maintain contact with Minerva."

"Bad idea." The foster mother's voice grew stern. "Letters and cards, that's all. No visits. Otherwise, the child never gets a chance to heal."

Right then, the domestic adoption community at large believed the more contact a child could have with her birth family, the better. Fewer questions and less confusion and emotional pain when she entered adolescence. But what if the birth parents had essentially abused their child from the moment they conceived her? Did they have any right to monthly, or even yearly, visitation? And if they were addicts living on the streets, what damage might mandatory visits do to a kiddo . . . and to her adoptive parents?

I heard a baby wailing in the background, shrill as a sharp-shinned hawk. "That's Minerva now, needing to be changed. I'd better go now. Good luck to you, dear."

I called up Marissa and related the conversations with the foster mom and pediatrician. "I don't think we're ready to take on an autistic child."

"If she were autistic," Marissa retorted, "it'd appear in her file. I see a kid with some difficulties who would thrive in your home. There's no reason to withdraw your application at this point."

"She said one more thing before I said good-bye," I told Jonathan at dinner.

He set a bowl of vegetable soup in front of me and sat down. "Okay . . ."

"She said, 'You may be the best people for her, but is she good for you?'"

On the morning we went to committee for Minerva, Laurin called. "Are you two available? There's a red-tail just off Highway 99. We need someone to go pick it up."

"Hit by a car, she thinks, but still alive." I petitioned Jonathan: "Can you be late to work?"

His brow shot up. "Bird rescue? Of course. C'mon, boys!"

We loaded up the dogs into the back of the truck, and he threw a box and gloves and his camera into the front. "Let's go!"

You never know what you're going to find on a bird emergency call. Sometimes the raptor is where a caller said it was—stunned by car collision at the side of the road, or stuck in barbed wire on someone's ranch. Other times it's recovered enough to fly or hobble away and you have to search for it. Regardless, it's important to get to the designated spot quickly, to make an attempt to rescue the bird.

Jonathan raced down Jefferson and blew through a stop sign. Instantly, a police car appeared behind us, lights flashing.

"Damn." He pulled over, and an officer appeared at his window. I leaned over, manic from too much caffeine and adrenaline.

"I'm sorry, sir!" I said. "We're on our way to rescue an injured hawk. We're from the raptor center, see?" I reached for the pet carrier and the gloves, found a book of matches and pushed them under the seat.

He looked from me to Jonathan, registered the tattoo on my husband's arm and the owl pellets on the dashboard. "Okay," he said. "Go get your bird, but hey . . ." He handed Jonathan his license. "Obey the stop signs, okay?"

"I will."

He pulled away, and I collapsed against the door in wild laughter. My mirth lasted all the way past the airport. "You got away without a ticket!"

"Thanks to you. Hey, help me look for this hawk."

Sometimes you go on a bird rescue and the raptor has vanished completely. Though Jonathan and I walked around and around the fields bordering Highway 99, searching through tall, wet grass for an injured red-tail, we found nothing. "Must've flown away," he said.

I peered into the cottonwoods around us. "I hope it's okay. I hate to think of it suffering."

His cell phone rang. He answered it and mouthed, "Marissa."

I froze. In the excitement of the raptor emergency, I'd forgotten about Minerva.

"Uh-huh. Yeah? Okay, well, thanks for telling us." He hung up. "The committee made their decision."

The members of a DHS committee look at several factors when choosing a family for a child—the parents' experience with special-needs kids, particularly if a baby has been born drug addicted or a child shows signs of disability; ethnicity and race; the presence of pets in the home if the child has allergies; the willingness of adoptive parents to comply with birth parents' desires for visits or correspondence. They look at whether the parents have other children—a plus in many social workers' books— and at how long the parents have been waiting to adopt.

To DHS social workers it looked as though Jonathan and I had been waiting only a few months for a child. They didn't factor in the years we'd spent involved with China and Vietnam.

"Our lack of previous children concerned them, as well." In the wet field Jonathan put his arms around me. "Another family who'd been wait-ing longer got Minerva."

"Oh. Okay."

The dogs scratched at the windows of the truck bed and whined. Cars rushed by on the highway. One truck driver honked at us. Still, I held onto Jonathan and closed my eyes, full of relief.

25

Always a Hidden Story

MOTHER'S DAY LOOMED ON A GRAY, RAINY SUNDAY, FRAUGHT WITH manufactured meaning that I nevertheless bought into completely.

My younger sister called me after brunch, her four-month-old son cooing in the background. "The whole family's here, celebrating my first time being a mom."

"Congratulations!" I stood and gazed into my empty nursery. Then I drove up to the raptor center, let myself into Bodhi's mew, and bawled.

He clacked his beak and shifted on his perch. I held out my gloved arm to him. He stepped onto my wrist, and I walked with him to the covered entryway.

I knew that Buddhist practitioners incorporate mindfulness into everything possible—sitting, brushing their teeth, washing the dishes. I'd learned from working with the owls that such a practice could deliver one from depression. Determined to escape the endless hellish circling of my thoughts, I lifted Bodhi to nose level and inhaled the smell of grain, felt the softness of his feathers tickle my nostrils. Low in his throat, he hooted, a guttural sound like a purr.

I rubbed my fingertips on his scalp, feeling the stiff feather shafts, the slippery skin. Rain pelted the fiberglass roof above us. He looked up at the sound, and his dark eyes met mine. "I'm not your mother, bird," I told him, "but I'm the closest thing to it. Happy Mother's Day to us."

❧

"Go skiing." Kat ordered me out of self-pity on our Saturday run. "For God's sake, go out to bars. Do everything you want to while you still can, without shelling out forty dollars a night for a babysitter."

Instead, Jonathan and I remodeled our bathroom—knocked the entire thing down to the studs and started over.

There's little more therapeutic than strapping on a pair of goggles, wielding a crowbar, and tearing down walls. Jonathan and I took turns deconstructing, so one of us wouldn't accidentally give the other a concussion in the tiny room. In the late afternoon we carted away all the plaster and lath in the truck, then loaded up the dogs and headed for Buford Park, the two-thousand-acre wilderness area that graces Eugene's backyard and is flanked by a fork of the Willamette River. We threw tennis balls, and the dogs raced down a paved path, stopping to pee on lichen-strewn maples. Above us we heard the familiar peep of osprey and craned our necks to look.

"What's it got? A fish?" I peered up at the black-and-white bird peeping in a slow circle above us; it clutched something long and skinny in its talons.

"It think it's a stick. That's the male, from the size of him, nest-building. But where's the nest?"

A fir towered above a ramshackle barn. Jonathan liked to explore there, pilfering the bones of a deceased cow for his photography projects. I pointed high above the sagging roof. "Is that the nest?"

"Good eye." He trained his binoculars on the mass wedged between two branches of the enormous fir.

Osprey nests can weigh up to four hundred pounds and may measure three feet deep and four feet wide, lined with sticks, bark, and leaves. The birds sometimes incorporate human detritus into their creation. David Gessner, in his book *Return of the Osprey*, describes a nest he once found that contained a naked Barbie doll.

We assumed that after the male above us dropped his stick onto his nest, he'd fly down to the ground to retrieve another. Instead, he launched himself toward a forest of firs and yanked another long stick from a branch with his talons. "I didn't know they did that." Jonathan adjusted his binoculars, mesmerized.

From the nest the female spread her wings and filled the air with encouraging chirps. "I like their division of labor." I tossed soggy tennis balls for the dogs, attempted a smile. "The male does all the work while the female sits and orders him around."

"Yeah, yeah." Jonathan kissed my head and we sat down, dogs panting at our feet, to watch. Eventually, the female took a turn at nest-building, too, flying off toward the river and returning with another stick. "She's so much larger than the male." Jonathan pointed up at the bird. "But females also have brown feathers that circle their breast like a necklace. See?"

Lately, I'd been bringing the center's resident injured osprey her trout during my shift. On the ground she looked awkward, hunched over on her curved, scaly toes unsuited to the mew's gravel floor. But in the air the species morphed into something magnificent.

"They'll be around all summer." Jonathan helped me to my feet. "We'll get to watch them sitting on the nest, and maybe even see their fledglings."

I walked with him hand in hand back to the car, dogs dancing around us. I picked up a stick and cracked it in two over my knee, hard.

"Bet the osprey have babies before we do."

———

"A child is a guest in the house, to be loved and respected—never possessed."

I paraphrased a line from one of J. D. Salinger's novellas on our way to the center the next day. "That's how I'd like to approach our child, if we ever get one."

"I'll have to think on that a while." He parked, and we walked up the driveway.

The education director waved at us from the lawn. "Melissa, I need to see you for a minute."

"Clock me in, love?" I walked over to her. "What's up?"

"Sit down." She motioned to the picnic table and stood beside me. "We believe Archimedes isn't working to his full potential."

I glanced toward the director's apartment. "Okay . . ."

"He's so intelligent—we think he can fly from one handler's glove to another, or even to a perch from someone's arm the way the birds do at the Oregon Zoo."

I'd watched her work with another handler and a red-tailed hawk on a creance—a long cord attached to the bird's jesses to allow trainers to teach it to fly from glove to glove, or glove to perch, without fear of a fly-off. I didn't know how to use a creance, and suddenly, rather than look-ing forward to the challenge, I found myself resenting the intrusion into my uninspired training plan. Still, I didn't want to give up control.

"Archimedes still bates and hangs sometimes," I told her. "Maybe we should wait until he's more solid on the glove."

She pursed her lips. "Why don't you let me take a crack at it with Jean. I'm not saying we're going put him in a flight show, but visitors would love to see him doing more than just sitting on a perch."

I knew in my heart that creance training would offer Archimedes enrichment and the opportunity to really fly, if only twenty feet. But how could I give him up to other handlers?

"I really think it's best if I just keep working with him."

"I'm sorry, Melissa, but we've made our decision. I'll write up a feed-ing schedule. You can still work with him a few days a week."

The snowy wasn't mine. The bond I felt for him when he sat on my glove and I scratched his eyelids might very well be one-sided. Raptor training isn't a Disney movie, after all, and at a nonprofit with volunteers appearing and disappearing as life schedules dictated, it made sense to ensure that the bird would work for as many handlers as possible.

"Loved and respected," I muttered on my way down to Bodhi's mew, "but never possessed."

The barred owl had grown into a bizarre-looking creature. His head remained tiny, and he had a tendency to hold his wings back at an awk-ward angle, so his flight feathers appeared freakishly long. He hooted when he saw me and flew to his perch. I got him on the glove and walked into the clinic to put balm on his foot pads.

A new volunteer, a smooth-skinned beauty with giant black earrings distorting her lobes, widened her eyes at me. "Aren't you afraid he'll punc-ture you with his talons?"

"He's done it before. It's not a big deal."

I walked Bodhi into the bathroom to get a paper towel. Instantly, he spread his wings backward and arched his neck. Every feather stood on end, and he clacked his beak in apparent fury.

Bewildered, I hollered to Jonathan in the treatment room. "Love, hurry! I think Bodhi's having a seizure!"

Jonathan rushed to the bathroom door. He stared and then laughed. "He's looking at himself in the mirror. He thinks he sees another barred owl—that's his defensive posture."

"I haven't seen it since he was a baby. Looks freakish with all his adult feathers."

I backed out of the bathroom. Bodhi's eyes stayed riveted on his reflection. In the clinic he relaxed and his feathers sank into their at-ease position. I stepped back toward the mirror. Again, he stuck out his feathers, wings stretched and head arched. "Who's a big, tough bird?" I teased.

Five minutes later, I found myself striking a defensive posture of my own when Darcy walked in and pointed out a sizable hole in my leather glove. "Wow. Who did that?"

My shoulders tensed toward my ears. "Oh, that's just Bodhi. He's taken to biting the glove."

"That's not good. It's a sign he's anxious. What's your training plan?"

My plan for Bodhi resembled the one I'd written for Archimedes—enter the mew with a full bits box, bait a perch, wait for the owl to fly over and step up on my glove, then walk him around the center or stand in the ed pavilion for a lecture while rewarding calm behavior with more bits. If the bird and I were alone with no visitors, I scratched his head.

Darcy scowled. "Something's not right. A good ed bird doesn't rip up the glove. Maybe I should work with him a while, and we'll see if we can extinguish that behavior between the two of us."

She was a senior handler, whereas I'd been working this gig only a short time. Still, I protested. "I'm not sure that's a good idea for Bodhi."

She turned on the heel of her rubber boot. "I'll talk with the ed director, see what she says. Wouldn't hurt to have a couple of us trained to work with Bodhi. You're not gonna be around forever, Mom."

Mom. Someone had clipped a short essay I'd published about Jonathan's and my decision to adopt domestically from Oregon and tacked it on the bulletin board above the hot water dispenser. Since then, fellow volunteers had clamored for updates; rumor had it they were planning a baby shower for Jonathan and me. Still, Darcy's audacity infuriated me.

"She can't just take my bird," I fumed to Jonathan.

He responded with silence, lips compressed.

At home my irritation remained. To distract myself I logged into my e-mail and discovered a fan letter from a stranger who had read my adoption essay.

I'm sending you this e-mail to extend a thank you for sharing with readers your personal story about your adoption decisions.

He went on to describe how he and his wife had adopted four children through the Department of Human Services.

I know there are many good-hearted people who go to a foreign land to adopt, and I understand intentions are often wanting to save children from desperate situations. But given the number of children in our country who might be eligible for adoption and that the longer children are in foster care, the less likely they will be to experience healthy development, I think it is a tragically sad decision to leave this country to adopt a child from a foreign land.

I read the letter to Jonathan when he returned home from the post office bearing a package from his mother. "Everyone's an adoption expert. Everyone's got an opinion, have you noticed?"

I told him how, earlier that day, I'd walked down to our little neighborhood market and the cashier behind the counter asked me if I intended to breast-feed our adopted child.

"There's special medication you can take to lactate." His eyes, behind frameless glasses, sought mine. "You don't want to miss out on that crucial bond between mother and child, Melissa."

"I almost told him to take the medication himself, and we'd walk our daughter down to the store a couple times a day so he could breast-feed her." I scowled at Jonathan. "Kat says when she was pregnant, strangers on the street stopped to offer her advice about child rearing. They'd actually put a hand on her stomach and tell her what kind of crib to buy, and what music to play while Andi was in utero."

"That's just weird."

He unwrapped the package from his mother and read the note inside. "Huh. My mom says she's been knitting the same baby sweater for the past twenty years, ever since the first grandchild was born." He chuckled. "But right now, she's doing a series of paintings for a land trust fundraiser, and she doesn't have time to knit. Instead, she sent this."

He reached into the box and opened a swath of bubble wrap to reveal a cat skull. "I think this was one of my childhood pets. She told me to photograph it." He turned over the card and read the back. "Also, she wants us to fly to Gettysburg for a family reunion in July."

The prospect of travel excited me until I realized we'd be the only couple without kids. I pictured myself milling about old cannons and gravestones, stalking my Korean niece and nephew, at war with myself for rejecting a handsome, healthy Vietnamese boy when, by now, we might have been packing our suitcases to head for Ho Chi Minh City and our son.

I felt slightly better after I read an AP story about how Vietnam had decided to halt all US adoptions following allegations of baby selling and fraud. "Hospitals are accused of selling infants whose moms can't pay their bills." I read the article to Jonathan. "Apparently, brokers are going to villages, looking for babies to hawk overseas. In one case a grandma gave away her grandkid without telling the baby's mother."

He shook his head. "There are no guarantees, not even adopting through the state. There's a guy sitting out on West Eleventh right now with a cardboard sign that says 'DHS ruined my family.'"

"What does that mean?"

He held the cat skull at eye level, as if asking for guidance. "There's always a hidden story," he said.

———

At Buford Park the next morning, we walked toward the old barn and the osprey nest. "Look!" Jonathan trained his binoculars on the nest in the fir tree. "Are those babies?"

Through the lenses I could just see two fuzzy heads peering over the mammoth pile of sticks. The female perched on the edge of the nest, flapping her wings and chirping. The male osprey sailed toward his new family with a fish in his talons.

I pressed my fists to my chest. "Even the osprey have babies now."

"Maybe it's a sign of hope."

"It's a sign of breeding season."

I sat down cross-legged on the warm cement and raised my binoculars. We spent a long time peering up at the babies and watching the parents minister to them with piercing chirps. Jonathan turned to me. "I read that males sometimes eat only the head and tail of a fish, leaving the nutritious parts in the middle for the female and their offspring."

He gazed into my eyes with mock earnestness. "I'd eat the head and tail of a fish for you."

"Thanks, dork."

Our romance had been restored—of this, I was certain.

And then the truth crashed down.

We returned home from Buford Park, and Jonathan leashed up Cody. He liked to walk him several times a day, separate from our trips to the dog park. "He won't poop in the backyard," he told me. "I want to make sure he doesn't get constipated."

Usually, he took his cell phone, but on this day, he forgot it on the counter. As he headed off down the street, it rang. Recognizing his mother's number, I ran out to the porch with it in time to see him pull out a pack of cigarettes from his coat pocket and light one.

I sat down on the doormat, head swimming.

He's smoking?

I thought of all the times over the past years that I'd smelled cigarettes, asked him about them, wondered aloud if he still got nicotine cravings. "No, no," he'd assured me. "I stood next to a coworker who smoked on our break. I chew gum, and that kills the cravings. I told you I'd quit, and I did."

"You *lied* to me," I said when he returned with his dog. I pointed at his pocket. "I saw you."

He slumped on the couch, head bowed. "I'm addicted," he said. "I tried. These two years have been . . . stressful."

Stress, I could understand. Addiction, I could imagine. But years of dishonesty?

My mind went to Tony, my first husband, who had lied about everything from financial income to relationships with other women. What other falsehoods had Jonathan told me . . . and why?

"I'm going out."

I leashed up my dogs and put them in the VW, drove blindly back to Buford Park and got out. Nauseated and shaking, I stumbled down the maple-lined path to the osprey nest, sat down, and stared up into the trees.

I couldn't see the mother or the babies. I didn't spot the male immediately, either. With dry eyes and a parched throat, I watched until he appeared at last. On crooked wings he hurled himself toward a tree and grasped a stick in his talons, shrieking as he approached the nest. But the thing proved too unwieldy, long and crooked, heavier than he'd likely suspected. He dropped it, and it fell at my feet, splintering into pieces.

26

Destiny Child

LEAVING WOULD HAVE BEEN SO EASY—PACK THE VW BEETLE, LOAD UP
Marley and Kawliga and Alger Hiss, write a kind but firm note, and drive
away. Find another home, another city, another college at which to teach,
another raptor center at which to volunteer.

Love is exhausting. I wanted to sleep.

Instead, I walked through the Buford Park wilderness unseeing,
clutching two dog leashes like a lifeline.

But Marley and Kawliga had led me to Jonathan.

My husband. I thought of all the times he'd looked me in the eye and
lied. He, my beloved, my best friend. How could I return home to him?

—•—

"You're being a drama queen." At the dog park later, Kat chastised me.
"You two have a great thing going. Let it go."

"I can't go home."

Early summer sun had brought out a crowd of dogs with their people;
Marley and Kawliga ran and sniffed and frolicked in the new grass. Their
crass exuberance disgusted me. "He lied, Kat. He promised to stop smoking, and he didn't."

She flung a Frisbee back to her daughter; Andi caught it, long legs
flashing in denim cutoffs. "He lied because he was ashamed. You're not
blameless, yourself."

I shot her an angry look. She held up a mollifying hand. "None of us
are, Melissa. Search your own conscience, then go home. Kiss and make
up."

I went home, but I didn't kiss Jonathan when he met me with a funereal face at our front door. "Where were you?" He looked at my muddy ankles, my red-rimmed eyes. "Are you hungry?"

"I need to be alone."

I let myself into his photography studio and sat cross-legged on the floor. Buddhist practitioners say that the first guideline, when doing lovingkindness meditation, is to say the words for oneself.

May I be happy, I thought in the half-darkness. *May my body be happy. May I be free of suffering. . . .*

Sentient beings experience anguish in their lifetime. That's a given, and the Buddha's first Noble Truth. I knew the nature of my own suffering well. But did I know Jonathan's? Had I even considered it?

There'd been truth in Darcy's assertion that I was too sensitive. To protect me Jonathan had remained stoic, strong. I'd marveled, these past two years, at his ability to embrace serenity in the midst of loss and confusion. He'd embraced me, comforted me hundreds of times as I lamented children we didn't get to parent, owls I didn't get to retain as my own. What had such efforts cost him?

May my mind be happy. I tried, in lotus position on a rug littered with fir needles and sheltie fur, to imagine how I'd feel if Jonathan had asked me to give up running or, worse, dessert—especially in the midst of a stressful adoption process. Would I jog on the sly, hide pints of Ben & Jerry's behind bags of corn and broccoli in the freezer, hedge when he pointed out chocolate streaked across my face?

I might.

May I be at peace.

Over and over I said the prayer in my head, praying for tranquility. Buddhists suggest that after we say it for ourselves a while, we then say it for someone we adore. I said it for Jonathan.

By the time I walked back in our house that night, I could look him in the eye, even sit next to him on the couch and eat the strawberry-rhubarb pie I'd baked and watch *Arrested Development*.

But I couldn't kiss him.

Right before the term ended, I biked over to the university to hear *New York Times* journalist Peggy Orenstein discuss *Waiting for Daisy*, a memoir about her quest to become a mother. In the back of a hall full of polished wood and elegant rugs, I marveled at Orenstein's candor. She admitted to a large audience of professors and students that over years of trying to get pregnant, suffering the indignities of fertility treatments and adoption mishaps, she'd turned into a shrew.

I bought her book. Then, entranced by her honesty, encouraged by her happy ending, I e-mailed her.

> *My husband and I have been trying to adopt a child in a long and heinous process. After listening to you and reading your book, I have much more hope for my adoption. Thank you.*

She wrote back immediately, two sentences worth more than any advice I might pay a therapist to give:

> *The process is stressful, competitive, time consuming, expensive, often humiliating, falls through constantly (the adoption equivalent of a miscarriage) and generally, as you say, heinous. I hope you get through the thicket quickly and can move on to the joys and trivialities of parenting.*

Sometimes just the affirmation that a situation sucks can turn a mood around and inspire strength and optimism. Instead of returning to my computer and my grading that afternoon, I drove up to the raptor center. "I know it's not my day," I told the ed director, who stood on the lawn with a hawk, "but I'd like to work with Archimedes."

She shrugged. "It's okay for more than one person to work with him each day. Just make sure you know who's feeding him, so you don't double up or, worse, forget his prey."

I pulled on my glove and tucked a mouse into my jacket pocket. Archimedes, when he saw me, flew to his perch. I let myself into the mew and walked over, placed my arm parallel to the Astroturf so he could step up. "Good bird." I handed him the mouse, and he threw back his head and swallowed it down, grunting as if he'd just done a shot of some particularly fine whiskey.

"You crack me up, bird." I swiveled and leashed him, and we stepped out of the mew. I didn't feel like walking him to the ed pavilion, didn't want to chat with any visitors or other volunteers just then. My motive for taking him out struck me as purely selfish, therapeutic . . . and that was okay.

Under the maple trees, sun streaking through with the promise of summer warmth, Archimedes sat quietly on my glove. Chickadees called around us. From his mew Bodhi gave a low hoot. I nuzzled my nose into the snowy owl's head feathers and closed my eyes.

That afternoon, I called my mother and planned a weekend in San Francisco. "I need a few days away," I told Jonathan as we drove to his first Nicotine Anonymous meeting. "I miss my mom."

He reached for my hand. "Whatever you need," he said. "Let me know how I can help."

We sat in the meeting and ate chocolate cake and listened to other people's stories about fighting addiction. At last I began to glimpse the power and pull of cigarettes, why they might have caused Jonathan to do what he'd done. Again, I thought about how I'd feel if he asked me to give up the slice of cake in front of me. Even knowing the health benefits of foregoing sugar and caffeine, I'd be pissed, resentful. Add to that the ongoing adoption trauma, and I'd be high-tailing it for Sweet Life Patisserie the moment his back was turned.

"I'm sorry," I said to him in the car after the meeting. "I didn't understand."

His arms went around me, his cheek next to mine. "I'm sorry I didn't tell you the truth."

I let him kiss me.

Beside us my cell phone rang. Marissa dispensed with hello and got straight to the point.

"I'm sending you two bulletins—a Roxy and a Maia."

"Great." I wiped my eyes on my sleeve and smiled weakly at Jonathan. "We're out right now—can you put them in our mailbox?"

"Yep. Remember, don't get excited."

The social workers from DHS had told us that parents sometimes went to seven or eight committees before they got a child. "Detach with love," I reminded Jonathan when we got home and walked down the hill to the mailbox under the cedar.

There were the bulletins—one for a cherubic blond child, and one for a round-faced tot with a head full of curly brown hair and a toothy grin that could only be described as shit-eating.

"Roxy's Anglo . . . born addicted to meth . . . has mild global delays." Jonathan skimmed the bulletins and read me the salient points. "Maia's half-Latina . . . she seems fine except for weak trunk muscles."

I studied the second kid's round brown face and alert dark eyes. "She looks like an adorable little russet potato."

"If we get her, we can call her Spud."

"Or Tater Tot. Ah, we shouldn't even be joking about nicknames. A hundred families'll apply for these little girls—families who've been waiting longer than we have. We don't have a chance."

"I'll bet we get a kid in a month." Jonathan unlocked the door and waded through an onslaught of animals. "In the meantime you're going to San Francisco with your mom, and then we're flying to see my family in Gettysburg in July."

He shouldered his camera bag and headed for the back door. "I'm going out to the studio. Gotta prep to take pictures of a little girl who has this enormous collection of stuffed cats—we're displaying them in the kids' section of the museum." He reached for his camera bag. "There's a reason some photographers refuse to work with children and animals."

"What is it?"

"They're both incredibly unpredictable."

⌒‿⌒

My mother and I like to meet halfway between our homes, in San Francisco, once a year. We stay in an inexpensive hotel in the Hayes Valley district and entertain ourselves on the cheap with ten-dollar standing-room tickets at the opera and cable car rides to Chinatown. In late June we reserved two tiny floral-themed rooms—ruffles wherever there could be ruffles—with a shared loo down the hall.

Our first morning there, I sat in the sunny breakfast room eating blueberry muffins and reading the *Chronicle*, waiting for my mother to finish her writing project on her laptop and join me. A middle-aged Anglo couple walked in with a lanky teenage Chinese girl in blue-and-green checkered shorts and long black braids. The trio sat down beside me with muffins and fruit and began to chat, as strangers sometimes do at bed-and-breakfasts, dispensing with small talk and getting straight to the good stuff.

"We're here from DC." The woman was petite, with blond-white hair and tiny features; already, her daughter looked to be half a foot taller. "We're visiting relatives our daughter, Amelia, hasn't seen in eleven years."

The girl sat bent over an English muffin, intent on knifing butter into every nook and cranny. "Are your relatives from China?" I asked her.

She nodded.

"What's that like, to meet family you haven't seen in so long?"

The girl looked up, and I saw that she had a quick, merry smile and snapping, sardonic brown eyes. She snorted. "They'll probably say, 'Oh, she's so tall,' and I'll be like, 'Duh, I'm fourteen.'"

Her mother patted her arm. "And you have boobs now."

"Mom." The girl rolled her eyes. "*Please.*"

Her father chuckled over his croissant. After half an hour and another cup of coffee, I learned that Amelia represented the couple's fourth try at a child. "Our agency assigned us one eleven years ago." The mother perched on the edge of her antique chair like a bright, pretty songbird and trilled out their tale. "Then our social worker called to say they'd accidentally assigned the same child to someone else who'd been waiting longer. The next child they gave us was a six-year-old boy."

The father set down his coffee cup and stroked his beard, sending a shower of croissant crumbs to the ruffled floral placemat. "What's wrong with *that* picture?"

I shook my head. "I . . . I'm not sure . . ."

"China *never* gives up boys."

"The social worker said it was a red flag for her, too, so we had to take a pass." The woman flashed a fond smile at her daughter. "And then we got Amelia, our destiny child."

She'd said the girl represented their fourth attempt. But the couple skipped the story about the third child. Did it have a schizophrenic family? Ambiguous genitalia? Did it die?

I didn't ask. Their daughter—the child who was meant for them—sat there, sassy and funny in her checkered shorts and braces, rolling her eyes at her parents. This was the kind of girl Jonathan and I had hoped for when we began our adventure. Who would we end up with? I had no idea.

I said good-bye to the family and left them joking with each other in the breakfast room. Upstairs, I put an ear to my mother's door and heard the sounds of frantic keyboarding; assuming the muse had spoken louder than her stomach, I went back to my room and let her work on her mystery novel. My cell phone lay on the rose-patterned pillow sham; I picked it up and saw that Marissa had called and left a message on my voice mail.

"Call me right back," she said.

I punched in her numbers.

"You and Jonathan have been selected to go to committee for Roxy *and* Maia."

"Maia? Is that the kid who looks like a potato? If we get her, we're going to call her Spud."

"She's beautiful. The committees meet next week. But most people don't get a kid on their second or third try, so don't get your hopes up."

"I won't."

Still, I called Jonathan at work and related the news.

"It's funny," he said. "I feel ambivalent. These children have no major issues. Roxy's medical stuff we can handle. Maia's tiny, but her bio says she's resilient, friendly, and curious, just like what we want. Maybe I just don't want to get my heart broken one more time."

I stared at myself in the mirror. I looked exhausted, a middle-age woman in a careless blue T-shirt and khaki shorts—a wan, wrinkled tourist bedraggled by the journey. I hadn't considered that my husband might be travel weary, too. Throughout the past two and a half years, he'd remained stoic and steadfast, mopping up my tears, ministering to my mourning, overlooking my angry outbursts. I'd forgotten that he might be grieving, as well.

I attempted optimism. "Maybe we'll actually get one of them. We should get the nursery ready."

His tone grew curt, distracted; he'd told me that when he felt the need for a cigarette, he had to pull away and concentrate on work, or he'd find himself down at the 7-Eleven petitioning for a pack of American Spirits. "We'll wait and see," he said. "I've gotta get back to photography."

"Don't worry, love," I said before I hung up, quoting the family from the breakfast room that morning. "We're going to get our *destiny child*."

I tried to forget about anything related to adoption that weekend. My mother and I walked all over Chinatown and Japantown and ended up at last where we felt most comfortable, in the Castro, laughing over T-shirts in a pricey boutique. "'I have two mommies.' Oh, Mom, you've gotta get that for your poodle!"

I spotted a toddler-size T-shirt, blue with red sleeves: "My dad rocks." I carried it up to the counter and bought it for Jonathan.

Over crepes that evening, I didn't tell my mother about his smoking. I related very little about Maia and Roxy, only allowing that if we got the former child, we'd already picked out a nickname, and if we got the latter, I'd learn the words to the song "Roxie" from *Chicago* and belt it out as I pushed her in the baby jogger.

"I hope you get one of those girls." She passed me the bread basket, her eyes full of concern. "You've been waiting so long."

I glanced up at a couple of drag queens sashaying by in feathers and pumps. Distracted, I reminded her of a previous trip to the city for a writer's conference; we'd found ourselves sharing the Sir Francis Drake Hotel with a contingent of drag queens who mingled with the authors in the lobby on Sunday morning, everyone in little black dresses and enigmatic eyeliner.

"We *have* been waiting a long time." I returned to the original conversation. The way I saw it, I had two choices in this Castro creperie. I could cry and confess my two-year angst, or I could get a grip, as my mother had so long ago when she had to relinquish custody of her children, and move on.

I thought of the Helen Keller quote we'd seen on a risqué fuchsia T-shirt at the boutique. "Life," I quoted, "is either a daring adventure, or nothing."

~ ~

When I returned from San Francisco, Jonathan and I worked a substitute shift for another couple at the raptor center. I took Bodhi his quail and asked him to step on the glove. He hooted as he hopped up, and I rubbed the tiny feathers, still like the petals of some soft, tawny marigold, ringing his eyes.

Volunteers had constructed a sort of raptor playground beside the ed pavilion, with low perches and an overturned log for volunteers to sit on. In the warm summer evening, I clipped Bodhi to a low perch and sat on the stump across from him, reaching occasionally to scratch his head. All was quiet except for a woodpecker knocking a fir. Abruptly, Bodhi craned his neck upward and triangulated, peering into the trees.

"What is it?" I followed his wide brown gaze. Two juvenile barred owls sat on a limb fifteen feet above us. One of them screeched a begging cry, and Bodhi's body shot into a thin, narrow arrow.

From where I sat I could see the owls' fluffy heads. Bodhi had looked like them a year ago, a dandelion puff on my glove. Maturity had given him flight feathers, but he'd retained his oddly small head and his drooping wing.

"Who cooks for you?" he called over and over.

"It's okay, little guy." My fingers returned to his head, and I felt my breath grow slow and steady, my muscles relax. I liked to think of myself as someone devoted to helping vulnerable creatures for purely altruistic reasons. The truth is, they restored me.

Bodhi's hoots took on a more urgent tone. I looked to up find him staring at a different tree. Above us, silent and watching, sat an enormous adult barred owl.

We locked eyes, and she puffed up her feathers, opened her beak, and screamed.

In an instant I had Bodhi unclipped from the ground perch and on my glove, safe under the covered pavilion.

310

"Jonathan!" I called up the hill. "I need you to run interference!"

He loped down to play bodyguard, and we walked together to the clinic with the wild owls still shrieking and begging in the trees.

On my glove Bodhi craned his neck and spread his wings and bated, trying to fly upward. His jesses caught him and he struggled a moment, then flew back to my arm, his enormous black eyes wide and searching.

———

I went for a six-mile run early the next day and walked back into the house as my cell phone rang. Sweaty and panting, shoes untied, I answered.

My literary agent at the time spoke in her breathy, high-pitched voice. "I've had an offer on your book, *Gringa*, and it looks really good. If the terms are acceptable to you, we've made a sale. It's a feminist press out of Berkeley, and the editor adores your manuscript."

I forced myself to sound calm and professional. We discussed the contract and the editor's request for revision. Then I thanked my agent quietly, hung up the phone, and screamed.

Writing a book, like waiting for a child or training a raptor, is unpredictable, an act of faith. You work and work, sometimes for years on end with no feedback and no reward beyond the process itself, without a definite outcome. When success hits it's heady stuff, more satisfying for the years of challenges and disappointments and mind-numbing, endless drudgery.

Hopping up and down with excitement, I called Jonathan. "I sold *Gringa*, love! They're giving me an advance!"

"That's wonderful. Let's have a party tonight. I'll e-mail everyone. They won't mind a last-minute invitation when they hear what's happened."

I blew off work the rest of the day and shopped for wine and beer and salmon burgers, and cleaned the house. I was kneeling in ratty cutoffs and an old raptor center T-shirt, scrubbing our white brick hearth with a toothbrush, when Jonathan walked in.

I glanced at the clock. "You're early. Have you come to help clean?" I beamed up at him.

He looked strange, biting his lip and holding his hands behind his back.

"Did you bring me flowers? That's so nice of you!"

He shook his head. In the sunlight streaming in from the newly washed windows, I saw tears shining in his hazel eyes.

"Marissa called me at work an hour ago. Remember, she went to committee today? Heck of a meeting, I guess—social workers from three families, Maia's case worker, some impartial folks from DHS . . ."

In the excitement of my book sale, I'd forgotten about the meeting. I couldn't remember if it was for Roxy or Maia. Didn't matter anyway—as Marissa had said, we'd likely not get a child on our second or third try.

I put down the toothbrush. "They said no, right? Well, no worries. Now I'll be so busy editing for a while that I won't even—"

"Melissa?" Jonathan held out his hands. In them he cradled a large sweet potato wearing a child's flowered sunhat. "Melissa . . . we got the Spud."

Epilogue

"Are you *sure* you want to do this?"

I crunched down the gravel path in worn running shoes, past Lorax's mew and Bodhi's, to where Maia stood—motionless, for once—in front of Archimedes. He sat on his stump, bright white against a backdrop of firs and yellowing maples. I thought, as he swiveled his head to look at me, that he might recognize my stocking cap and braids, even after my four-year absence. He opened his beak wide and honked so we could see inside his pink throat.

"I want to do this, Mommy."

Maia looked up at me, brown eyes earnest under her mop of spiral curls. "I never, *ever* spend my allowance. I want to adopt the snowy owl."

We'd been in the visitors' center watching another girl—also a first grader—as she sorted out a handful of birthday checks and crumpled bills she'd saved to adopt one of the screech owls. The volunteer on duty introduced Maia to a resident peregrine tethered to a perch. "You could have your seventh birthday party here," she told her. "We'll bring a bird out on the glove for you."

Maia grinned, exhibiting a gap where two adult incisors had just started to poke through. "I turned two here," she told the volunteer. "I had a snowy owl cake and people gave me bird books and an owl puppet." She pointed out the window to the windmill towering above the mews. "My parents had a wedding right there."

The volunteer's eyes widened at us. "Oh, you're the two who met here and got married."

Jonathan and I smiled. "We met at the dog park," he said.

I reached for his hand. "And we fell in love at the raptor center."

"Mama? Dad?" Maia tugged the sleeve of my jacket. "About that snowy owl . . ."

We held a family meeting under the trio of owl skeletons, who looked on like cheerleaders. Jonathan and I agreed that we'd help contribute to

Archimedes' adoption if Maia chipped in part of her allowance earned for feeding our cats.

The volunteer held up a hand. "Now, you know you can't take him home. The money will go toward his food for a year, and you can come visit him whenever you want."

Maia nodded. "*I'm* adopted," she confided, "but my parents got to take me home."

I thought of that first day we'd glimpsed her tottering around the corner of her foster mother's house in a peach pantsuit, curls slicked back and eyes sparkling with mischief. We'd recognized the shit-eating grin from her DHS photo and—as per the foster mom's suggestion—handed her a brownie. "Hi," we'd said. "We're your parents."

At eighteen months old she could say one word—"meow"—and she said it in her car seat over and over down the I-5 as we headed for our home and her nursery with its owl-print curtains and snowy owl quilt. She said it over Jonathan's shoulder, tucked into a toddler backpack, as he stood in the treatment room holding an injured great horned owl in his arms while another volunteer tube-fed the bird.

"Owl," Maia whispered then. "Owl."

Five years later, she walked back down to Archimedes' mew to study his slitted yellow eyes, his prodigious fluffy feet, the jesses dangling from his feathered ankles. "My mother used to train him," she said to a couple of families who wandered down to look at him, and the bird opened his beak again and squealed.

He didn't recognize me; I felt sure of it. I was just one of a handful of trainers who'd worked with him over the years.

I walked over to look at Lorax, perched close to the side of her mew. She clacked her beak, placid, though her feather tufts stood at attention. "Hello, beautiful," I whispered. In the mew below Bodhi dozed in a beam of sunlight. I clicked my tongue against my teeth, and one dark eye opened slightly.

"Who's that?" Maia said at my elbow.

"That's the barred owl," I told her. "He's exactly your age. After he was born I trained him while Daddy and I looked for you."

She stepped closer to his mew, and his eyes widened. "So he's your baby, too. May I pet him?"

My own fingers ached to bury themselves in his feathers again, to scratch the slippery skin around his eyes. I longed to breathe in his grain-sweet scent once more, but I shook my head. "He's a wild bird, Sweet Potato Pie," I said, using the nickname that had morphed out of Spud. "See how he puffs up his body so that his feathers stick out? He's nervous."

"We won't hurt him." She remained still another moment, crooned a made-up love song to the owl. Then she took off, fluttering from mew to mew in her bright pink coat. "C'mon, Mommy!"

She beckoned me with one small hand, and I let Bodhi be and followed her.

Jonathan, Author, and Maia
BRITT MYERS

Acknowledgments

This book emerged from my desire to share what I learned about birds of prey while volunteering at the Cascades Raptor Center in Eugene. The more I delved into the hands-on study of raptor conservation and education while waiting to adopt my daughter, the more I became struck by the similarities between injured and orphaned wildlife and children. Thousands of volunteers dedicate an incredible amount of time and money to protecting these vulnerable demographics worldwide. I hope this book conveys the gratitude I feel for their work.

Specifically, I'd like to thank Louise Shimmel, Laurin Huse, Kit Lacy, Jean Daugherty, Peggy McConnell, and all the volunteers who shared Sunday morning and Thursday evening shifts with Jonathan and me at our raptor center. I appreciate your patience and kindness, especially in the early days of my volunteering, when I couldn't tell a hawk from a falcon or pick up a mealworm with my bare fingers. Thanks, too, to Steve Martin and to members of IAATE for their encouragement and support. My deepest gratitude goes to the birds themselves, who act as ambassadors for their species. Lorax, Bodhi, Archimedes . . . you taught me about mindfulness, compassion, and tenacity.

A special thanks to Christy Obie-Barrett, whose commitment to finding forever homes for foster children through the Heart Gallery of Lane County inspired Jonathan and me on our journey. Thanks, as well, to the dedicated social workers who held our hands and talked us down off numerous ledges as we moved through the sometimes-tumultuous adoption process.

I'm grateful to my first readers, Hope Lyda and Laura White, for their encouragement and advice on rough drafts of this manuscript. Thank you to my agent, Jennifer Unter, for seeing the worth in my book proposal and for making me laugh. I'm indebted to my editor, Anna Bliss, for her magnificent insight and her commitment to this story.

There would be no story without my husband, Jonathan—my partner in adventure these past thirteen years. I call myself "beloved on the earth," thanks to you and to our sweet potato, Maia.

Appendix

A SELECTION OF RAPTOR CENTERS OPEN DAILY OR WEEKLY TO THE PUBLIC

Alaska Raptor Center
1000 Raptor Way
Sitka, AK 99835
(800) 643-9425
www.alaskaraptor.org

Audubon Florida Center for Birds of Prey
444 Brickell Ave., Ste. 850
Miami, FL 33131-2403
(305) 371-6399
http://fl.audubon.org/audubon-center-birds-prey

California Raptor Center
1340 Equine Ln.
Davis, CA 95616
(530) 752-6091
www.vetmed.ucdavis.edu/calraptor

Carolina Raptor Center
6000 Sample Rd.
Huntersville, NC 28079
(704) 875-6521
www.carolinaraptorcenter.org

Cascades Raptor Center
32275 Fox Hollow Rd.
Eugene, OR 97405
(541) 485-1320
www.eraptors.org

The Center for Birds of Prey
Avian Conservation Center
4872 Seewee Rd.
Awendaw, SC 29429
(843) 971-7474
www.thecenterforbirdsofprey.org

Donald M. Kerr Birds of Prey Center
High Desert Museum
59800 South Hwy. 97
Bend, OR 97702
(541) 382-4754
www.highdesertmuseum.org

Hawk Mountain Sanctuary
1700 Hawk Mountain Rd.
Kempton, PA 19529
(610) 756-6961
www.hawkmountain.org

Nature and Raptor Center of Pueblo
5200 Nature Center Rd.
Pueblo, CO 81003
(719) 549-2414
http://natureandraptor.org

The Raptor Center
University of Minnesota College of Veterinary Medicine
1920 Fitch Ave.
St. Paul, MN 55108
(612) 624-4745
www.raptor.cvm.umn.edu

Raptor Center at Glen Helen Ecology Institute
405 Corry St.
Yellow Springs, OH 45387
(937) 769-1902
http://glen.antiochcollege.org/glen_helen/raptor_center/visit

Raptor Center at Great Bend Zoo
2123 Main St.
Great Bend, KS 67530
(620) 793-4226
www.greatbendks.net/index.aspx?NID=35

Sardis Raptor Center
7472 Valley View Rd.
Ferndale, WA 98248
(360) 366-3863
http://sardisraptor.org

Shaver's Creek Environmental Center
3400 Discovery Rd.
Petersburg, PA 16669-2114
(814) 863-2000
http://shaverscreek.org

Teton Raptor Center
5450 West Hwy. 22
Wilson, WY 83014
(307) 203-2551
www.tetonraptorcenter.org

Vermont Institute of Natural Science
6565 Woodstock Rd.
Quechee, VT 05059
(802) 359-5000
www.vinsweb.org

Wild Wings
27 Pond Rd.
Honeoye Falls, NY 14472
(585) 334-7790
www.wildwingsinc.org

Wildlife Care Center
Audubon Society of Portland
5151 NW Cornell Rd.
Portland, OR 97210
(503) 292-6855
http://audubonportland.org/wcc

World Center for Birds of Prey
5668 West Flying Hawk Ln.
Boise, ID 83709
(208) 362-8687
www.peregrinefund.org/world-center

OTHER RAPTOR-RELATED WEBSITES OF INTEREST

HawkWatch International
www.hawkwatch.org

The Peregrine Fund
www.peregrinefund.org

Raptor Research Foundation
www.raptorresearchfoundation.org

ADOPTION RESOURCES

Domestic

AdoptUSKids
www.adoptuskids.org

Center for Adoption Policy
www.adoptionpolicy.org

Heart Gallery of America
www.heartgalleryofamerica.org

National Adoption Center
www.adopt.org

US Department of Health and Human Services
Child Welfare Information Gateway
www.childwelfare.gov/adoption/adoptive/foster_care.cfm

Voice for Adoption
www.voice-for-adoption.org

International

Alliance for Children
www.allforchildren.org

Children's Hope International
www.childrenshopeint.org

Families Thru International Adoption
www.ftia.org

Holt International Children's Services
www.holtinternational.org/adoption

About the Author

Melissa Hart is an essayist and author from Eugene, Oregon. Her work has appeared in the *Washington Post*, the *Los Angeles Times*, the *Chronicle of Higher Education*, *High Country News*, *Orion*, *Hemispheres*, the *Advocate*, and numerous other magazines and newspapers. She's the author of the memoir *Gringa: A Contradictory Girlhood*. She teaches at the School of Journalism and Communication, University of Oregon. In her free time she loves to run, hike, kayak, and travel with her husband—photographer Jonathan B. Smith—and their daughter. Learn more at www.melissahart.com.

JONATHAN B. SMITH